500 JUMBO CHRISTMAS ACTIVITIES

PaRragon

Bath · New York · Cologne · Melbourne · Delhi
Hong Kong · Shenzhen · Singapore

This edition published by Parragon Books Ltd in 2016 and distributed by

Parragon Inc.
440 Park Avenue South, 13th Floor
New York, NY 10016
www.parragon.com

Copyright © Parragon Books Ltd 2016

Individual Puzzles © Any Puzzle Media

ISBN 978-1-4748-5837-3

Printed in China

1. FITWORD

Place each of the following words into the empty squares, crossword-style.

3 Letters
Urn

4 Letters
Acne
Anon
Idea
Offs

5 Letters
Globe
Heart
Leers
Lover

Metro
Raise
Tiara
Utter

6 Letters
Orange
Toggle

7 Letters
Advance
Algebra
Bananas
Bishops

Founded
Pronoun

8 Letters
Eventual
Troubles

12 Letters
Bureaucratic
Illumination

2. PATH HUNTER

Join dots with horizontal and vertical lines to form a single path which does not touch or cross itself at any point. The start and end of the path are given. Numbers outside the grid specify the number of dots in their row or column that are visited by the path.

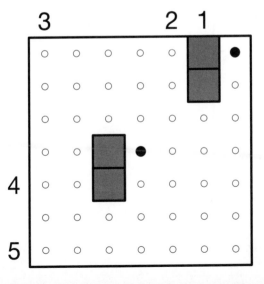

3. TOUCHY

Place A to F once each in every row and column such that two identical letters never touch—not even diagonally.

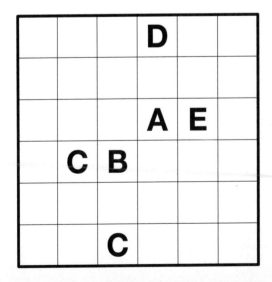

4. SUDOKU

Place 1 to 9 once each into every row, column, and bold-lined 3 × 3 square.

		5	7		8	1		
	3						8	
8		4				5		7
1			6					2
		2	4	7				
4			3					6
3		7				2		1
	4						6	
		8	4		1	3		

5. BRIDGES

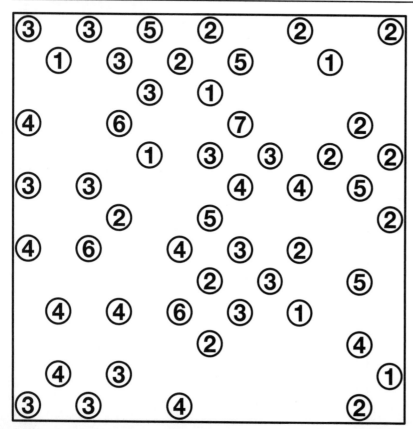

Join circled numbers with horizontal or vertical lines. Each number must have as many lines connected to it as are specified by its value.

No more than two lines may join any pair of numbers, and no lines may cross.

The finished layout must connect all numbers, so you can travel between any pair of numbers by following one or more lines.

6. BRIDGE MAZE

Find a path from the entrance at the top of the maze to the exit at the bottom of the maze. The path may cross over or under itself by using the marked bridges.

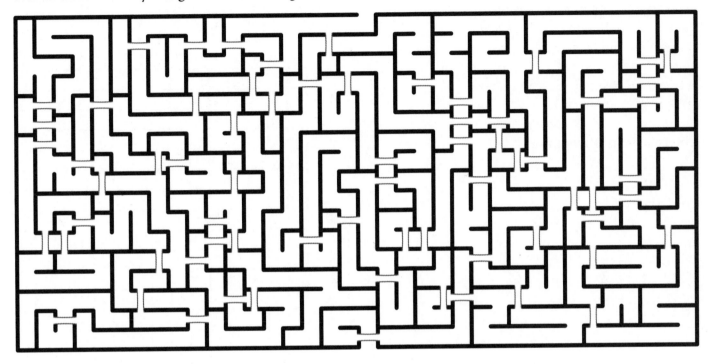

7. WORD CHAIN

Can you complete this word chain, in order to convert the word at the top into the word at the bottom?

At each step you may change only one letter so as to form a new English word, and you may not rearrange any of the letters.

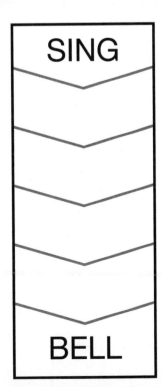

SING

BELL

8. LETTER CIRCLE

How many words can you find in this letter circle? Every word must use the center letter plus two or more of the other letters. No letter can be used more than once in a single word. There is one eight-letter seasonal word to find.

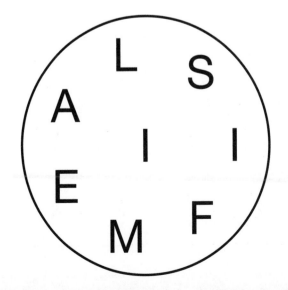

9. PICROSS

Shade in squares in the grid to reveal a picture. Numbers at the start of each row or column reveal, in order from left to right or top to bottom, the length of each consecutive run of shaded squares. There must be a gap of at least one empty square between each run of shaded squares in the same row or column.

Clue: Christmas shopping

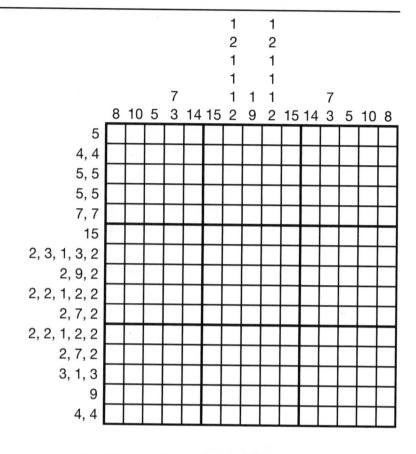

10. WORD RECTANGLE

Can you find the 12-letter word hidden in this Word Rectangle? Find words by moving from letter to touching letter, including diagonally, and without revisiting a square in a single word. How many other words can you find?

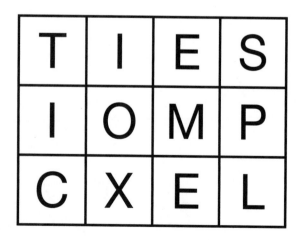

11. BRAIN CHAINS

Without using a calculator or making any written notes, solve these brain chains as quickly as you can. Write the solution in the "Result" box.

12. CROSSWORD

Solve the clues to complete the crossword grid.

Across

1 Adulation (6)
4 Appoint by force (6)
9 Increase in rank (9)
10 Arrest (3)
11 Novel, *The Catcher in the ___* (3)
12 Fungal fruiting body (9)
13 DC subway (5)
15 iPhone maker (5)
20 One who maims and kills for a cause (9)
22 NBC sketch show (inits) (3)
23 Travelers often need these (abbr) (3)
24 Principally (2,3,4)
25 Emotional shock (6)
26 Situation (6)

Down

1 Warhol's genre (3,3)
2 Solo (5)
3 Moped (7)
5 Tends (5)
6 Score against yourself, in soccer (3,4)
7 Mummify (6)
8 Greek elder god (5)
14 Europe and Asia combined (7)
16 Happy to wait (7)
17 Severe (6)
18 Beethoven's Choral symphony (5)
19 Aircraft (6)
21 Strong dislike (5)
22 Sting (5)

13. DOMINOES

Draw solid lines to divide the grid to form a complete set of standard dominoes, with exactly one of each domino. A "0" represents a blank on a traditional domino.

Use the checkoff chart to help you keep track of which dominoes you've placed.

0	6	5	5	2	2	6	3
5	1	6	1	6	4	4	2
5	2	3	4	1	3	0	4
0	3	3	3	4	1	0	4
1	1	0	5	5	3	5	2
1	4	0	6	6	6	6	2
1	0	5	4	3	2	0	2

	0	1	2	3	4	5	6	
								0
								1
								2
								3
								4
								5
								6

14. KILLER SUDOKU

Place the digits 1 to 9 once each into every row, column, and bold-lined 3 × 3 square.

Each dashed-line cage must contain digits that add up to the given number.

No digit can repeat within a dashed-line cage.

15. SNAKE

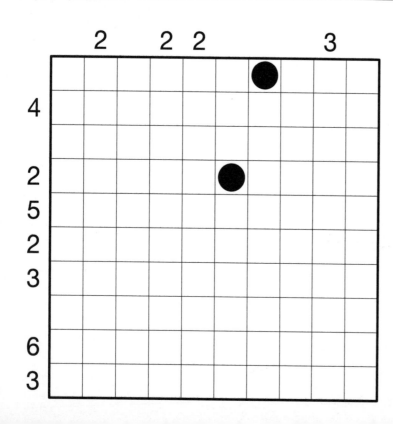

Shade some squares to form a snake that starts and ends at the given squares.

A snake is a single path of adjacent squares that does not branch or cross over itself.

The snake does not touch itself—not even diagonally.

Numbers outside the grid specify the number of squares in their row or column that contain part of the snake.

16. WORD SEARCH—CHRISTMASTIDE

Can you find all of these words or phrases in the grid? They may be written in any direction, including diagonally.

ANGEL
CARDS
CHURCH
DECORATIONS
ELVES
FAMILY
GIFTS
LIGHTS

NOEL
PARTIES
PRESENTS
SANTA
SNOW
STARS
STOCKINGS
TREE

D	L	I	G	H	T	S	S	N	G	G	M	N	E	R
C	Y	M	N	H	E	S	E	E	A	I	T	R	E	E
A	L	N	P	R	C	O	R	H	O	N	F	A	A	E
R	I	L	R	S	C	R	C	A	O	N	S	T	L	C
D	M	E	E	S	G	C	U	E	T	N	T	V	S	E
S	A	L	S	T	E	T	L	H	O	S	E	E	F	W
C	F	A	E	O	F	I	I	I	C	S	S	T	P	G
P	O	I	N	T	T	O	T	R	E	A	C	E	D	R
D	S	O	T	K	P	A	L	R	T	C	L	A	K	H
C	R	S	S	A	R	L	G	C	A	G	H	S	S	I
S	E	S	N	O	A	F	A	E	T	P	T	L	T	A
E	E	G	C	W	O	N	S	S	E	A	G	F	E	T
I	E	E	I	T	T	Y	O	A	T	N	A	S	H
L	D	R	C	P	E	R	S	Y	T	S	Y	S	S	G
R	L	A	S	L	S	G	N	I	K	C	O	T	S	G

17. CIRCULAR MAZE

Can you find a route from the gap at the top to the gap at the bottom of this circular maze?

18. CODEWORD

A codeword is a coded crossword in which every letter has been replaced by a number, indicated by the small digits in the top left corner of each crossword square.

Work out which number represents each letter of the alphabet and use this information to complete the crossword grid.

Use the letters outside the grid, and the empty squares beneath the grid, to keep track of your deductions.

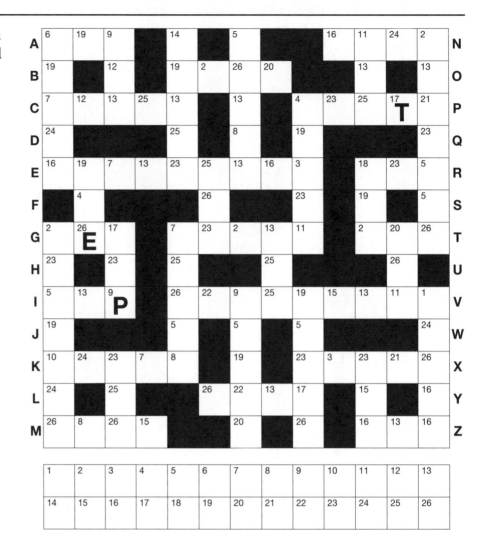

1	2	3	4	5	6	7	8	9	10	11	12	13
14	15	16	17	18	19	20	21	22	23	24	25	26

19. CHRISTMAS GIFT BOXES

Can you rearrange these gift boxes into their correct order? Once properly aligned they will spell out a word associated with Christmas.

20. KAKURO

Place a digit from 1 to 9 into each white square.

Each horizontal run of white squares adds up to the total above the diagonal line to the left of the run, and each vertical run of white squares adds up to the total below the diagonal line above the run.

No digit can be used more than once in any run.

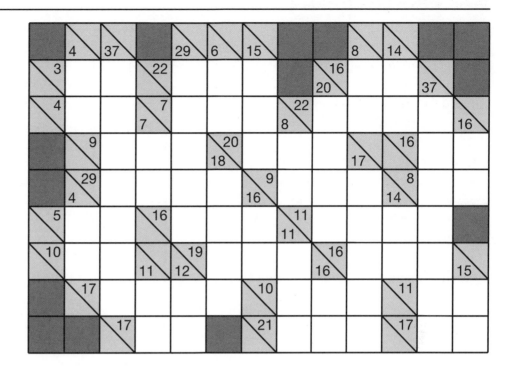

21. SLITHERLINK

Draw a single loop by connecting some dots with horizontal and vertical lines so that each numbered square has the specified number of adjacent line segments.

The loop cannot cross or touch itself.

```
  2 3           3
3         1 3   2     3
    0   3     1 2   2 3
  2 1   0         0
  3 1   2     1
          3     1   0 1
      0         2     2 2
  3 1   3 1     1   2
  1   0   2 3         3
        1           2 1
```

22. RECTANGLES

Draw borders along some grid lines to divide the grid into a set of rectangles, such that each rectangle contains exactly one number.

All grid squares must be contained within exactly one rectangle.

The number inside each rectangle must be exactly equal to the number of grid squares that the rectangle contains, so for example a "4" could only be in a 1 × 4, 2 × 2, or 4 × 1 rectangle.

Note that the term "rectangle" also includes squares.

	6					3			
	6						21		
5									
				5	4			4	
	4				6				
		8						6	
	4							3	9
				3					3

23. CALCUDOKU

Place the numbers 1 to 6 once each into every row and column of the grid, while obeying the region clues.

The value at the top left of each bold-lined region must be obtained when all of the numbers in that region have the given operation (+, -, ×, ÷) applied between them. For - and ÷ operations, begin with the largest number in the region and then subtract or divide by the other numbers in the region in any order.

1−	11+		6×		
	6÷		3−		14+
5÷		12+			
3÷				5×	
	1−		18×		3+
9+			1−		

24. SLANTED SUMS

Place 1 to 6 once each in every row and column.

Numbers outside the grid give the total of the indicated diagonals.

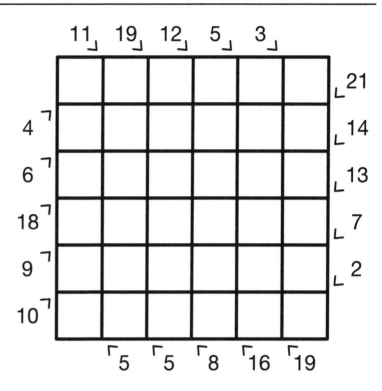

25. QUIZ

Test your knowledge of a specialist subject with this quiz.

Christmas

1. There are two places called "Christmas Island." Which two oceans are they in?

2. The Three Wise Men brought gifts of gold, frankincense, and myrrh—but what exactly *is* myrrh?

3. Which former *American Idol* winner had a hit in 2013 with her *Wrapped in Red* Christmas album?

4. What was the name of the 1942 movie that was the first to feature Bing Crosby's *White Christmas*?

5. On what calendar date is the feast of the Epiphany?

26. FUTOSHIKI

Place 1 to 7 once each into every row and column while obeying the inequality signs.

Greater than (>) signs between some squares indicate that the value in one square is greater than that in another as indicated by the sign. The sign always points toward the smaller number.

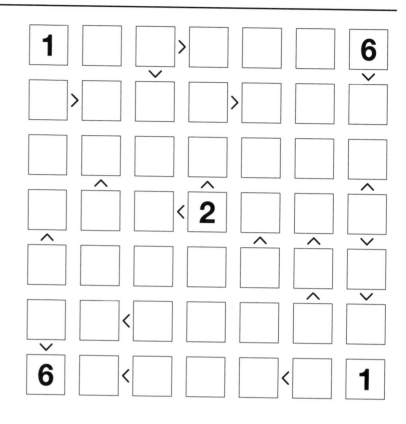

27. NUMBER LINK

Draw a series of separate paths, each connecting a pair of identical numbers.

No more than one path can enter any grid square, and paths can only travel horizontally or vertically, and never diagonally.

28. ARROWWORD

Complete this crossword where all of the clues are given within the grid.

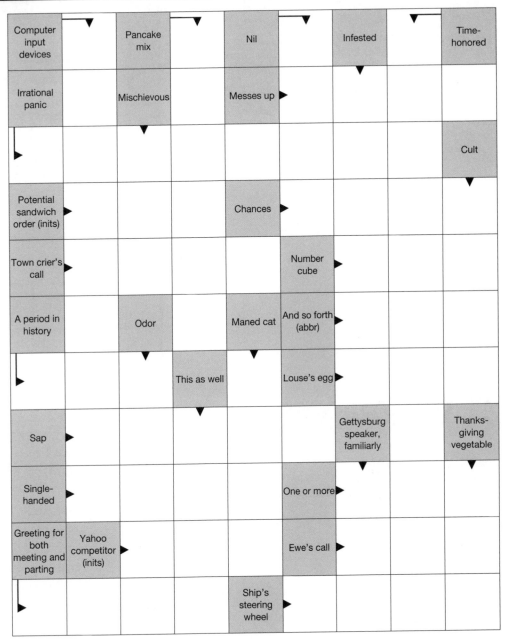

29. CHRISTMAS JUMBLE

Rearrange the following letters to reveal something associated with Christmas.

G G GONE

30. JIGSAW LETTERS

Place A to H once each in every row, column, and bold-lined region.

31. SKYSCRAPERS

Place 1 to 6 once each into every row and column of the grid.

Place digits in the grid in such a way that each given clue number outside the grid represents the number of digits that are "visible" from that point, looking along that clue's row or column.

A digit is visible unless there is a higher digit preceding it, reading in order along that row or column. For example, if a row was "215346" then the 2, 5, and 6 would be visible from the left end (giving a clue of "3" visible digits), since 1 is obscured by the preceding higher 2, and both 3 and 4 are obscured by the preceding higher 5. A clue at the right-hand end of the same row would be "1," since only the 6 would be visible.

32. FITWORD

Place each of the following words into the empty squares, crossword-style.

3 Letters
Cry
Lie

4 Letters
Drop
Dyed
Eave
Rows

5 Letters
Alibi
Cameo

Gawks
Upset

6 Letters
Drives
Scampi
Smiles
Waving

7 Letters
Arrived
Eclipse
Trinity
Undergo

8 Letters
Synonyms
Teaching
Terminal
Unusable

9 Letters
Admirable
Allowance

13 Letters
Objectionable

33. PATH HUNTER

Join dots with horizontal and vertical lines to form a single path which does not touch or cross itself at any point. The start and end of the path are given. Numbers outside the grid specify the number of dots in their row or column that are visited by the path.

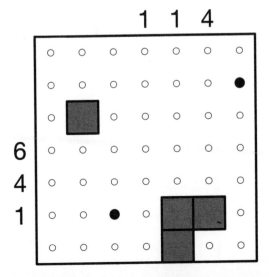

34. TOUCHY

Place A to F once each in every row and column such that two identical letters never touch—not even diagonally.

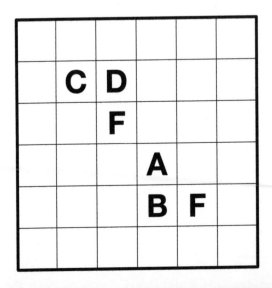

35. SUDOKU

Place 1 to 9 once each into every row, column, and bold-lined 3 × 3 square.

	9						7	
6				9				2
		2	8			6	9	
		1	4			2	5	
	4						1	
		6	9			5	4	
		9	3			1	2	
3				8				5
	2						4	

36. BRIDGES

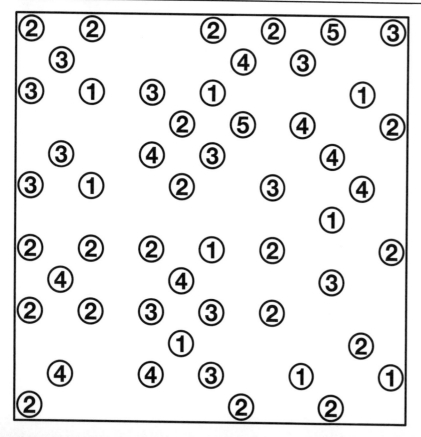

Join circled numbers with horizontal or vertical lines. Each number must have as many lines connected to it as specified by its value.

No more than two lines may join any pair of numbers, and no lines may cross.

The finished layout must connect all numbers, so you can travel between any pair of numbers by following one or more lines.

37. BRIDGE MAZE

Find a path from the entrance at the top of the maze to the exit at the bottom of the maze. The path may cross over or under itself by using the marked bridges.

38. WORD CHAIN

Can you complete this word chain, in order to convert the word at the top into the word at the bottom?

At each step you may change only one letter so as to form a new English word, and you may not rearrange any of the letters.

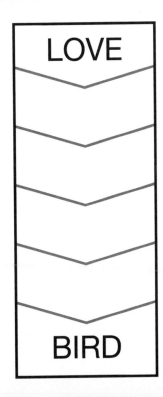

LOVE

BIRD

39. LETTER CIRCLE

How many words can you find in this letter circle? Every word must use the center letter plus two or more of the other letters. No letter can be used more than once in a single word. There is one eight-letter seasonal word to find.

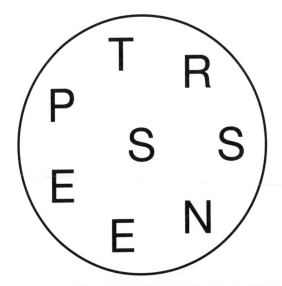

40. PICROSS

Shade in squares in the grid to reveal a picture. Numbers at the start of each row or column reveal, in order from left to right or top to bottom, the length of each consecutive run of shaded squares. There must be a gap of at least one empty square between each run of shaded squares in the same row or column.

Clue: A closer look

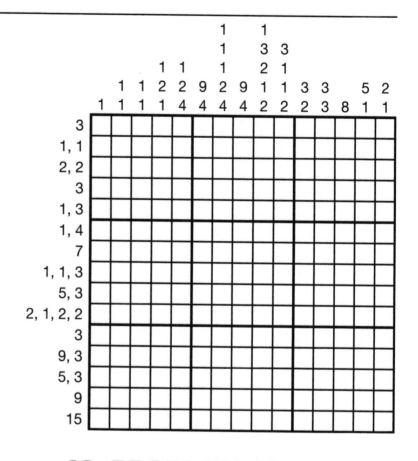

41. WORD RECTANGLE

Can you find the 12-letter word hidden in this Word Rectangle? Find words by moving from letter to touching letter, including diagonally, and without revisiting a square in a single word. How many other words can you find?

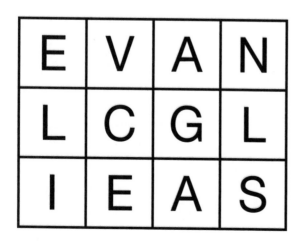

42. BRAIN CHAINS

Without using a calculator or making any written notes, solve these brain chains as quickly as you can. Write the solution in the "Result" box.

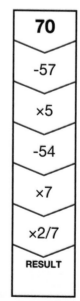

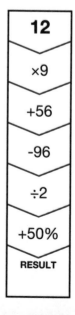

43. CROSSWORD

Solve the clues to complete the crossword grid.

Across

7 Common area of interest (7)
9 Extend a subscription (5)
10 2011 animated movie (3)
11 Noticing (9)
12 Makes (5)
14 Burrows (7)
16 Easily broken (7)
18 Chocolate substitute (5)
19 Association (9)
20 Harden (3)
21 Is in flames (5)
22 Astute (7)

Down

1 Pronoun for the solver of this puzzle (8)
2 Mexican monetary unit (4)
3 Inundates (6)
4 Rehearsal (3,3)
5 Machine designer (8)
6 Drink in large gulps (4)
8 Shift an obligation (4,3,4)
13 Comfort; encourage (8)
15 Deliberate damage (8)
17 Chilliest (6)
18 Statements of belief (6)
19 International book number (inits) (4)
20 Mix a liquid (4)

44. DOMINOES

Draw solid lines to divide the grid to form a complete set of standard dominoes, with exactly one of each domino. A "0" represents a blank on a traditional domino.

Use the checkoff chart to help you keep track of which dominoes you've placed.

1	2	4	5	0	2	1	0
3	3	6	5	1	1	5	2
6	6	2	6	0	0	3	3
3	1	4	6	5	4	3	2
3	2	2	2	6	5	0	1
5	4	4	1	3	0	6	5
0	0	4	6	4	5	1	4

	0	1	2	3	4	5	6	
								0
								1
								2
								3
								4
								5
								6

45. KILLER SUDOKU

Place the digits 1 to 9 once each into every row, column, and bold-lined 3 × 3 square.

Each dashed-line cage must contain digits that add up to the given number.

No digit can repeat within a dashed-line cage.

46. SNAKE

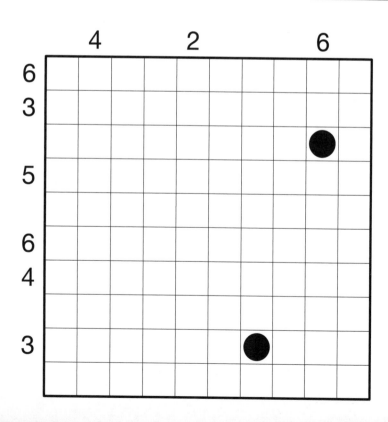

Shade some squares to form a snake that starts and ends at the given squares.

A snake is a single path of adjacent squares that does not branch or cross over itself.

The snake does not touch itself—not even diagonally.

Numbers outside the grid specify the number of squares in their row or column that contain part of the snake.

47. WORD SEARCH—CHRISTMAS DINNER

Can you find all of these words or phrases in the grid? They may be written in any direction, including diagonally.

APPLE PIE
BEEF
BOILED CUSTARD
CANDY CANE
CARROTS
CHESTNUTS
COOKIES
CRANBERRY SAUCE

FRUITCAKE
GINGERBREAD
GRAVY
HAM
MASHED POTATO
PUMPKIN PIE
STUFFING
TURKEY

C	C	P	I	N	P	U	M	P	K	I	N	P	I	E
M	B	H	K	U	A	O	A	U	E	K	D	C	C	C
C	A	D	E	C	I	S	A	Y	E	K	R	U	T	O
M	O	S	A	S	F	C	V	C	I	C	A	O	P	O
F	E	O	H	E	T	A	A	A	G	S	T	U	I	K
R	R	U	E	E	R	N	I	E	Y	O	S	T	D	I
G	I	B	C	G	D	B	U	R	S	E	U	P	F	E
A	L	F	A	Y	U	P	R	T	P	I	C	I	B	S
P	N	E	C	I	O	E	O	E	S	Y	D	G	E	T
P	S	A	D	U	B	R	A	T	G	A	E	E	E	U
L	N	N	A	N	R	G	O	F	A	N	L	A	A	F
E	N	C	A	A	T	E	K	A	C	T	I	U	R	F
P	E	R	C	E	D	T	N	P	E	G	O	G	S	I
I	C	D	B	I	M	O	O	P	R	B	B	M	D	N
E	T	O	C	Y	N	P	R	T	N	N	O	E	A	G

48. CIRCULAR MAZE

Can you find a route from the gap at the top to the gap at the bottom of this circular maze?

49. CODEWORD

A codeword is a coded crossword in which every letter has been replaced by a number, indicated by the small digits in the top left corner of each crossword square.

Work out which number represents each letter of the alphabet and use this information to complete the crossword grid.

Use the letters outside the grid, and the empty squares beneath the grid, to keep track of your deductions.

Codeword grid (row labels A–M on the left, N–Z on the right):

A	8	■	24	■	26	■	6	■		18	24	6	■
B	21	3	11	7	6	24	16	8	■		17	■	8
C	18	■	26	■	8	■	18		19	18	10	16	
D	■	21	18	24	23	8	■	9	11	11		3	
E	■	6	■	11	■		18	10	18	■		17	
F	5	18	8	8	17	4	6	15	25	■	11	18	23
G	18	■	10	■		6	■	22	■	3 (R)		6	
H	17	4	25	■	26	17	8	18	8	16 (T)	6	3	8
I	15	■		14	20	13	■		9		11	■	
J	19	■	9	6	19	■		12	20	11	16	6	■
K	11	25	6	2	■	24	■	8		9	■	18	
L	1	■	15	■	21	11	9	6	3	17	13	22	
M	■	11	15	26 (D)	■	13	■	8		22	■	11	

Letter/number key:

1	2	3	4	5	6	7	8	9	10	11	12	13

14	15	16	17	18	19	20	21	22	23	24	25	26

50. CHRISTMAS GIFT BOXES

Can you rearrange these gift boxes into their correct order? Once properly aligned they will spell out a word associated with Christmas.

G · HO · S · IN · PP

51. KAKURO

Place a digit from 1 to 9 into each white square.

Each horizontal run of white squares adds up to the total above the diagonal line to the left of the run, and each vertical run of white squares adds up to the total below the diagonal line above the run.

No digit can be used more than once in any run.

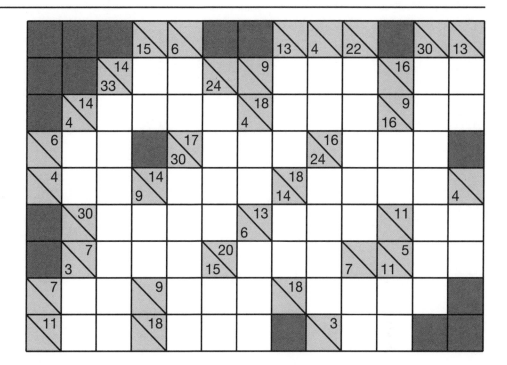

52. SLITHERLINK

Draw a single loop by connecting some dots with horizontal and vertical lines so that each numbered square has the specified number of adjacent line segments.

The loop cannot cross or touch itself.

53. RECTANGLES

Draw borders along some grid lines to divide the grid into a set of rectangles, such that each rectangle contains exactly one number.

All grid squares must be contained within exactly one rectangle.

The number inside each rectangle must be exactly equal to the number of grid squares that the rectangle contains, so for example a "4" could only be in a 1 × 4, 2 × 2, or 4 × 1 rectangle.

Note that the term "rectangle" also includes squares.

	16					2			
							5		
				3	4				
5									8
	3								
	8					2			
	3								
	6						8		12
3			12						

54. CALCUDOKU

2−	72×		2÷	2÷	
		20×		10×	
3+				2−	
9+		12×	9+	4×	
10×				36×	15×
4×					

Place the numbers 1 to 6 once each into every row and column of the grid, while obeying the region clues.

The value at the top left of each bold-lined region must be obtained when all of the numbers in that region have the given operation (+, -, ×, ÷) applied between them. For - and ÷ operations, begin with the largest number in the region and then subtract or divide by the other numbers in the region in any order.

55. SLANTED SUMS

Place 1 to 6 once each in every row and column.

Numbers outside the grid give the total of the indicated diagonals.

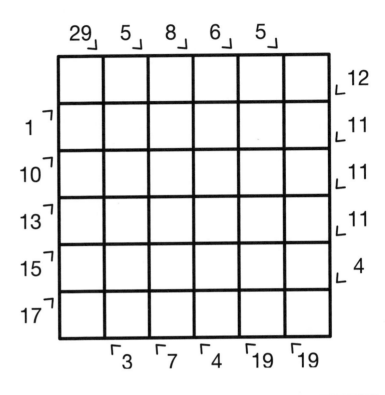

56. QUIZ

Test your knowledge of a specialist subject with this quiz.

Ancient Greece

1. How many Muses were there in Greek mythology?

2. Who was the Parthenon in Athens built to honor?

3. In ancient Greece, what was an "obol"?

4. If you went to the "agora," where would you be?

5. Which Greek mathematician first calculated the value of "pi"?

57. FUTOSHIKI

Place 1 to 7 once each into every row and column while obeying the inequality signs.

Greater than (>) signs between some squares indicate that the value in one square is greater than that in another as indicated by the sign. The sign always points toward the smaller number.

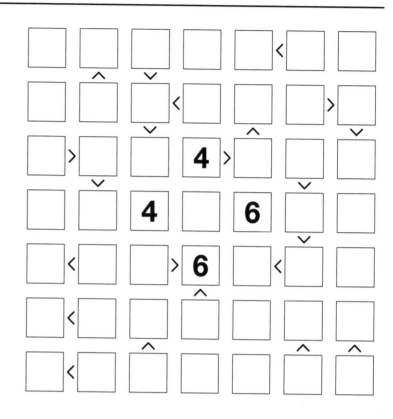

58. NUMBER LINK

1	2							3
	4			5				5
								3
			6	7				
	4				8	9		
			2			7		
10			1			11		
	8	6						
							9	
				10	11			

Draw a series of separate paths, each connecting a pair of identical numbers.

No more than one path can enter any grid square, and paths can only travel horizontally or vertically, and never diagonally.

59. ARROWWORD

Complete this crossword where all of the clues are given within the grid.

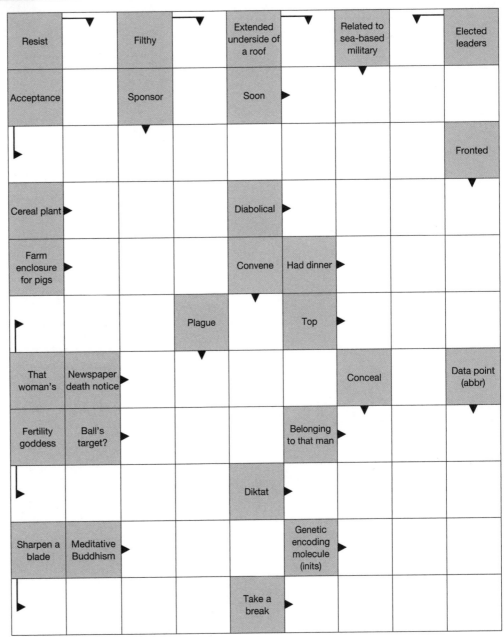

60. CHRISTMAS JUMBLE

Rearrange the following letters to reveal something associated with Christmas.

CASUAL TANS

61. JIGSAW LETTERS

Place A to H once each in every row, column, and bold-lined region.

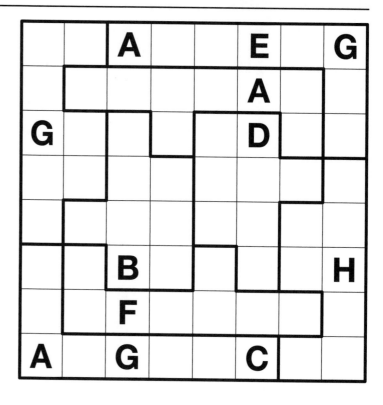

62. SKYSCRAPERS

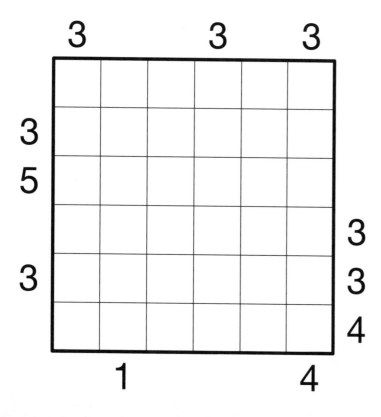

Place 1 to 6 once each into every row and column of the grid.

Place digits in the grid in such a way that each given clue number outside the grid represents the number of digits that are "visible" from that point, looking along that clue's row or column.

A digit is visible unless there is a higher digit preceding it, reading in order along that row or column. For example, if a row was "214356" then the 2, 4, 5, and 6 would be visible from the left end (giving a clue of "5" visible digits), since 1 is obscured by the preceding higher 2, and 3 is obscured by the preceding higher 4. A clue at the right-hand end of the same row would be "1," since only the 6 would be visible.

63. FITWORD

Place each of the following words into the empty squares, crossword-style.

4 Letters
Dash
Itch
Plus
Pure

Iodine
Lessen
Needle
Oxygen
Tomato

Snobbery
Verbatim

11 Letters
Environment
Transplants

5 Letters
Glory
Order

7 Letters
Doctors
Unlucky

6 Letters
Angora
Eureka
Gossip

8 Letters
Friendly
Nonsense

64. PATH HUNTER

Join dots with horizontal and vertical lines to form a single path which does not touch or cross itself at any point. The start and end of the path are given. Numbers outside the grid specify the number of dots in their row or column that are visited by the path.

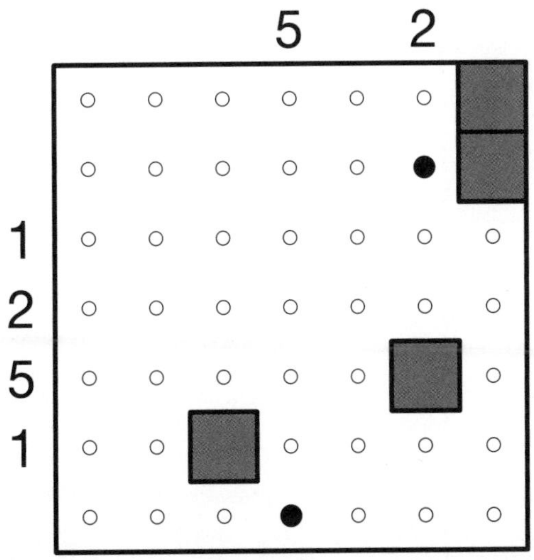

65. TOUCHY

Place A to F once each in every row and column such that two identical letters never touch—not even diagonally.

66. SUDOKU

Place 1 to 9 once each into every row, column, and bold-lined 3 × 3 square.

8			2		1			3
	2	1	3		8	9	4	
	6		7		5		2	
3	1	4				7	6	8
2	5	7				4	1	9
	4		5		9		8	
	3	5	8		6	1	7	
1			4		7			6

67. BRIDGES

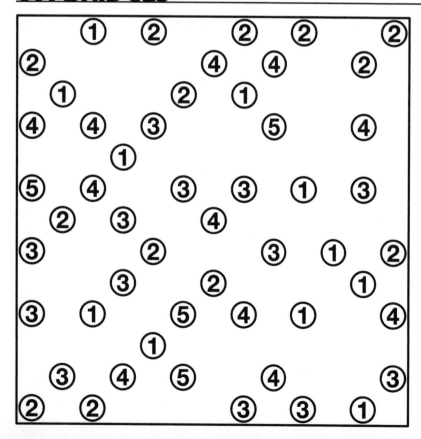

Join circled numbers with horizontal or vertical lines. Each number must have as many lines connected to it as specified by its value.

No more than two lines may join any pair of numbers, and no lines may cross.

The finished layout must connect all numbers, so you can travel between any pair of numbers by following one or more lines.

68. BRIDGE MAZE

Find a path from the entrance at the top of the maze to the exit at the bottom of the maze. The path may cross over or under itself by using the marked bridges.

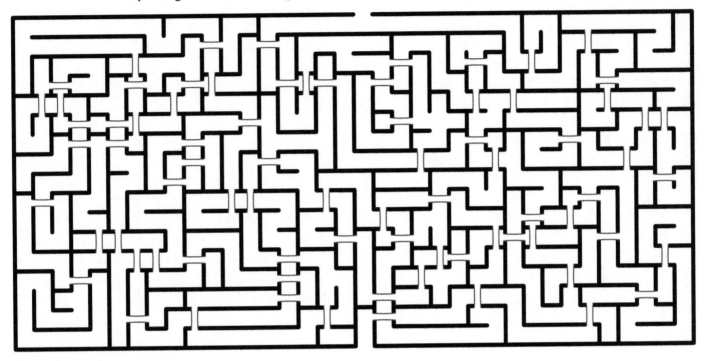

69. WORD CHAIN

Can you complete this word chain, in order to convert the word at the top into the word at the bottom?

At each step you may change only one letter so as to form a new English word, and you may not rearrange any of the letters.

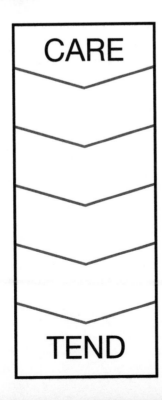

CARE

TEND

70. LETTER CIRCLE

How many words can you find in this letter circle? Every word must use the center letter plus two or more of the other letters. No letter can be used more than once in a single word. There is one eight-letter seasonal word to find.

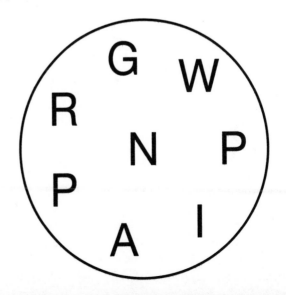

71. PICROSS

Shade in squares in the grid to reveal a picture. Numbers at the start of each row or column reveal, in order from left to right or top to bottom, the length of each consecutive run of shaded squares. There must be a gap of at least one empty square between each run of shaded squares in the same row or column.

Clue: Seasonal decoration

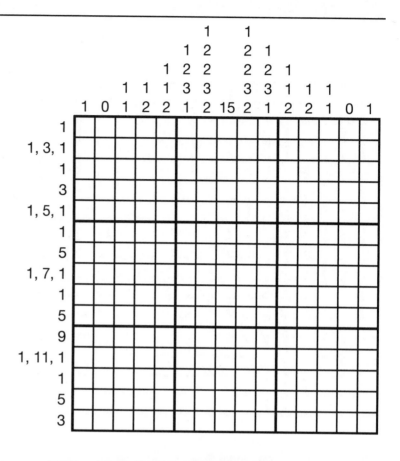

72. WORD RECTANGLE

Can you find the 12-letter word hidden in this Word Rectangle? Find words by moving from letter to touching letter, including diagonally, and without revisiting a square in a single word. How many other words can you find?

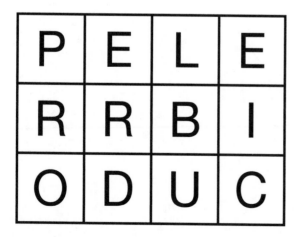

P	E	L	E
R	R	B	I
O	D	U	C

73. BRAIN CHAINS

Without using a calculator or making any written notes, solve these brain chains as quickly as you can. Write the solution in the "Result" box.

50
÷2
√
+60%
×1/2
×11
RESULT

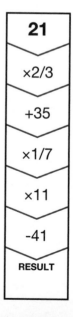

21
×2/3
+35
×1/7
×11
−41
RESULT

74. CROSSWORD

Solve the clues to complete the crossword grid.

Across
1 Guided (7)
5 Give off (4)
9 Knock down with a vehicle (3,4)
10 Baseball targets (5)
11 Obvious (5)
12 Mythical sea monster (6)
14 Straying from accepted standards (6)
16 Artist's room (6)
18 Influence (6)
19 Gradually disappears (5)
22 Worth; goodness (5)
23 Ailment (7)
24 Cheek (4)
25 Use again (7)

Down
2 Uptight (5)
3 The natural world (11)
4 "I've worked it out!" (6)
6 Deceive (7)
7 Examination (4)
8 Chirping insect (7)
10 Attractively (11)
13 Own (7)
15 Institutional fixes (7)
17 Delete or cross out (6)
20 Inhabit (5)
21 Large, flightless birds (4)

75. DOMINOES

Draw solid lines to divide the grid to form a complete set of standard dominoes, with exactly one of each domino. A "0" represents a blank on a traditional domino.

Use the checkoff chart to help you keep track of which dominoes you've placed.

0	1	1	5	2	1	6	1
4	6	6	1	5	0	3	0
4	3	3	3	6	0	0	6
2	6	2	2	1	5	2	5
5	4	0	2	3	6	4	5
2	0	4	4	3	6	4	1
2	3	4	5	3	1	5	0

	0	1	2	3	4	5	6	
								0
								1
								2
								3
								4
								5
								6

76. KILLER SUDOKU

Place the digits 1 to 9 once each into every row, column, and bold-lined 3 × 3 square.

Each dashed-line cage must contain digits that add up to the given number.

No digit can repeat within a dashed-line cage.

77. SNAKE

Shade some squares to form a snake that starts and ends at the given squares.

A snake is a single path of adjacent squares that does not branch or cross over itself.

The snake does not touch itself—not even diagonally.

Numbers outside the grid specify the number of squares in their row or column that contain part of the snake.

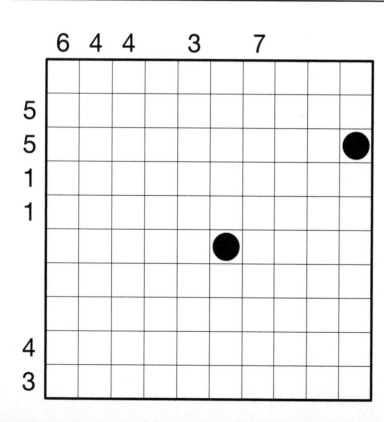

78. WORD SEARCH—CHRISTMAS DECORATIONS

Can you find all of these words or phrases in the grid? They may be written in any direction, including diagonally.

CANDLES
CANDY CANES
CHOCOLATES
CHRISTMAS TREE
GARLANDS
GLASS
INFLATABLES
MISTLETOE

NATIVITY SCENE
OUTDOOR LIGHTS
REINDEER
STARS
STOCKINGS
TINSEL
TOYS
WREATHS

S	R	A	T	E	C	N	C	D	T	T	E	C	N	S
H	E	C	A	N	D	Y	C	A	N	E	S	A	C	C
A	E	O	T	E	L	T	S	I	M	E	S	O	H	E
S	D	C	G	C	H	T	B	N	I	K	S	O	R	T
F	N	O	T	S	E	I	S	C	N	O	C	S	I	S
C	I	N	U	Y	Y	S	S	Y	F	O	A	T	S	R
W	E	O	U	T	D	O	O	R	L	I	G	H	T	S
G	R	C	S	I	I	T	T	A	A	N	G	A	M	G
G	A	E	S	V	E	N	T	C	T	T	S	H	A	N
I	S	R	A	I	U	E	S	A	A	S	S	V	S	I
A	T	S	L	T	S	O	S	E	B	N	N	L	T	K
L	O	H	G	A	H	R	T	C	L	C	D	E	R	C
G	G	O	A	N	N	S	L	D	E	G	T	L	E	O
S	I	I	S	A	T	D	C	H	S	I	E	T	E	T
R	O	E	C	C	S	C	S	I	I	A	S	D	T	S

79. CIRCULAR MAZE

Can you find a route from the gap at the top to the gap at the bottom of this circular maze?

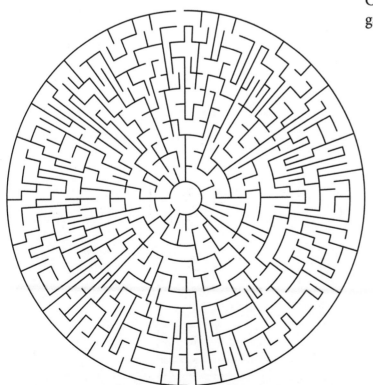

80. CODEWORD

A codeword is a coded crossword in which every letter has been replaced by a number, indicated by the small digits in the top left corner of each crossword square.

Work out which number represents each letter of the alphabet and use this information to complete the crossword grid.

Use the letters outside the grid, and the empty squares beneath the grid, to keep track of your deductions.

The grid letters down the right-hand side read: N O P Q R S T U V W X Y Z

Given letters in the grid: 19 = A, 3 = N, 23 = I

1	2	3	4	5	6	7	8	9	10	11	12	13

14	15	16	17	18	19	20	21	22	23	24	25	26

81. CHRISTMAS GIFT BOXES

Can you rearrange these gift boxes into their correct order? Once properly aligned they will spell out a word associated with Christmas.

NE

YF

SS

JO

UL

82. KAKURO

Place a digit from 1 to 9 into each white square.

Each horizontal run of white squares adds up to the total above the diagonal line to the left of the run, and each vertical run of white squares adds up to the total below the diagonal line above the run.

No digit can be used more than once in any run.

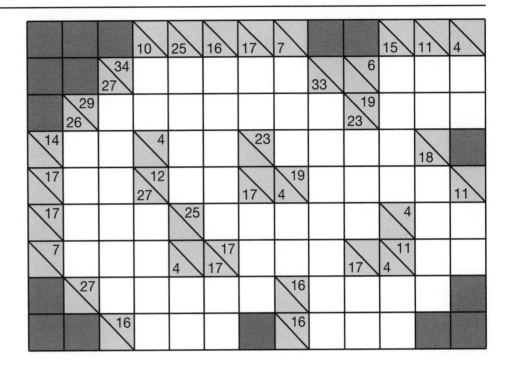

83. SLITHERLINK

Draw a single loop by connecting some dots with horizontal and vertical lines so that each numbered square has the specified number of adjacent line segments.

The loop cannot cross or touch itself.

84. RECTANGLES

Draw borders along some grid lines to divide the grid into a set of rectangles, such that each rectangle contains exactly one number.

All grid squares must be contained within exactly one rectangle.

The number inside each rectangle must be exactly equal to the number of grid squares that the rectangle contains, so for example a "4" could only be in a 1 × 4, 2 × 2, or 4 × 1 rectangle.

Note that the term "rectangle" also includes squares.

4						4			
	4				2	2			
			12		4				
									18
			14				4		
		6			6		4		
3				8					
		3				2			

85. CALCUDOKU

Place the numbers 1 to 6 once each into every row and column of the grid, while obeying the region clues.

The value at the top left of each bold-lined region must be obtained when all of the numbers in that region have the given operation (+, -, ×, ÷) applied between them. For - and ÷ operations, begin with the largest number in the region and then subtract or divide by the other numbers in the region in any order.

6÷		36×		2×	11+
10×		1-			
1-			60×	4-	
6+				1-	
24×	5+	8+		3÷	
				9+	

86. SLANTED SUMS

Place 1 to 6 once each in every row and column.

Numbers outside the grid give the total of the indicated diagonals.

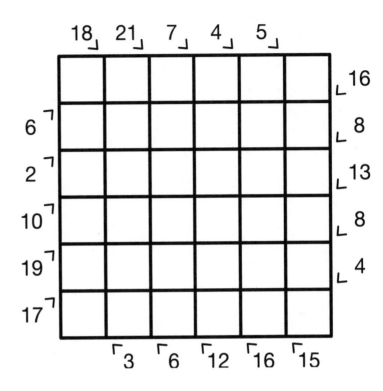

87. QUIZ

Test your knowledge of a specialist subject with this quiz.

Music

1. Which state is most associated with the ukulele?

2. What other common name is used to refer to timpani percussion?

3. Which musical features the song *Defying Gravity*?

4. Which Queen song, famously featured in *Wayne's World*, has the lyric, "Mama, just killed a man"?

5. Which composer wrote the music for *West Side Story*?

88. FUTOSHIKI

Place 1 to 7 once each into every row and column while obeying the inequality signs.

Greater than (>) signs between some squares indicate that the value in one square is greater than that in another as indicated by the sign. The sign always points toward the smaller number.

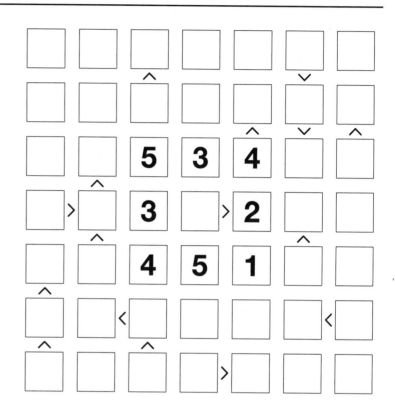

89. NUMBER LINK

Draw a series of separate paths, each connecting a pair of identical numbers.

No more than one path can enter any grid square, and paths can only travel horizontally or vertically, and never diagonally.

			1					
	2	3			2	4		
	1					5		3
6								
7			7			8		
6								
9				9	10			
	11				11	5		4
						10		8

90. ARROWWORD

Complete this crossword where all of the clues are given within the grid.

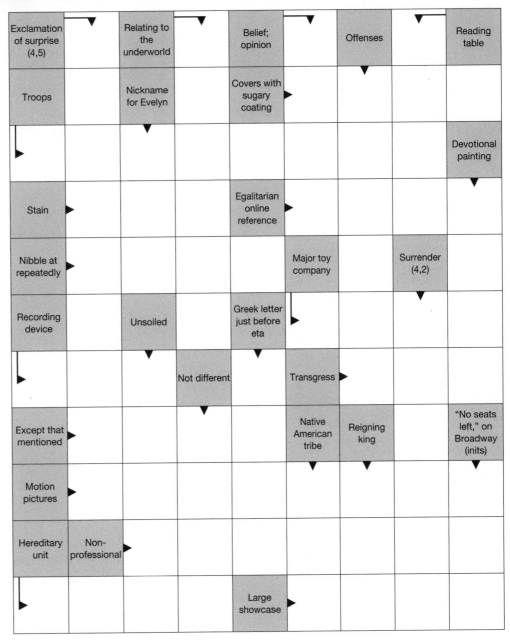

Exclamation of surprise (4,5)	▼	Relating to the underworld	▼	Belief; opinion		Offenses		▼	Reading table
Troops		Nickname for Evelyn		Covers with sugary coating	▶		▼		
◣			▼						Devotional painting
Stain	▶			Egalitarian online reference	▶				▼
Nibble at repeatedly	▶					Major toy company		Surrender (4,2)	
Recording device		Unsoiled		Greek letter just before eta		▶		▼	
◣			▼	Not different		Transgress	▶		
Except that mentioned	▶			▼		Native American tribe	Reigning king		"No seats left," on Broadway (inits)
Motion pictures	▶						▼		▼
Hereditary unit	Non-professional	▶							
◣				Large showcase	▶				

91. CHRISTMAS JUMBLE

Rearrange the following letters to reveal someone associated with Christmas.

RINGLESS KIRK

92. JIGSAW LETTERS

Place A to H once each in every row,
column, and bold-lined region.

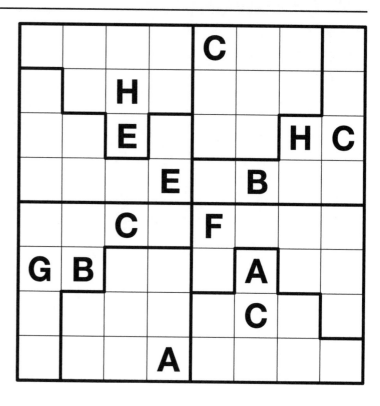

93. SKYSCRAPERS

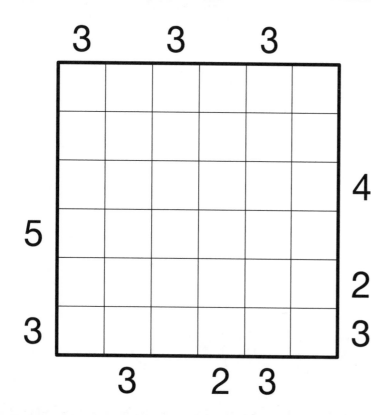

Place 1 to 6 once each into every row and
column of the grid.

Place digits in the grid in such a way that
each given clue number outside the grid
represents the number of digits that are
"visible" from that point, looking along that
clue's row or column.

A digit is visible unless there is a higher
digit preceding it, reading in order along
that row or column. For example, if a row
was "214356" then the 2, 4, 5, and 6 would
be visible from the left end (giving a clue of
"5" visible digits), since 1 is obscured by the
preceding higher 2, and 3 is obscured by
the preceding higher 4. A clue at the right-
hand end of the same row would be "1,"
since only the 6 would be visible.

94. FITWORD

Place each of the following words into the empty squares, crossword-style.

3 Letters
Ads
Eel
Ego
Oil

5 Letters
Alone
Evade
Igloo
Opera
Repel
Style

6 Letters
Animal
Arenas
Ascend
Likely
Messes
Raised

7 Letters
Indulge
Network
Rotates
Sampler

9 Letters
Amusement
Discounts
Promotion
Uniformly

11 Letters
Citizenship
Unnecessary

95. PATH HUNTER

Join dots with horizontal and vertical lines to form a single path which does not touch or cross itself at any point. The start and end of the path are given. Numbers outside the grid specify the number of dots in their row or column that are visited by the path.

96. TOUCHY

Place A to F once each in every row and column such that two identical letters never touch—not even diagonally.

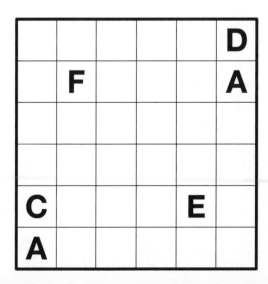

97. SUDOKU

Place 1 to 9 once each into every row, column, and bold-lined 3 × 3 square.

		8	5			4	9		
	7		6			2		8	
4				9					7
2	4							6	5
		7					8		
8	3							4	9
1				5					6
	2		1			6		9	
		5	2			9	4		

98. BRIDGES

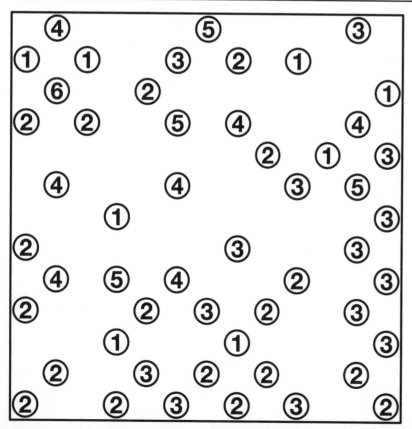

Join circled numbers with horizontal or vertical lines. Each number must have as many lines connected to it as specified by its value.

No more than two lines may join any pair of numbers, and no lines may cross.

The finished layout must connect all numbers, so you can travel between any pair of numbers by following one or more lines.

99. BRIDGE MAZE

Find a path from the entrance at the top of the maze to the exit at the bottom of the maze. The path may cross over or under itself by using the marked bridges.

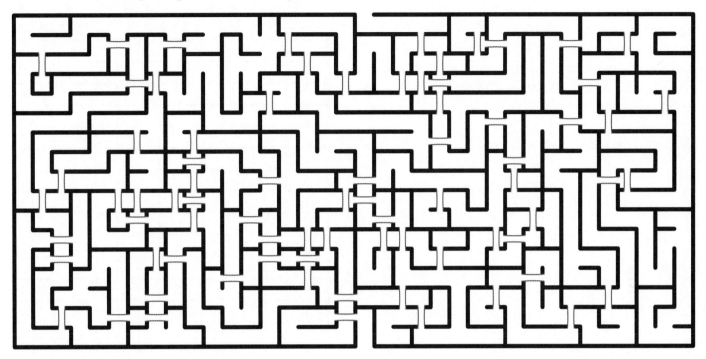

100. WORD CHAIN

Can you complete this word chain, in order to convert the word at the top into the word at the bottom?

At each step you may change only one letter so as to form a new English word, and you may not rearrange any of the letters.

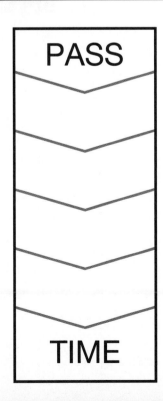

PASS

TIME

101. LETTER CIRCLE

How many words can you find in this letter circle? Every word must use the center letter plus two or more of the other letters. No letter can be used more than once in a single word. There is one eight-letter seasonal word to find.

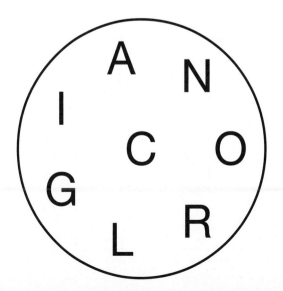

102. PICROSS

Shade in squares in the grid to reveal a picture. Numbers at the start of each row or column reveal, in order from left to right or top to bottom, the length of each consecutive run of shaded squares. There must be a gap of at least one empty square between each run of shaded squares in the same row or column.

Clue: Wake-up call

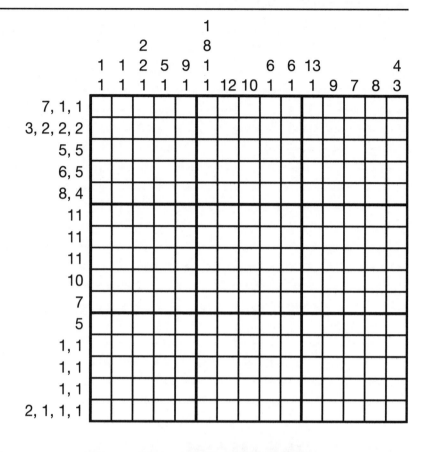

103. WORD RECTANGLE

Can you find the 12-letter word hidden in this Word Rectangle? Find words by moving from letter to touching letter, including diagonally, and without revisiting a square in a single word. How many other words can you find?

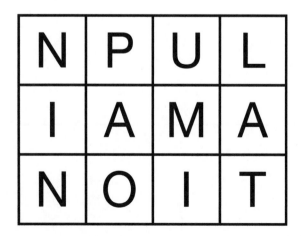

104. BRAIN CHAINS

Without using a calculator or making any written notes, solve these brain chains as quickly as you can. Write the solution in the "Result" box.

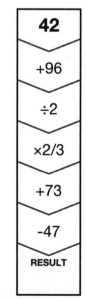

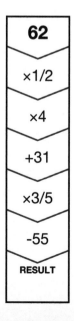

105. CROSSWORD

Solve the clues to complete the crossword grid.

Across

- **1** Noises (6)
- **4** "Stay still!" (6)
- **9** Putrefy (3)
- **10** Abrasive polishing sheet (9)
- **11** Distance units (5)
- **12** Advanced in years (7)
- **14** Surplus to requirements (11)
- **17** Clothed (7)
- **18** *Pacman* and *Mario Bros* (5)
- **20** Pocket money, perhaps (9)
- **22** Female rabbit (3)
- **23** Nun (6)
- **24** Written papers (6)

Down

- **1** Squirts (6)
- **2** Articulate (5)
- **3** Calamities (9)
- **5** Congressman (abbr) (3)
- **6** Ruler of multiple countries (7)
- **7** Before the expected time (5)
- **8** Self-contained (11)
- **13** Planners (9)
- **15** Provokes (7)
- **16** Evaluate (6)
- **17** Calls (5)
- **19** TV, radio, print, and so on (5)
- **21** Triangle of railway track (3)

106. DOMINOES

Draw solid lines to divide the grid to form a complete set of standard dominoes, with exactly one of each domino. A "0" represents a blank on a traditional domino.

Use the checkoff chart to help you keep track of which dominoes you've placed.

0	3	4	5	1	0	5	6
0	0	1	6	1	3	0	2
4	0	6	6	3	3	1	5
2	6	1	6	2	5	4	5
3	3	1	3	2	2	4	0
2	0	4	1	5	5	2	4
1	5	6	3	2	4	6	4

0	1	2	3	4	5	6	
							0
							1
							2
							3
							4
							5
							6

107. KILLER SUDOKU

Place the digits 1 to 9 once each into every row, column, and bold-lined 3 × 3 square.

Each dashed-line cage must contain digits that add up to the given number.

No digit can repeat within a dashed-line cage.

108. SNAKE

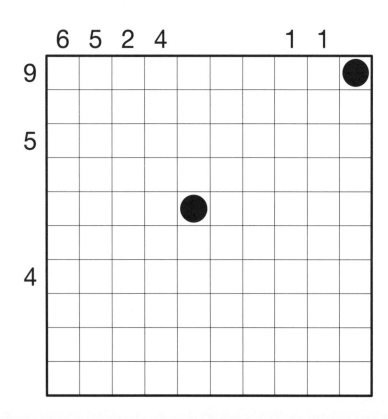

Shade some squares to form a snake that starts and ends at the given squares.

A snake is a single path of adjacent squares that does not branch or cross over itself.

The snake does not touch itself—not even diagonally.

Numbers outside the grid specify the number of squares in their row or column that contain part of the snake.

109. WORD SEARCH—CHRISTMAS SONGS

Can you find all of these words or phrases in the grid? They may be written in any direction, including diagonally.

BLUE CHRISTMAS
COOL YULE
DECK THE ROOFTOP
FELIZ NAVIDAD
HAPPY HOLIDAY
LET IT SNOW
LITTLE SAINT NICK
MARY'S BOY CHILD
MUST BE SANTA
MY ONLY WISH
RUN RUDOLPH RUN
SANTA BABY
SILVER BELLS
SLEIGH RIDE
SUZY SNOWFLAKE
WHITE CHRISTMAS

L	S	I	Y	Y	T	I	L	F	R	C	P	Y	A	W
G	I	A	P	A	I	I	R	E	L	O	N	S	O	E
I	L	T	O	D	B	M	A	L	E	O	U	A	E	L
O	V	N	T	I	L	A	M	I	K	L	R	M	D	D
S	E	A	F	L	U	R	A	Z	A	Y	H	T	I	M
H	R	S	O	O	E	Y	Y	N	L	U	P	S	R	Y
S	B	E	O	H	C	S	B	A	F	L	L	I	H	O
E	E	B	R	Y	H	B	A	V	W	E	O	R	G	N
H	L	T	E	P	R	O	B	I	O	T	D	H	I	L
A	L	S	H	P	I	Y	A	D	N	I	U	C	E	Y
N	S	U	T	A	S	C	T	A	S	T	R	E	L	W
Y	N	M	K	H	T	H	N	D	Y	S	N	T	S	I
I	H	R	C	G	M	I	A	H	Z	N	U	I	V	S
D	A	O	E	F	A	L	S	I	U	O	R	H	C	H
R	W	L	D	O	S	D	E	E	S	W	E	W	K	K

110. CIRCULAR MAZE

Can you find a route from the gap at the top to the gap at the bottom of this circular maze?

111. CODEWORD

A codeword is a coded crossword in which every letter has been replaced by a number, indicated by the small digits in the top left corner of each crossword square.

Work out which number represents each letter of the alphabet and use this information to complete the crossword grid.

Use the letters outside the grid, and the empty squares beneath the grid, to keep track of your deductions.

	1	2	3	4	5	6	7	8	9	10	11	12	13	
A	16	18	6	9	■	25	■	12	■	18	24	20	23	N
B	6	■	1	■	20	21	6	22	11	■	18 (O)	■	6	O
C	15	8	4	16	■	6	■	4	■	9	24	22	4	P
D	25	■	8	6	26	8	■	20	3	6	25	■	20	Q
E	■	11	■	26	■	26	6 (U)	3	■	5	■	26	■	R
F	3	8	4	6	26	20	■	8	19	8	1	20	8	S
G	■	25	■	■	20	■	■	■	18	■	■	13	■	T
H	25	10	20	1	2	20	■	3 (M)	18	25	8	22	12	U
I	■	8	■	18	■	3	18	8	■	10	■	16	■	V
J	25	■	17	18	26	20	■	25	9	8	16	■	8	W
K	14	20	1	11	■	26	■	25	■	3	18	5	25	X
L	22	■	20	■	18	16	1	20	25	■	24	■	14	Y
M	9	8	7	22	■	20	■	25	■	18	4	6	25	Z

1	2	3	4	5	6	7	8	9	10	11	12	13
14	15	16	17	18	19	20	21	22	23	24	25	26

112. CHRISTMAS GIFT BOXES

Can you rearrange these gift boxes into their correct order? Once properly aligned they will spell out a place associated with Christmas.

113. KAKURO

Place a digit from 1 to 9 into each white square.

Each horizontal run of white squares adds up to the total above the diagonal line to the left of the run, and each vertical run of white squares adds up to the total below the diagonal line above the run.

No digit can be used more than once in any run.

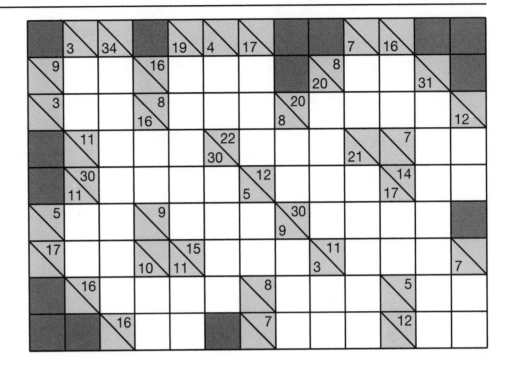

114. SLITHERLINK

Draw a single loop by connecting some dots with horizontal and vertical lines so that each numbered square has the specified number of adjacent line segments.

The loop cannot cross or touch itself.

115. RECTANGLES

Draw borders along some grid lines to divide the grid into a set of rectangles, such that each rectangle contains exactly one number.

All grid squares must be contained within exactly one rectangle.

The number inside each rectangle must be exactly equal to the number of grid squares that the rectangle contains, so for example a "4" could only be in a 1 × 4, 2 × 2, or 4 × 1 rectangle.

Note that the term "rectangle" also includes squares.

			5			5			
				5				3	
							2		
3				10					
				6		4			
								6	4
	8			12				2	
							3	3	3
		4			4				
		3			5				

116. CALCUDOKU

Place the numbers 1 to 6 once each into every row and column of the grid, while obeying the region clues.

The value at the top left of each bold-lined region must be obtained when all of the numbers in that region have the given operation (+, -, ×, ÷) applied between them. For - and ÷ operations, begin with the largest number in the region and then subtract or divide by the other numbers in the region in any order.

8+	12×		7+		6+
	6×	2-		24×	
24×		1-			
		2×		20×	
2-		15×			4-
	8+		5-		

117. SLANTED SUMS

Place 1 to 6 once each in every row and column.

Numbers outside the grid give the total of the indicated diagonals.

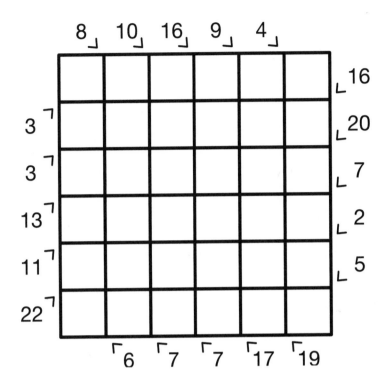

118. QUIZ

Test your knowledge of a specialist subject with this quiz.

Literature

1. Who wrote the novel *The Da Vinci Code*?

2. What do the C and S stand for in the name of *The Lion, the Witch and the Wardrobe* author, "C. S. Lewis"?

3. What is the full title of the third *Harry Potter* book?

4. Anna Sewell is most famous for writing which classic 1877 novel about animal welfare?

5. What is the title of Harper Lee's second published novel, published 55 years after *To Kill a Mockingbird*?

119. FUTOSHIKI

Place 1 to 7 once each into every row and column while obeying the inequality signs.

Greater than (>) signs between some squares indicate that the value in one square is greater than that in another as indicated by the sign. The sign always points toward the smaller number.

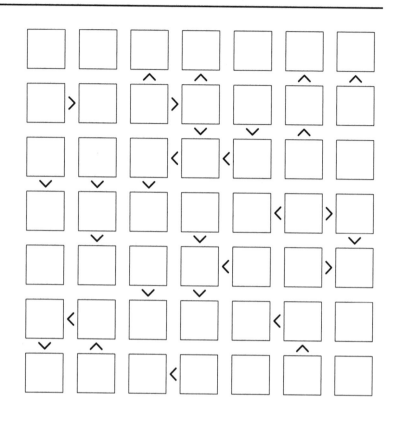

120. NUMBER LINK

1	2	3		4			
				3	5		6
						4	
7		2		6		1	
8					9		
	8	7				9	
			10				
	11		11		5		
			10				

Draw a series of separate paths, each connecting a pair of identical numbers.

No more than one path can enter any grid square, and paths can only travel horizontally or vertically, and never diagonally.

121. ARROWWORD

Complete this crossword where all of the clues are given within the grid.

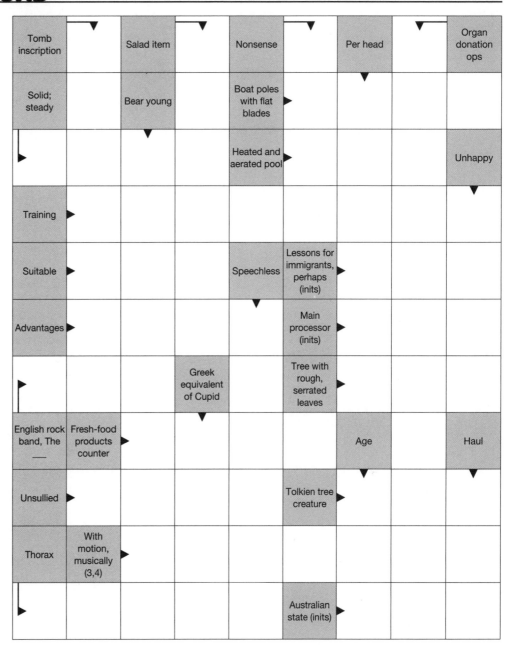

122. CHRISTMAS JUMBLE

Rearrange the following letters to reveal something associated with Christmas.

MERRIEST CHATS

123. JIGSAW LETTERS

Place A to H once each in every row, column, and bold-lined region.

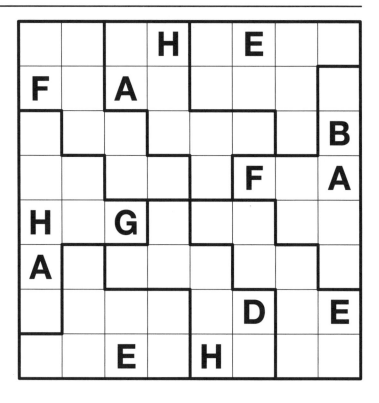

124. SKYSCRAPERS

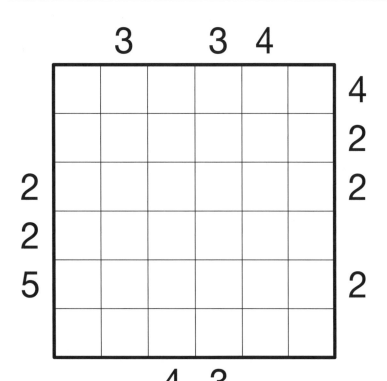

Place 1 to 6 once each into every row and column of the grid.

Place digits in the grid in such a way that each given clue number outside the grid represents the number of digits that are "visible" from that point, looking along that clue's row or column.

A digit is visible unless there is a higher digit preceding it, reading in order along that row or column. For example, if a row was "214356" then the 2, 4, 5, and 6 would be visible from the left end (giving a clue of "5" visible digits), since 1 is obscured by the preceding higher 2, and 3 is obscured by the preceding higher 4. A clue at the right-hand end of the same row would be "1," since only the 6 would be visible.

125. FITWORD

Place each of the following words into the empty squares, crossword-style.

3 Letters
Bar
Set

4 Letters
Used
Yard

5 Letters
Abyss
Bases
Edges
Enemy
Ensue

Lying
Paste
Pilot
Stash
Weigh

6 Letters
Absent
Apathy
Delays
Obeyed

7 Letters
Improve

Orbital
Suggest
Tableau

9 Letters
Designers
Economics

11 Letters
Contentious
Recognition

126. PATH HUNTER

Join dots with horizontal and vertical lines to form a single path which does not touch or cross itself at any point. The start and end of the path are given. Numbers outside the grid specify the number of dots in their row or column that are visited by the path.

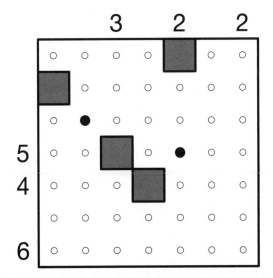

127. TOUCHY

Place A to F once each in every row and column such that two identical letters never touch—not even diagonally.

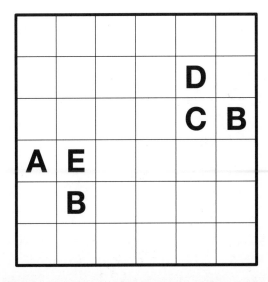

128. SUDOKU

Place 1 to 9 once each into every row, column, and bold-lined 3 × 3 square.

	2						4	
9		5				3		1
	6	7	4		1	9	2	
		9		3		8		
		1		7				
		2		4		7		
	5	1	9		3	4	8	
2		4				6		5
	8						7	

129. BRIDGES

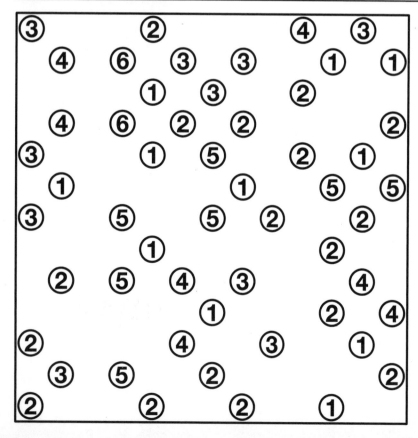

Join circled numbers with horizontal or vertical lines. Each number must have as many lines connected to it as specified by its value.

No more than two lines may join any pair of numbers, and no lines may cross.

The finished layout must connect all numbers, so you can travel between any pair of numbers by following one or more lines.

130. BRIDGE MAZE

Find a path from the entrance at the top of the maze to the exit at the bottom of the maze. The path may cross over or under itself by using the marked bridges.

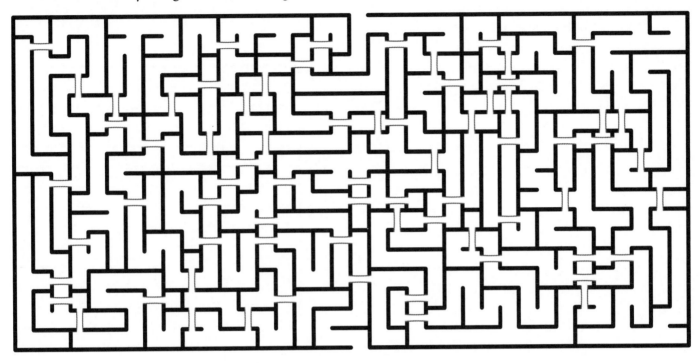

131. WORD CHAIN

Can you complete this word chain, in order to convert the word at the top into the word at the bottom?

At each step you may change only one letter so as to form a new English word, and you may not rearrange any of the letters.

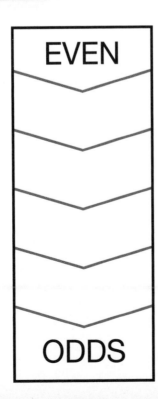

EVEN

ODDS

132. LETTER CIRCLE

How many words can you find in this letter circle? Every word must use the center letter plus two or more of the other letters. No letter can be used more than once in a single word. There is one eight-letter seasonal word to find.

133. PICROSS

Shade in squares in the grid to reveal a picture. Numbers at the start of each row or column reveal, in order from left to right or top to bottom, the length of each consecutive run of shaded squares. There must be a gap of at least one empty square between each run of shaded squares in the same row or column.

Clue: Christmas dinner

Column clues (left to right, each read top to bottom):

2 2 2 5 | 1 1 1 2 3 | 2 3 1 | 1 1 1 1 | 2 2 1 2 1 1 | 1 1 2 3 1 | 1 2 1 | 1 3 1 1 | 2 2 2 1 1 1 | 1 1 2 1 1 1 | 1 2 1 1 | 1 3 1 1 | 1 2 2 3 | 2 1 4 | 2

Row clues (top to bottom):

2, 2
1, 2, 1, 2
1, 1
2, 2
1, 2, 1
1, 2
2, 4, 1, 2
1, 4, 2, 1
2, 1, 3
2, 2, 1, 3
1, 1, 2, 3, 2
1, 1, 2, 2
15
2, 2
12

134. WORD RECTANGLE

Can you find the 12-letter word hidden in this Word Rectangle? Find words by moving from letter to touching letter, including diagonally, and without revisiting a square in a single word. How many other words can you find?

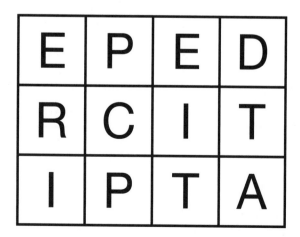

E	P	E	D
R	C	I	T
I	P	T	A

135. BRAIN CHAINS

Without using a calculator or making any written notes, solve these brain chains as quickly as you can. Write the solution in the "Result" box.

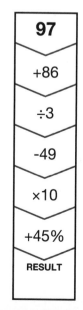

97
+86
÷3
-49
×10
+45%
RESULT

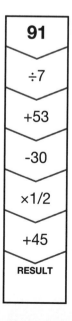

91
÷7
+53
-30
×1/2
+45
RESULT

136. CROSSWORD

Solve the clues to complete the crossword grid.

Across
7 Eerie (6)
8 Chore (6)
9 Without (4)
10 In an appropriate manner (8)
11 Liberal; tolerant (5-6)
14 Weather condition (11)
18 Drivel (8)
19 Colored part of the eye (4)
20 Strand (6)
21 Nefarious computer user (6)

Down
1 Emerges (7)
2 Lego and Barbie (4)
3 Hydrated calcium sulfate (6)
4 Territory (6)
5 Largest (8)
6 Slant (5)
12 Animosity (8)
13 Reached the end of a journey (7)
15 Sports trading cards company (6)
16 Repeat again (6)
17 *Mr Bean* star, Atkinson (5)
19 Urge (4)

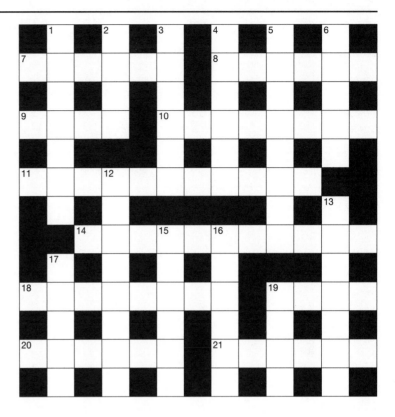

137. DOMINOES

Draw solid lines to divide the grid to form a complete set of standard dominoes, with exactly one of each domino. A "0" represents a blank on a traditional domino.

Use the checkoff chart to help you keep track of which dominoes you've placed.

6	6	2	0	5	5	1	5
0	0	2	4	3	2	1	0
2	6	4	0	5	0	6	0
5	1	1	6	4	3	1	3
5	1	5	3	2	4	4	6
3	3	1	6	5	3	4	2
6	4	2	3	2	1	4	0

0	1	2	3	4	5	6	
							0
							1
							2
							3
							4
							5
							6

138. KILLER SUDOKU

Place the digits 1 to 9 once each into every row, column, and bold-lined 3 × 3 square.

Each dashed-line cage must contain digits that add up to the given number.

No digit can repeat within a dashed-line cage.

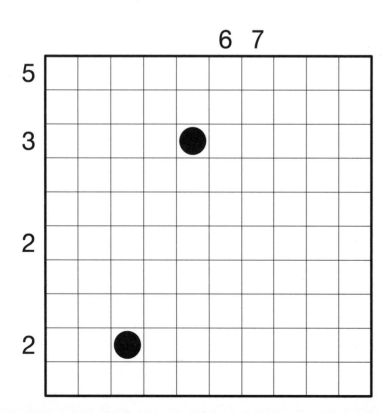

139. SNAKE

Shade some squares to form a snake that starts and ends at the given squares.

A snake is a single path of adjacent squares that does not branch or cross over itself.

The snake does not touch itself—not even diagonally.

Numbers outside the grid specify the number of squares in their row or column that contain part of the snake.

140. WORD SEARCH—CHRISTMAS GIFTS

Can you find all of these words or phrases in the grid? They may be written in any direction, including diagonally.

ART SUPPLIES
BOARD GAME
BOOKS
CELL PHONE
CHOCOLATES
CLOTHES
COOKWARE
GIFT CARDS

JEWELRY
MOVIES
PERFUME
PET
PLANT
SOCKS
TABLET
TOYS

T	T	E	L	B	A	T	L	S	S	P	L	B	E	M
S	T	R	L	A	S	L	C	P	O	E	T	O	Y	S
M	H	C	O	O	E	H	H	O	L	R	I	S	S	T
C	C	L	A	S	S	M	S	S	O	F	K	V	P	M
P	T	L	T	R	A	E	A	O	P	U	L	A	O	P
P	I	E	O	N	T	E	T	G	V	M	R	T	S	M
E	A	S	N	T	A	S	S	A	D	E	G	O	E	R
C	P	D	N	O	H	L	U	E	L	R	E	L	E	P
O	K	R	S	S	H	E	P	P	Y	O	A	P	R	G
O	R	A	N	T	K	P	S	R	P	Y	C	O	G	V
K	R	C	E	F	A	C	L	U	M	L	C	O	B	D
W	H	T	B	L	L	E	O	L	E	F	I	W	H	H
A	E	F	S	E	W	S	I	S	E	W	L	E	A	C
R	T	I	T	E	C	S	E	E	I	C	W	T	S	C
E	O	G	J	S	K	O	O	B	O	S	I	S	O	Y

141. CIRCULAR MAZE

Can you find a route from the gap at the top to the gap at the bottom of this circular maze?

142. CODEWORD

A codeword is a coded crossword in which every letter has been replaced by a number, indicated by the small digits in the top left corner of each crossword square.

Work out which number represents each letter of the alphabet and use this information to complete the crossword grid.

Use the letters outside the grid, and the empty squares beneath the grid, to keep track of your deductions.

143. CHRISTMAS GIFT BOXES

Can you rearrange these gift boxes into their correct order? Once properly aligned they will spell out a word associated with Christmas.

144. KAKURO

Place a digit from 1 to 9 into each white square.

Each horizontal run of white squares adds up to the total above the diagonal line to the left of the run, and each vertical run of white squares adds up to the total below the diagonal line above the run.

No digit can be used more than once in any run.

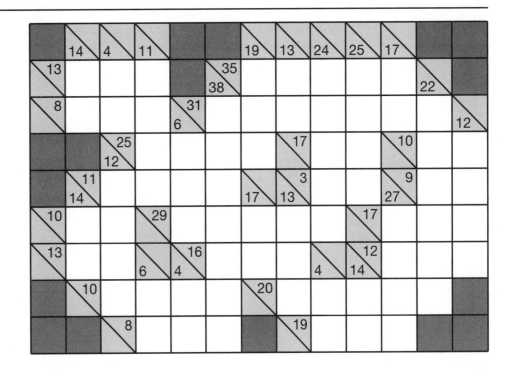

145. SLITHERLINK

Draw a single loop by connecting some dots with horizontal and vertical lines so that each numbered square has the specified number of adjacent line segments.

The loop cannot cross or touch itself.

146. RECTANGLES

Draw borders along some grid lines to divide the grid into a set of rectangles, such that each rectangle contains exactly one number.

All grid squares must be contained within exactly one rectangle.

The number inside each rectangle must be exactly equal to the number of grid squares that the rectangle contains, so for example a "4" could only be in a 1 × 4, 2 × 2, or 4 × 1 rectangle.

Note that the term "rectangle" also includes squares.

					8			
		2		2		4		
			3				8	
		3		3		4		
								7
18					6			
					6		8	
		8	3					
	4							3

147. CALCUDOKU

Place the numbers 1 to 6 once each into every row and column of the grid, while obeying the region clues.

The value at the top left of each bold-lined region must be obtained when all of the numbers in that region have the given operation (+, -, ×, ÷) applied between them. For - and ÷ operations, begin with the largest number in the region and then subtract or divide by the other numbers in the region in any order.

10+		20×		6×	
2÷			2-	1-	
5÷	8×				11+
	3-	4+	2-		
6+			12+	9+	
				9+	

148. SLANTED SUMS

Place 1 to 6 once each in every row and column.

Numbers outside the grid give the total of the indicated diagonals.

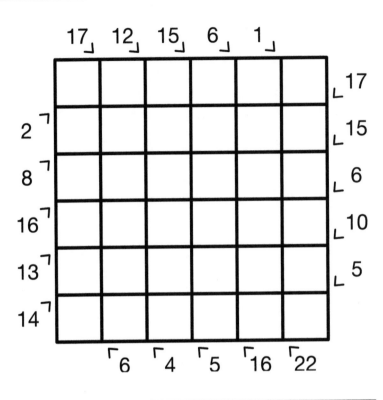

149. QUIZ

Test your knowledge of a specialist subject with this quiz.

Mathematics

1. What do you call a nine-sided polygon?

2. What is a "perfect number"?

3. The fraction 22/7 is close in value to which famous constant?

4. Is 2 a prime number?

5. What is 20% of 200%?

150. FUTOSHIKI

Place 1 to 7 once each into every row and column while obeying the inequality signs.

Greater than (>) signs between some squares indicate that the value in one square is greater than that in another as indicated by the sign. The sign always points toward the smaller number.

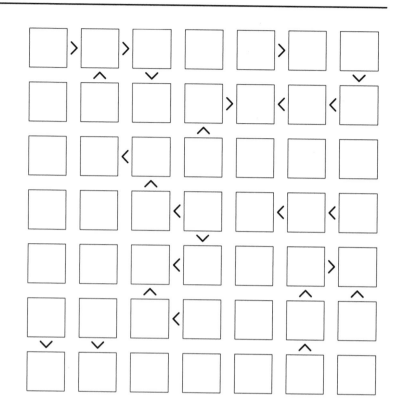

151. NUMBER LINK

Draw a series of separate paths, each connecting a pair of identical numbers.

No more than one path can enter any grid square, and paths can only travel horizontally or vertically, and never diagonally.

		1	2					
	2							
		1		3		4		
				5		6		
	7	8					4	
				7			9	
10	3		8				10	
	5						6	
					9			

152. ARROWWORD

Complete this crossword where all of the clues are given within the grid.

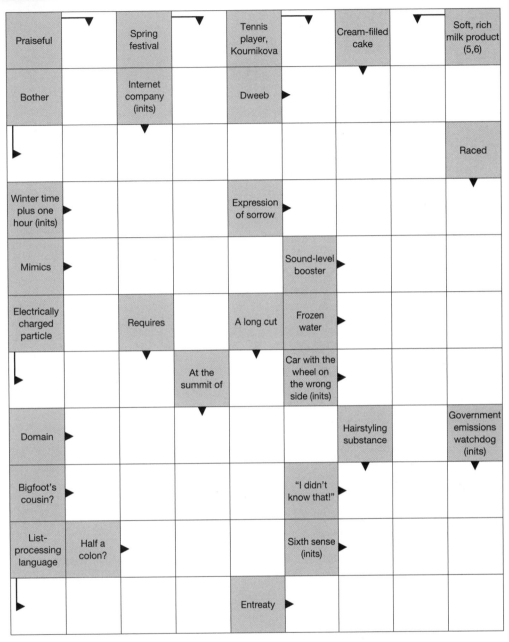

153. CHRISTMAS JUMBLE

Rearrange the following letters to reveal something associated with Christmas.

INN LOGS FLAW

154. JIGSAW LETTERS

Place A to H once each in every row,
column, and bold-lined region.

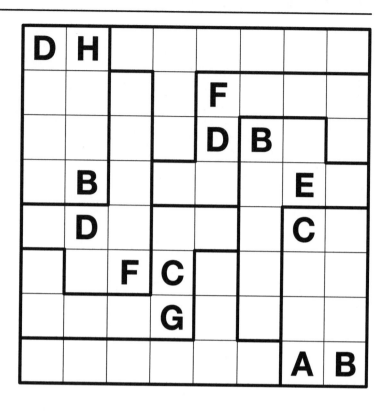

155. SKYSCRAPERS

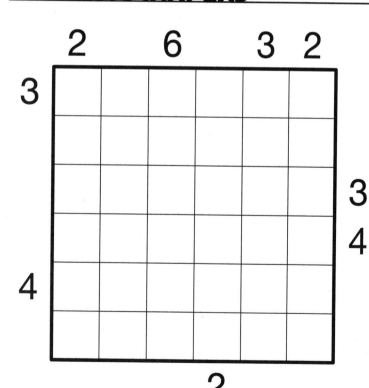

Place 1 to 6 once each into every row and
column of the grid.

Place digits in the grid in such a way that
each given clue number outside the grid
represents the number of digits that are
"visible" from that point, looking along that
clue's row or column.

A digit is visible unless there is a higher
digit preceding it, reading in order along
that row or column. For example, if a row
was "214356" then the 2, 4, 5, and 6 would
be visible from the left end (giving a clue of
"5" visible digits), since 1 is obscured by the
preceding higher 2, and 3 is obscured by
the preceding higher 4. A clue at the right-
hand end of the same row would be "1,"
since only the 6 would be visible.

156. FITWORD

Place each of the following words into the empty squares, crossword-style.

3 Letters
Rye

Nerve
Using

Satchel
Scherzo

4 Letters
Ogre
Pour
Sign
Torc

6 Letters
Camera
Effort
Essays
Priest

8 Letters
Entirely
Thorough

12 Letters
Achievements
Subterranean

5 Letters
Aroma
Early
Fired
Ideal

7 Letters
Chooses
Cleared
Gardens
Gorilla

157. PATH HUNTER

Join dots with horizontal and vertical lines to form a single path which does not touch or cross itself at any point. The start and end of the path are given. Numbers outside the grid specify the number of dots in their row or column that are visited by the path.

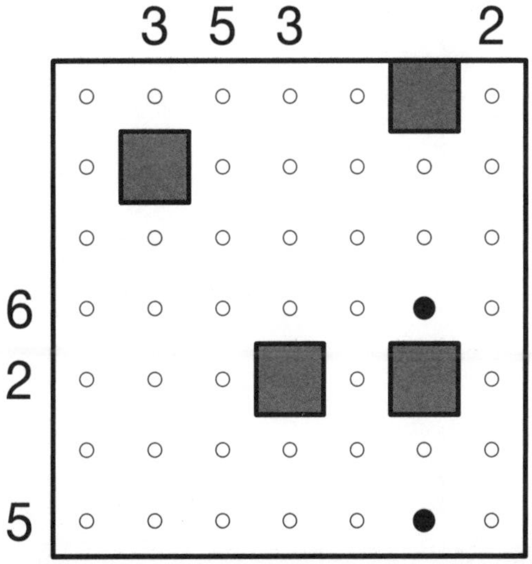

158. TOUCHY

Place A to F once each in every row and column such that two identical letters never touch—not even diagonally.

159. SUDOKU

Place 1 to 9 once each into every row, column, and bold-lined 3 × 3 square.

			4		7			
	9	6					3	7
	7			3			4	
7			6	2	1			3
		2	7		3	5		
6			9	4	5			7
	6			1			5	
	1	4				8	9	
			8		6			

160. BRIDGES

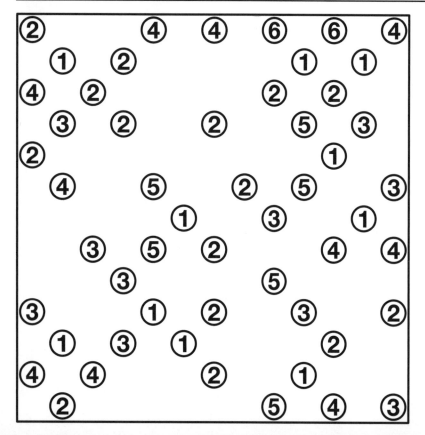

Join circled numbers with horizontal or vertical lines. Each number must have as many lines connected to it as specified by its value.

No more than two lines may join any pair of numbers, and no lines may cross.

The finished layout must connect all numbers, so you can travel between any pair of numbers by following one or more lines.

161. BRIDGE MAZE

Find a path from the entrance at the top of the maze to the exit at the bottom of the maze. The path may cross over or under itself by using the marked bridges.

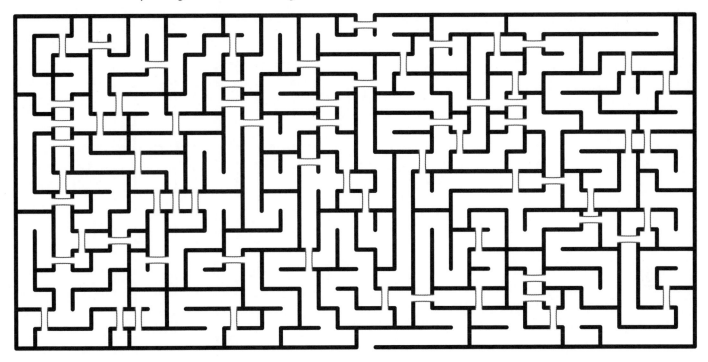

162. WORD CHAIN

Can you complete this word chain, in order to convert the word at the top into the word at the bottom?

At each step you may change only one letter so as to form a new English word, and you may not rearrange any of the letters.

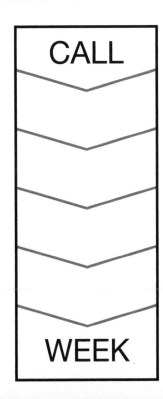

CALL

WEEK

163. LETTER CIRCLE

How many words can you find in this letter circle? Every word must use the center letter plus two or more of the other letters. No letter can be used more than once in a single word. There is one eight-letter seasonal word to find.

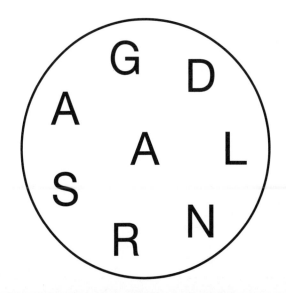

164. PICROSS

Shade in squares in the grid to reveal a picture. Numbers at the start of each row or column reveal, in order from left to right or top to bottom, the length of each consecutive run of shaded squares. There must be a gap of at least one empty square between each run of shaded squares in the same row or column.

Clue: Nut gatherer

Column clues (top to bottom):

```
        3  4  1        1
        1  1  2        1
     1  2  1  3  9     9  1        4  7     3  1
     2  1  2  1  3 15  1  9  7  6  3  1 13  7  4
```

Row clues:

```
         4
         4
   2, 3, 3
      6, 5
      6, 4
      3, 3
      8, 3
   1, 5, 3
      7, 3
   1, 5, 3
   1, 5, 3
      7, 3
      7, 3
1, 2, 4, 2
   3, 5, 2
```

165. WORD RECTANGLE

Can you find the 12-letter word hidden in this Word Rectangle? Find words by moving from letter to touching letter, including diagonally, and without revisiting a square in a single word. How many other words can you find?

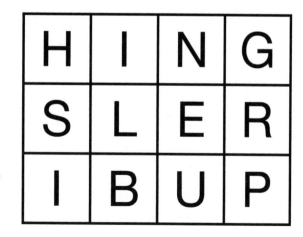

H	I	N	G
S	L	E	R
I	B	U	P

166. BRAIN CHAINS

Without using a calculator or making any written notes, solve these brain chains as quickly as you can. Write the solution in the "Result" box.

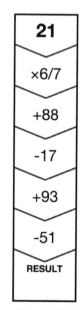

21
×6/7
+88
−17
+93
−51
RESULT

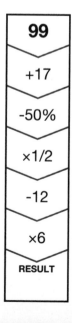

99
+17
−50%
×1/2
−12
×6
RESULT

167. CROSSWORD

Solve the clues to complete the crossword grid.

Across
1 Animal-viewing expedition (6)
5 Gimmick (6)
8 Bean curd (4)
9 Note to self (8)
10 A chocoholic, eg (6)
11 SLR, eg (6)
12 Online photo, perhaps (inits) (4)
14 Two hours before midday (3)
15 Man, informally (4)
16 Imperfections (6)
18 Allow to leave (6)
20 Sixth of a fluid ounce (8)
22 Units of electrical resistance (4)
23 Stellar (6)
24 Cause someone concern (6)

Down
2 Bypass (5)
3 What a funny joke is (7)
4 Annoys (9)
5 Block the flow of water (3)
6 Spider poison (5)
7 Erased; removed (7)
11 Sent to prison (9)
13 Supplications (7)
15 Medical practitioners (7)
17 Cutting light (5)
19 Ballroom dance (5)
21 Lubricate (3)

168. DOMINOES

Draw solid lines to divide the grid to form a complete set of standard dominoes, with exactly one of each domino. A "0" represents a blank on a traditional domino.

Use the checkoff chart to help you keep track of which dominoes you've placed.

0	0	0	2	4	6	5	4
3	2	5	3	4	1	3	2
4	5	2	3	6	6	2	4
5	6	2	1	3	3	6	0
1	6	1	1	1	2	0	3
0	0	5	1	4	3	6	5
2	4	1	5	4	0	6	5

0	1	2	3	4	5	6	
							0
							1
							2
							3
							4
							5
							6

169. KILLER SUDOKU

Place the digits 1 to 9 once each into every row, column, and bold-lined 3 × 3 square.

Each dashed-line cage must contain digits that add up to the given number.

No digit can repeat within a dashed-line cage.

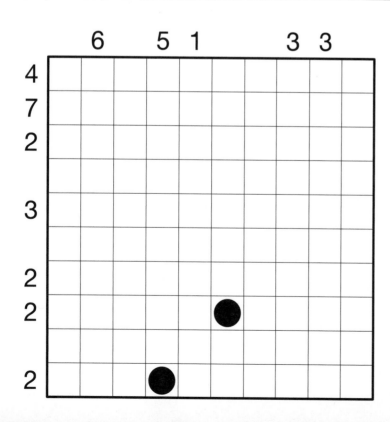

170. SNAKE

Shade some squares to form a snake that starts and ends at the given squares.

A snake is a single path of adjacent squares that does not branch or cross over itself.

The snake does not touch itself—not even diagonally.

Numbers outside the grid specify the number of squares in their row or column that contain part of the snake.

171. WORD SEARCH—CHRISTMAS CAROLS

Can you find all of these words or phrases in the grid? They may be written in any direction, including diagonally.

AWAY IN A MANGER
BLUE CHRISTMAS
CAROL OF THE BELLS
DECK THE HALL
FELIZ NAVIDAD
JINGLE BELL ROCK
JINGLE BELLS
JOY TO THE WORLD

MARY DID YOU KNOW
O CHRISTMAS TREE
O HOLY NIGHT
SILENT NIGHT
SILVER BELLS
SLEIGH RIDE
THE FIRST NOEL
WHAT CHILD IS THIS

```
C M A D L L A H E H T K C E D
M A R Y D I D Y O U K N O W H
H H R E G N A M A N I Y A W A
T G O O I E D I R H G I E L S
H C F E L I Z N A V I D A D M
G R L L D O H O L Y N I G H T
I O D J H E F W T I E D L C T
N O C H R I S T M A S T R E E
T S A M T S I R H C E U L B U
N K C O R L L E B E L G N I J
E M A F J I N G L E B E L L S
L T H E F I R S T N O E L H L
I E Y N S I L V E R B E L L S
S O J O Y T O T H E W O R L D
W H A T C H I L D I S T H I S
```

172. CIRCULAR MAZE

Can you find a route from the gap at the top to the gap at the bottom of this circular maze?

173. CODEWORD

A codeword is a coded crossword in which every letter has been replaced by a number, indicated by the small digits in the top left corner of each crossword square.

Work out which number represents each letter of the alphabet and use this information to complete the crossword grid.

Use the letters outside the grid, and the empty squares beneath the grid, to keep track of your deductions.

1	2	3	4	5	6	7	8	9	10	11	12	13
14	15	16	17	18	19	20	21	22	23	24	25	26

174. CHRISTMAS GIFT BOXES

Can you rearrange these gift boxes into their correct order? Once properly aligned they will spell out a word associated with Christmas.

175. KAKURO

Place a digit from 1 to 9 into each white square.

Each horizontal run of white squares adds up to the total above the diagonal line to the left of the run, and each vertical run of white squares adds up to the total below the diagonal line above the run.

No digit can be used more than once in any run.

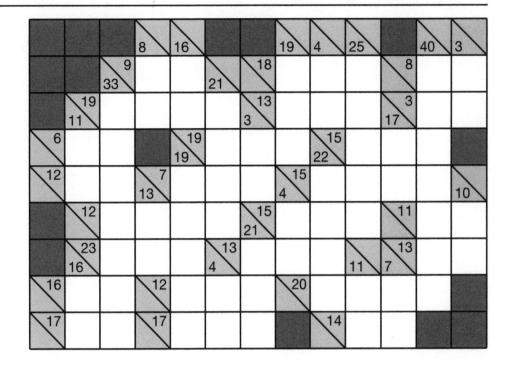

176. SLITHERLINK

Draw a single loop by connecting some dots with horizontal and vertical lines so that each numbered square has the specified number of adjacent line segments.

The loop cannot cross or touch itself.

177. RECTANGLES

Draw borders along some grid lines to divide the grid into a set of rectangles, such that each rectangle contains exactly one number.

All grid squares must be contained within exactly one rectangle.

The number inside each rectangle must be exactly equal to the number of grid squares that the rectangle contains, so for example a "4" could only be in a 1 × 4, 2 × 2, or 4 × 1 rectangle.

Note that the term "rectangle" also includes squares.

		10							
8									
			8				6		
	4					9		12	
		4	8						
		4							
				3					
			2						
	2		4	2			4		
	2		5				3		

178. CALCUDOKU

Place the numbers 1 to 6 once each into every row and column of the grid, while obeying the region clues.

The value at the top left of each bold-lined region must be obtained when all of the numbers in that region have the given operation (+, -, ×, ÷) applied between them. For - and ÷ operations, begin with the largest number in the region and then subtract or divide by the other numbers in the region in any order.

1−	16+		4×	2÷	
					11+
11+		20×		10×	
5÷		12×			
	8+		216×		5+
3÷					

179. SLANTED SUMS

Place 1 to 6 once each in every row and column.

Numbers outside the grid give the total of the indicated diagonals.

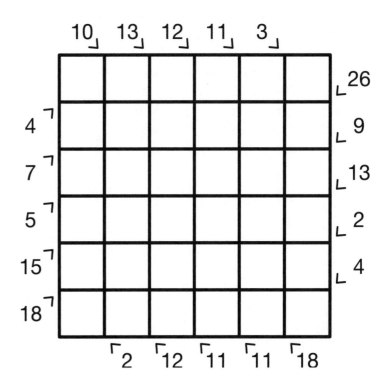

180. QUIZ

Test your knowledge of a specialist subject with this quiz.

Technology

1. Which computer company originally released the standard "PC"?

2. In what country is microprocessor design company ARM headquartered?

3. What is the name of the operating system on Google's mobile devices?

4. Which major version number of Apple's iOS introduced the App Store?

5. Which company brands its color e-book readers with the word *Fire*?

181. FUTOSHIKI

Place 1 to 7 once each into every row and column while obeying the inequality signs.

Greater than (>) signs between some squares indicate that the value in one square is greater than that in another as indicated by the sign. The sign always points toward the smaller number.

182. NUMBER LINK

Draw a series of separate paths, each connecting a pair of identical numbers.

No more than one path can enter any grid square, and paths can only travel horizontally or vertically, and never diagonally.

183. ARROWWORD

Complete this crossword where all of the clues are given within the grid.

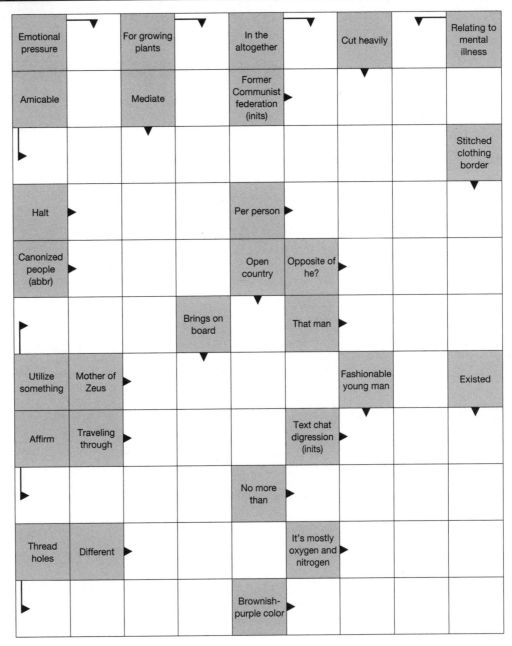

184. CHRISTMAS JUMBLE

Rearrange the following letters to reveal something associated with Christmas.

WATER WHITENER

185. JIGSAW LETTERS

Place A to H once each in every row, column, and bold-lined region.

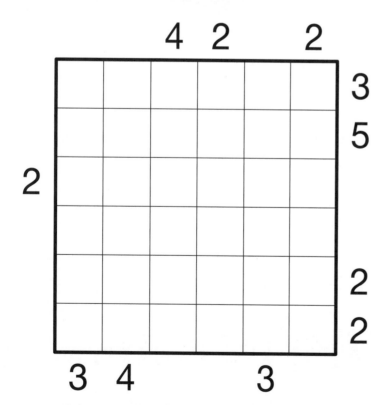

186. SKYSCRAPERS

Place 1 to 6 once each into every row and column of the grid.

Place digits in the grid in such a way that each given clue number outside the grid represents the number of digits that are "visible" from that point, looking along that clue's row or column.

A digit is visible unless there is a higher digit preceding it, reading in order along that row or column. For example, if a row was "214356" then the 2, 4, 5, and 6 would be visible from the left end (giving a clue of "5" visible digits), since 1 is obscured by the preceding higher 2, and 3 is obscured by the preceding higher 4. A clue at the right-hand end of the same row would be "1," since only the 6 would be visible.

187. FITWORD

Place each of the following words into the empty squares, crossword-style.

4 Letters
Anti
Area
Note
Rate

5 Letters
Major
Rifle

6 Letters
Common
Muesli
Obsess

Ravage
Revamp
Ruling
Sketch
Utopia

7 Letters
Baroque
Lettuce

8 Letters
Assembly
Calculus

Catacomb
Formally

11 Letters
Stereotyped
Susceptible

188. PATH HUNTER

Join dots with horizontal and vertical lines to form a single path which does not touch or cross itself at any point. The start and end of the path are given. Numbers outside the grid specify the number of dots in their row or column that are visited by the path.

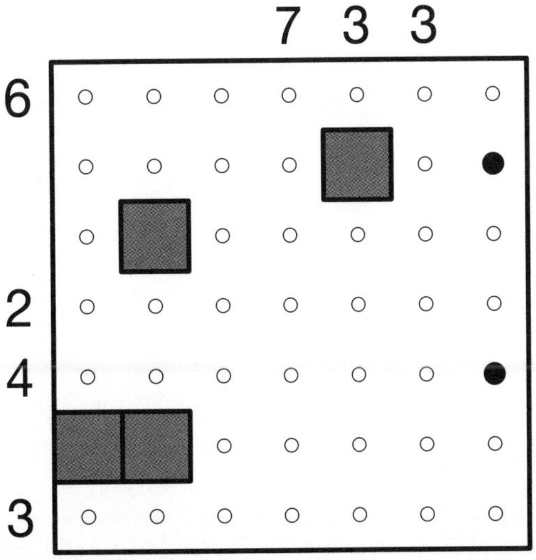

189. TOUCHY

Place A to F once each in every row and column such that two identical letters never touch—not even diagonally.

190. SUDOKU

Place 1 to 9 once each into every row, column, and bold-lined 3 × 3 square.

		3		7		8		
			1		2			
7		2				4		9
	5		8		6		9	
2								6
	6		7		4		8	
8		9				6		2
			2		3			
		4		6		1		

191. BRIDGES

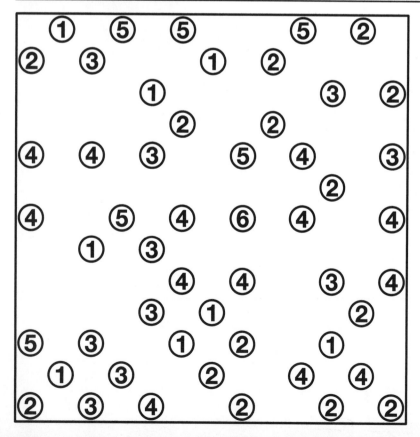

Join circled numbers with horizontal or vertical lines. Each number must have as many lines connected to it as specified by its value.

No more than two lines may join any pair of numbers, and no lines may cross.

The finished layout must connect all numbers, so you can travel between any pair of numbers by following one or more lines.

192. BRIDGE MAZE

Find a path from the entrance at the top of the maze to the exit at the bottom of the maze. The path may cross over or under itself by using the marked bridges.

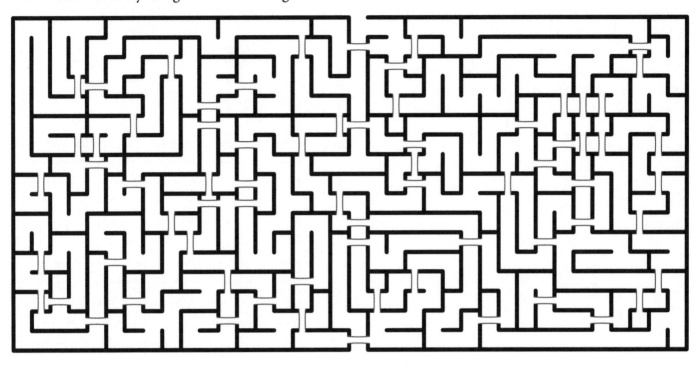

193. WORD CHAIN

Can you complete this word chain, in order to convert the word at the top into the word at the bottom?

At each step you may change only one letter so as to form a new English word, and you may not rearrange any of the letters.

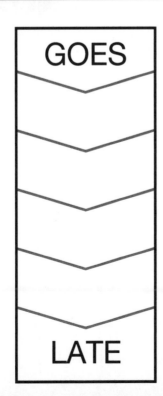

GOES

LATE

194. LETTER CIRCLE

How many words can you find in this letter circle? Every word must use the center letter plus two or more of the other letters. No letter can be used more than once in a single word. There is one eight-letter seasonal word to find.

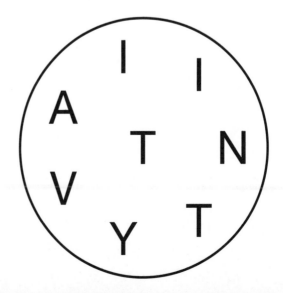

195. PICROSS

Shade in squares in the grid to reveal a picture. Numbers at the start of each row or column reveal, in order from left to right or top to bottom, the length of each consecutive run of shaded squares. There must be a gap of at least one empty square between each run of shaded squares in the same row or column.

Clue: Illumination

	2 2 1 1 2	1 1 1 1	1 1 1 1	0	2 5	2 3	1 1 4	3 1 2 1 2	1 1 4	2 3	2 5	0	1 1 1 1	1 1 1 1	2 2 1 1 2
1, 1, 1, 1, 1															
1, 1, 1, 1, 1															
3, 1, 3															
0															
1, 5, 1															
2, 2, 2, 2															
1, 1															
1, 1															
3, 1, 3, 1, 3															
2, 1, 2															
1, 1															
2, 5, 2															
1, 1															
1, 3, 1															
1, 1, 3, 1, 1															

196. WORD RECTANGLE

Can you find the 12-letter word hidden in this Word Rectangle? Find words by moving from letter to touching letter, including diagonally, and without revisiting a square in a single word. How many other words can you find?

O	C	S	N
R	V	A	O
P	O	I	T

197. BRAIN CHAINS

Without using a calculator or making any written notes, solve these brain chains as quickly as you can. Write the solution in the "Result" box.

63	**39**
÷7	+64
×2/3	-63
÷2	+40
×8	+25%
+75%	-16
RESULT	RESULT

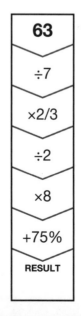

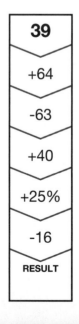

198. CROSSWORD

Solve the clues to complete the crossword grid.

Across
1 Declare (5)
4 Unfavorable (7)
9 Way of thinking (8)
10 Tussock (4)
11 Next to (6)
12 Welsh breed of dog (5)
13 Oppose (4)
15 Website address (inits) (3)
16 Width times length (4)
17 Afterwards (5)
19 Two-way switch (6)
21 Summit (4)
22 Ills (8)
23 Show-off (7)
24 Barely perceptible (5)

Down
2 Name (5)
3 Character in *The Matrix* (7)
5 Decrease in intensity (2-10)
6 Participate (5)
7 Fulfill (7)
8 Procedural (12)
14 Surpass (7)
16 Branch of mathematics (7)
18 Poisonous (5)
20 Type of public protest (3-2)

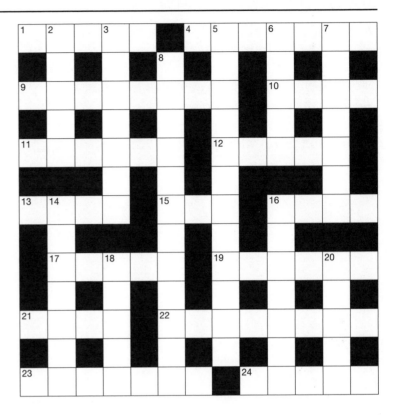

199. DOMINOES

Draw solid lines to divide the grid to form a complete set of standard dominoes, with exactly one of each domino. A "0" represents a blank on a traditional domino.

Use the checkoff chart to help you keep track of which dominoes you've placed.

2	4	2	4	6	6	4	1
2	5	6	4	0	1	5	6
1	5	0	3	6	4	0	3
1	5	1	2	2	3	0	3
1	2	4	4	2	3	5	5
3	0	5	0	6	1	5	4
0	6	1	0	6	2	3	3

0	1	2	3	4	5	6	
							0
							1
							2
							3
							4
							5
							6

200. KILLER SUDOKU

Place the digits 1 to 9 once each into every row, column, and bold-lined 3 × 3 square.

Each dashed-line cage must contain digits that add up to the given number.

No digit can repeat within a dashed-line cage.

201. SNAKE

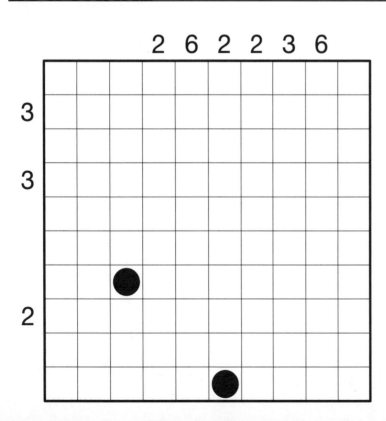

Shade some squares to form a snake that starts and ends at the given squares.

A snake is a single path of adjacent squares that does not branch or cross over itself.

The snake does not touch itself—not even diagonally.

Numbers outside the grid specify the number of squares in their row or column that contain part of the snake.

202. WORD SEARCH—COUNTRIES OF THE WORLD

Can you find all of these words or phrases in the grid? They may be written in any direction, including diagonally.

AFGHANISTAN
ARGENTINA
AUSTRALIA
CAMBODIA
EGYPT
ETHIOPIA
FIJI
FRANCE

INDIA
IRELAND
ISRAEL
ITALY
KENYA
PAKISTAN
ROMANIA
VIETNAM

R	L	O	Y	N	I	A	R	G	E	N	T	I	N	A
A	M	I	S	R	A	E	L	A	A	I	D	N	I	D
L	K	A	A	N	N	A	R	O	M	A	N	I	A	A
A	D	L	N	I	S	I	E	G	I	L	S	H	V	I
A	F	A	S	T	D	I	A	N	T	L	N	R	T	R
I	E	G	T	O	E	O	E	A	N	K	E	I	O	E
L	L	C	H	H	T	I	B	T	I	N	A	A	E	L
A	G	N	N	A	I	O	V	M	H	A	A	H	L	A
R	M	Y	A	A	N	I	E	I	A	I	I	A	A	N
T	E	N	L	T	R	I	F	G	G	C	O	B	A	D
S	A	R	N	A	S	F	S	I	Y	A	A	P	E	O
U	Y	O	E	Y	T	I	I	T	J	P	T	F	I	D
A	N	V	R	A	N	I	K	G	A	I	T	O	I	A
R	E	I	H	D	A	M	S	A	D	N	A	I	Y	S
N	K	E	N	I	H	L	E	U	P	O	P	T	R	A

203. CIRCULAR MAZE

Can you find a route from the gap at the top to the gap at the bottom of this circular maze?

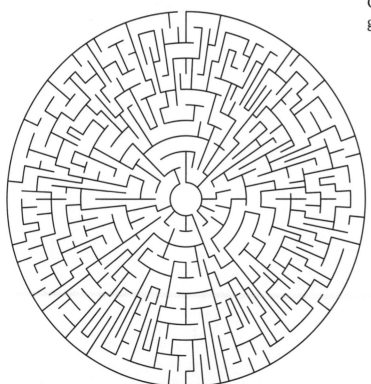

204. CODEWORD

A codeword is a coded crossword in which every letter has been replaced by a number, indicated by the small digits in the top left corner of each crossword square.

Work out which number represents each letter of the alphabet and use this information to complete the crossword grid.

Use the letters outside the grid, and the empty squares beneath the grid, to keep track of your deductions.

1	2	3	4	5	6	7	8	9	10	11	12	13
14	15	16	17	18	19	20	21	22	23	24	25	26

205. CHRISTMAS GIFT BOXES

Can you rearrange these gift boxes into their correct order? Once properly aligned they will spell out a word associated with Christmas.

206. KAKURO

Place a digit from 1 to 9 into each white square.

Each horizontal run of white squares adds up to the total above the diagonal line to the left of the run, and each vertical run of white squares adds up to the total below the diagonal line above the run.

No digit can be used more than once in any run.

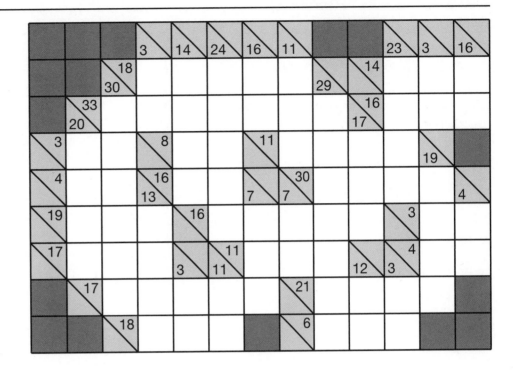

207. SLITHERLINK

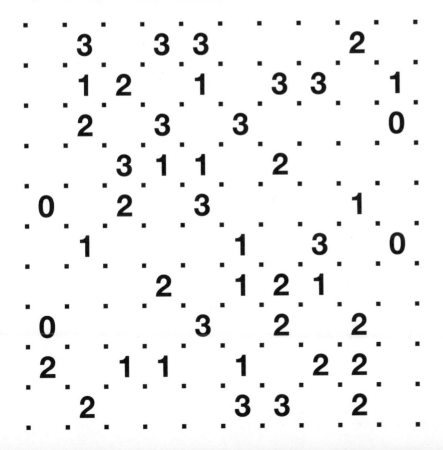

Draw a single loop by connecting some dots with horizontal and vertical lines so that each numbered square has the specified number of adjacent line segments.

The loop cannot cross or touch itself.

208. RECTANGLES

Draw borders along some grid lines to divide the grid into a set of rectangles, such that each rectangle contains exactly one number.

All grid squares must be contained within exactly one rectangle.

The number inside each rectangle must be exactly equal to the number of grid squares that the rectangle contains, so for example a "4" could only be in a 1 × 4, 2 × 2, or 4 × 1 rectangle.

Note that the term "rectangle" also includes squares.

		4						2	
							2		
		12						5	
				16					
			7						
						6			5
5									
				2				2	2
	15				3			2	
		3		4				3	

209. CALCUDOKU

11+	45×			2−	
	6+		23+	30×	
4÷					5+
	1÷			7+	
			288×		6+
3÷					

Place the numbers 1 to 6 once each into every row and column of the grid, while obeying the region clues.

The value at the top left of each bold-lined region must be obtained when all of the numbers in that region have the given operation (+, -, ×, ÷) applied between them. For - and ÷ operations, begin with the largest number in the region and then subtract or divide by the other numbers in the region in any order.

210. SLANTED SUMS

Place 1 to 6 once each in every row
and column.

Numbers outside the grid give the
total of the indicated diagonals.

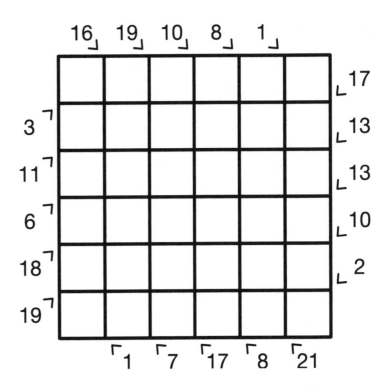

211. QUIZ

Test your knowledge of a specialist subject with this quiz.

Roman Gods

1. Which Roman god is the equivalent of the Greek god, Zeus?

2. Which is the only planet not named after a Roman god, other than Earth?

3. Who is the Roman god of the sea?

4. Which Roman god is often pictured on Saint Valentine's Day?

5. Who is the Roman goddess of love?

212. FUTOSHIKI

Place 1 to 7 once each into every row and column while obeying the inequality signs.

Greater than (>) signs between some squares indicate that the value in one square is greater than that in another as indicated by the sign. The sign always points toward the smaller number.

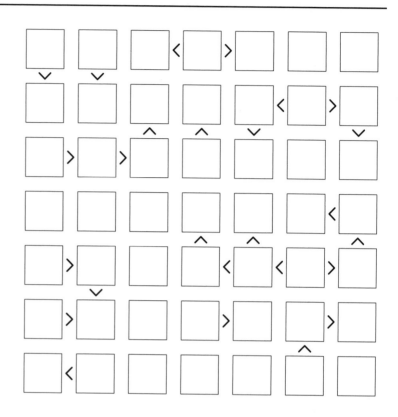

213. NUMBER LINK

1		2						
3				1	4			
	5					5		
		6						2
	4	3	7					
			8		8	7	9	6
				9				10
	11			12			12	
		10	11					

Draw a series of separate paths, each connecting a pair of identical numbers.

No more than one path can enter any grid square, and paths can only travel horizontally or vertically, and never diagonally.

214. ARROWWORD

Complete this crossword where all of the clues are given within the grid.

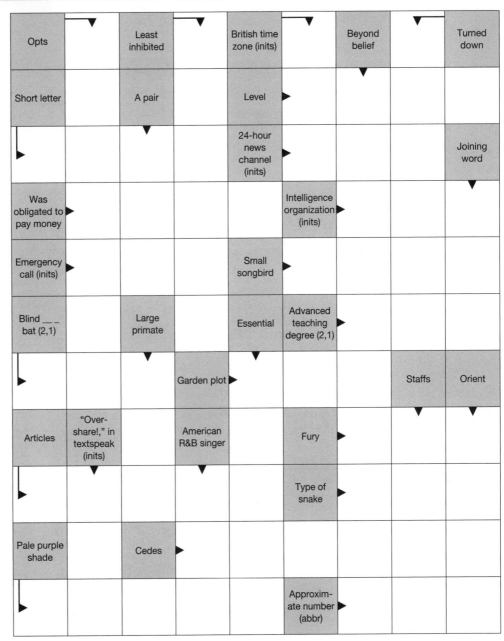

215. CHRISTMAS JUMBLE

Rearrange the following letters to reveal something associated with Christmas.

MAINLY FIGHTS RAGE

216. JIGSAW LETTERS

Place A to H once each in every row, column, and bold-lined region.

	G			H		
D						
A			G	B		F
F		D	G			A
						E
		A			H	

217. SKYSCRAPERS

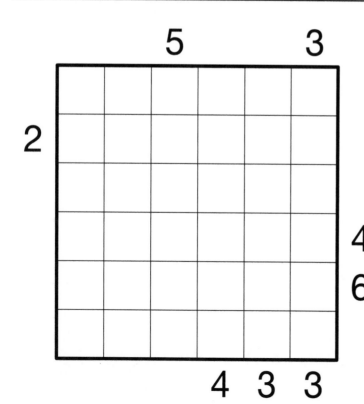

Place 1 to 6 once each into every row and column of the grid.

Place digits in the grid in such a way that each given clue number outside the grid represents the number of digits that are "visible" from that point, looking along that clue's row or column.

A digit is visible unless there is a higher digit preceding it, reading in order along that row or column. For example, if a row was "214356" then the 2, 4, 5, and 6 would be visible from the left end (giving a clue of "5" visible digits), since 1 is obscured by the preceding higher 2, and 3 is obscured by the preceding higher 4. A clue at the right-hand end of the same row would be "1," since only the 6 would be visible.

218. FITWORD

Place each of the following words into the empty squares, crossword-style.

4 Letters
Afar
Aver
Raps
Rare

5 Letters
About
Error
Felon
Later
Meant
Siren

6 Letters
Argali
Energy
Ground
Second
Settee
Violin

7 Letters
Article
Claimed
Educate
Mistake
Outlook

Overlap
Passive
Veranda

12 Letters
Inconsistent
Melodramatic

219. PATH HUNTER

Join dots with horizontal and vertical lines to form a single path which does not touch or cross itself at any point. The start and end of the path are given. Numbers outside the grid specify the number of dots in their row or column that are visited by the path.

220. TOUCHY

Place A to F once each in every row and column such that two identical letters never touch—not even diagonally.

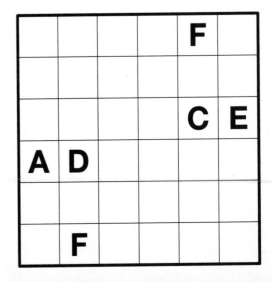

221. SUDOKU

Place 1 to 9 once each into every row, column, and bold-lined 3 × 3 square.

8				2				5
	1					7		
	7		1		6		9	
	7	8		2	5			
4				6				7
	9	7		4	6			
	2		9		3		1	
	8					3		
1				7				2

222. BRIDGES

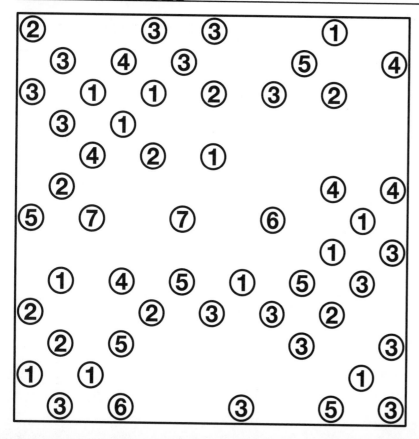

Join circled numbers with horizontal or vertical lines. Each number must have as many lines connected to it as specified by its value.

No more than two lines may join any pair of numbers, and no lines may cross.

The finished layout must connect all numbers, so you can travel between any pair of numbers by following one or more lines.

223. BRIDGE MAZE

Find a path from the entrance at the top of the maze to the exit at the bottom of the maze. The path may cross over or under itself by using the marked bridges.

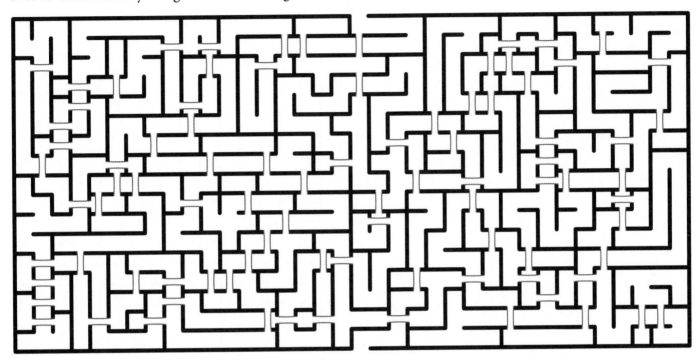

224. WORD CHAIN

Can you complete this word chain, in order to convert the word at the top into the word at the bottom?

At each step you may change only one letter so as to form a new English word, and you may not rearrange any of the letters.

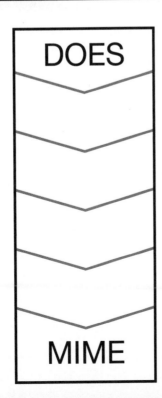

DOES

MIME

225. LETTER CIRCLE

How many words can you find in this letter circle? Every word must use the center letter plus two or more of the other letters. No letter can be used more than once in a single word. There is one nine-letter seasonal word to find.

226. PICROSS

Shade in squares in the grid to reveal a picture. Numbers at the start of each row or column reveal, in order from left to right or top to bottom, the length of each consecutive run of shaded squares. There must be a gap of at least one empty square between each run of shaded squares in the same row or column.

Clue: Time for cheese

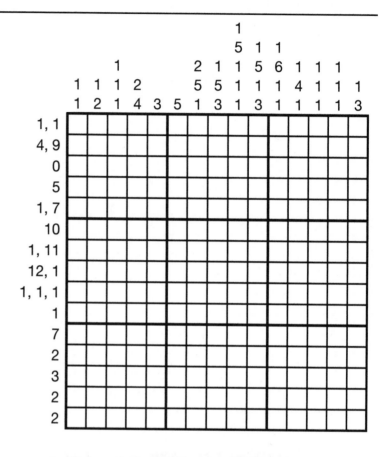

227. WORD RECTANGLE

Can you find the 12-letter word hidden in this Word Rectangle? Find words by moving from letter to touching letter, including diagonally, and without revisiting a square in a single word. How many other words can you find?

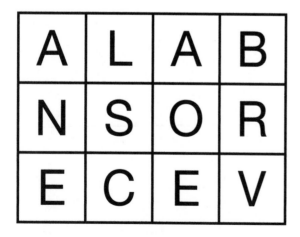

228. BRAIN CHAINS

Without using a calculator or making any written notes, solve these brain chains as quickly as you can. Write the solution in the "Result" box.

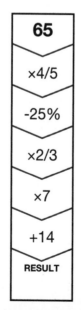

65
×4/5
-25%
×2/3
×7
+14
RESULT

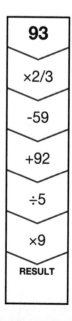

93
×2/3
-59
+92
÷5
×9
RESULT

229. CROSSWORD

Solve the clues to complete the crossword grid.

Across
1 Religious leader (6)
4 One after the first (6)
8 Pimple (3)
9 Vanish (9)
11 Without fat (4)
12 Unusual (8)
15 Long, stringy pasta (9)
18 Keyboard star (8)
19 Highest European volcano (4)
21 Dejects (9)
23 Public house (3)
24 Freshest (6)
25 Finished (6)

Down
1 A word search, perhaps (6)
2 On the way (2,7)
3 *Candy Crush* sequel suffix (4)
5 Deeds; feats (8)
6 Rock containing metal (3)
7 Audacity (6)
10 Making a whole out of parts (9)
13 Provides for (9)
14 Obstructions (8)
16 Forgive (6)
17 Won (6)
20 Part of an archipelago (4)
22 Dog's foot (3)

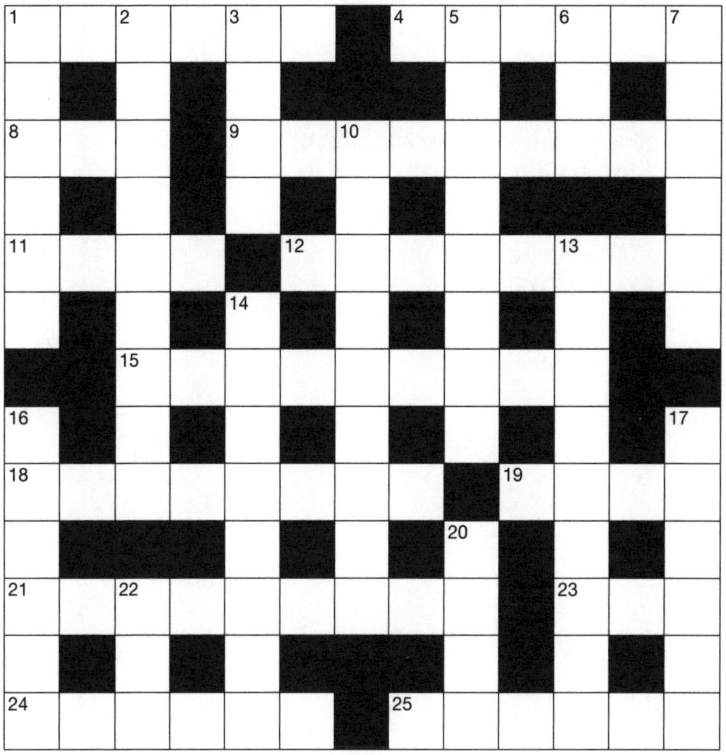

230. DOMINOES

Draw solid lines to divide the grid to form a complete set of standard dominoes, with exactly one of each domino. A "0" represents a blank on a traditional domino.

Use the checkoff chart to help you keep track of which dominoes you've placed.

2	0	1	1	0	1	2	0
4	4	3	5	5	5	3	5
1	2	3	0	5	5	6	2
5	4	6	3	1	3	4	4
3	1	4	6	6	4	2	1
6	6	0	1	0	5	6	3
2	2	0	4	2	3	6	0

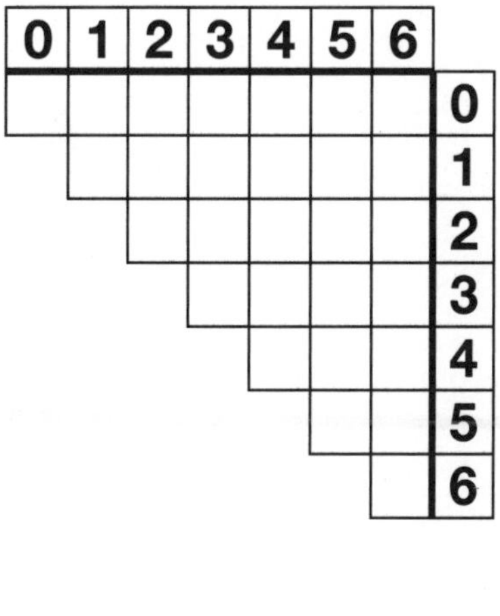

231. KILLER SUDOKU

Place the digits 1 to 9 once each into every row, column, and bold-lined 3 × 3 square.

Each dashed-line cage must contain digits that add up to the given number.

No digit can repeat within a dashed-line cage.

232. SNAKE

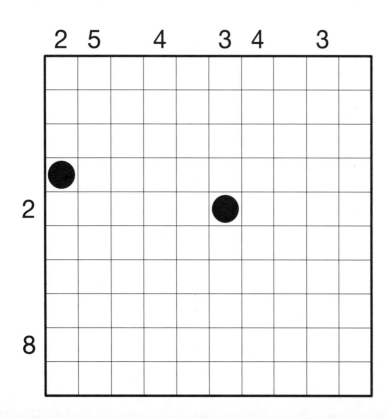

Shade some squares to form a snake that starts and ends at the given squares.

A snake is a single path of adjacent squares that does not branch or cross over itself.

The snake does not touch itself—not even diagonally.

Numbers outside the grid specify the number of squares in their row or column that contain part of the snake.

233. WORD SEARCH—EDIBLE FISH

Can you find all of these words or phrases in the grid? They may be written in any direction, including diagonally.

BASS
CARP
CATFISH
FLOUNDER
HADDOCK
HALIBUT
JOHN DORY
MACKEREL

MONKFISH
PLAICE
POLLACK
SALMON
SNAPPER
SOLE
TROUT
TUNA

```
N A A O R S S D E N F M P T T
H D A I L N K M N B O S C U I
A K A O A E O R P K L F R N N
E D L P B N C R E P I A C A P
O L P E K Y C I I D B A A E O
O E H F R I R L A K N A T L D
R A I A T E N O C L E U S P A
S S D P L O K A D P P J O S S
H F O O M I L C U N R T T L D
E P O L H L B O A S H R C A F
C E A P O C A U O M O O A A H
R S R P S D U S T U M A J D E
F A A P P A U O T O A U O L I
C N K S O L E C A T F I S H E
H A D D O C K K I H C L S C C
```

234. CIRCULAR MAZE

Can you find a route from the gap at the top to the gap at the bottom of this circular maze?

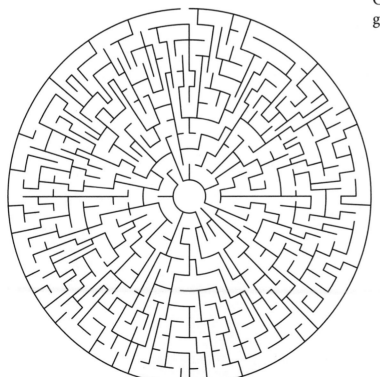

235. CODEWORD

A codeword is a coded crossword in which every letter has been replaced by a number, indicated by the small digits in the top left corner of each crossword square.

Work out which number represents each letter of the alphabet and use this information to complete the crossword grid.

Use the letters outside the grid, and the empty squares beneath the grid, to keep track of your deductions.

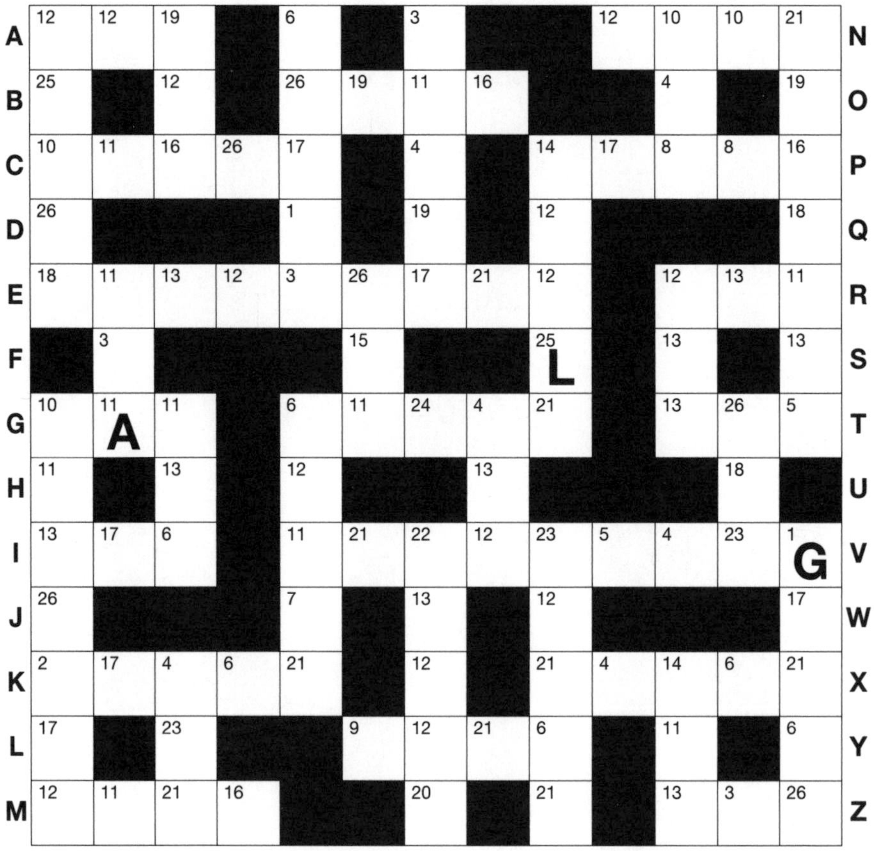

A 12	12	19	■	6	■	3	■	■	12	10	10	21
B 25	■	12	■	26	19	11	16	■	■	4	■	19
C 10	11	16	26	17	■	4	■	14	17	8	8	16
D 26	■	■	■	1	■	19	■	12	■	■	■	18
E 18	11	13	12	3	26	17	21	12	■	12	13	11
F ■	3	■	■	■	15	■	■	25 **L**	■	13	■	13
G 10	11 **A**	11	■	6	11	24	4	21	■	13	26	5
H 11	■	13	■	12	■	■	13	■	■	■	18	■
I 13	17	6	■	11	21	22	12	23	5	4	23	1 **G**
J 26	■	■	■	7	■	13	■	12	■	■	■	17
K 2	17	4	6	21	■	12	■	21	4	14	6	21
L 17	■	23	■	■	9	12	21	6	■	11	■	6
M 12	11	21	16	■	20	■	21	■	13	3	26	

Letters outside the grid (right side): N O P Q R S T U V W X Y Z

1	2	3	4	5	6	7	8	9	10	11	12	13
14	15	16	17	18	19	20	21	22	23	24	25	26

236. CHRISTMAS GIFT BOXES

Can you rearrange these gift boxes into their correct order? Once properly aligned they will spell out a word associated with Christmas.

237. KAKURO

Place a digit from 1 to 9 into each white square.

Each horizontal run of white squares adds up to the total above the diagonal line to the left of the run, and each vertical run of white squares adds up to the total below the diagonal line above the run.

No digit can be used more than once in any run.

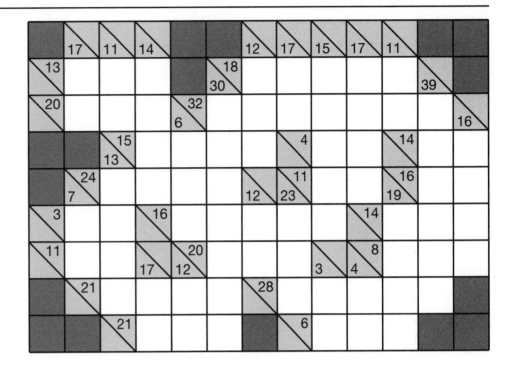

238. SLITHERLINK

Draw a single loop by connecting some dots with horizontal and vertical lines so that each numbered square has the specified number of adjacent line segments.

The loop cannot cross or touch itself.

239. RECTANGLES

Draw borders along some grid lines to divide the grid into a set of rectangles, such that each rectangle contains exactly one number.

All grid squares must be contained within exactly one rectangle.

The number inside each rectangle must be exactly equal to the number of grid squares that the rectangle contains, so for example a "4" could only be in a 1 × 4, 2 × 2, or 4 × 1 rectangle.

Note that the term "rectangle" also includes squares.

240. CALCUDOKU

Place the numbers 1 to 6 once each into every row and column of the grid, while obeying the region clues.

The value at the top left of each bold-lined region must be obtained when all of the numbers in that region have the given operation (+, -, ×, ÷) applied between them. For - and ÷ operations, begin with the largest number in the region and then subtract or divide by the other numbers in the region in any order.

241. SLANTED SUMS

Place 1 to 6 once each in every row and column.

Numbers outside the grid give the total of the indicated diagonals.

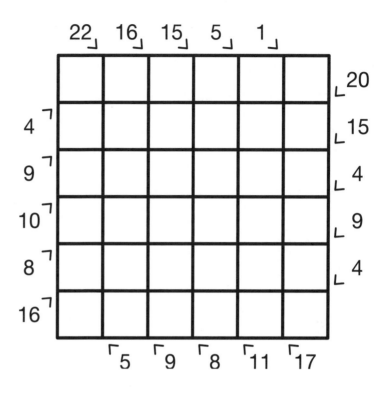

242. QUIZ

Test your knowledge of a specialist subject with this quiz.

Home Consoles

1. In what year did Sony first release the original PlayStation console in the United States?

2. Which company released the portable Game Boy system?

3. What was Sega's color portable console called?

4. What was the first successor to the original Xbox console called?

5. The Wii was the follow-up to which previous console?

243. FUTOSHIKI

Place 1 to 7 once each into every row and column while obeying the inequality signs.

Greater than (>) signs between some squares indicate that the value in one square is greater than that in another as indicated by the sign. The sign always points toward the smaller number.

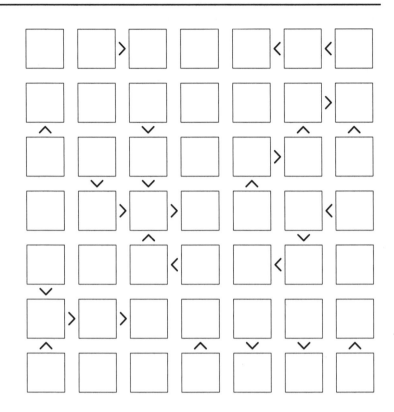

244. NUMBER LINK

Draw a series of separate paths, each connecting a pair of identical numbers.

No more than one path can enter any grid square, and paths can only travel horizontally or vertically, and never diagonally.

1				2	3		4
5		6		7			8
		9					
							10
		9					
	5						
	2		6	1		3		8	
				7	4		10	

245. ARROWWORD

Complete this crossword where all of the clues are given within the grid.

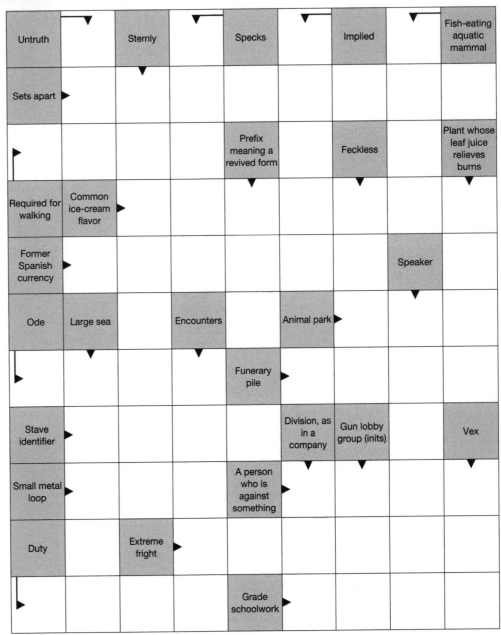

246. CHRISTMAS JUMBLE

Rearrange the following letters to reveal something associated with Christmas.

WARP PIG PER PAN

247. JIGSAW LETTERS

Place A to H once each in every row, column, and bold-lined region.

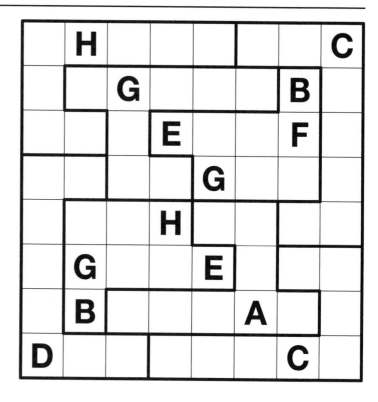

248. SKYSCRAPERS

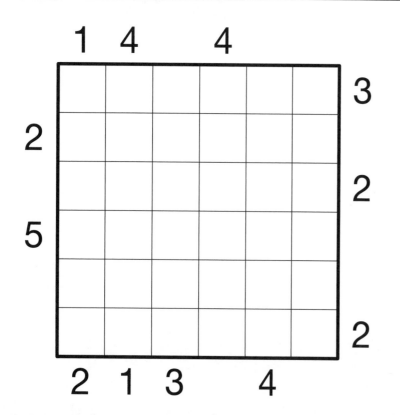

Place 1 to 6 once each into every row and column of the grid.

Place digits in the grid in such a way that each given clue number outside the grid represents the number of digits that are "visible" from that point, looking along that clue's row or column.

A digit is visible unless there is a higher digit preceding it, reading in order along that row or column. For example, if a row was "214356" then the 2, 4, 5, and 6 would be visible from the left end (giving a clue of "5" visible digits), since 1 is obscured by the preceding higher 2, and 3 is obscured by the preceding higher 4. A clue at the right-hand end of the same row would be "1," since only the 6 would be visible.

249. FITWORD

Place each of the following words into the empty squares, crossword-style.

3 Letters
Bow
Ewe

4 Letters
Baht
Idol
Snag
Tree

5 Letters
Clean
Dared

Odium
Sward

6 Letters
Axioms
Dreary
Putrid
Scrimp

7 Letters
Circuit
Diorama
Earthly
Expands

8 Letters
Accessed
Acoustic
Designer
Sideways

9 Letters
Institute
Remaining

11 Letters
Temperature

250. PATH HUNTER

Join dots with horizontal and vertical lines to form a single path which does not touch or cross itself at any point. The start and end of the path are given. Numbers outside the grid specify the number of dots in their row or column that are visited by the path.

251. TOUCHY

Place A to F once each in every row and column such that two identical letters never touch—not even diagonally.

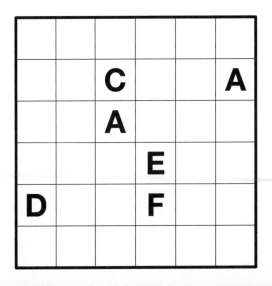

252. SUDOKU

Place 1 to 9 once each into every row, column, and bold-lined 3 × 3 square.

5	3		4	1	6		9	7
8								6
		7				3		
2			8		1			3
7								4
9			7		3			5
		5				4		
1								9
6	2		3	5	9		1	8

253. BRIDGES

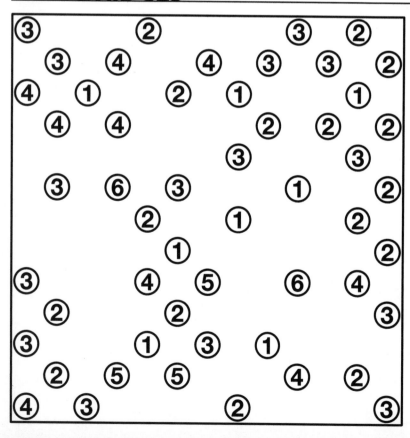

Join circled numbers with horizontal or vertical lines. Each number must have as many lines connected to it as specified by its value.

No more than two lines may join any pair of numbers, and no lines may cross.

The finished layout must connect all numbers, so you can travel between any pair of numbers by following one or more lines.

254. BRIDGE MAZE

Find a path from the entrance at the top of the maze to the exit at the bottom of the maze. The path may cross over or under itself by using the marked bridges.

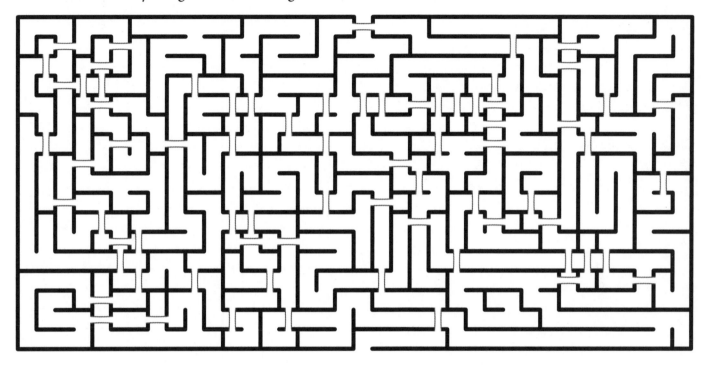

255. WORD CHAIN

Can you complete this word chain, in order to convert the word at the top into the word at the bottom?

At each step you may change only one letter so as to form a new English word, and you may not rearrange any of the letters.

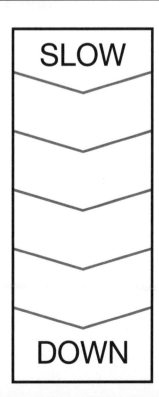

SLOW

DOWN

256. LETTER CIRCLE

How many words can you find in this letter circle? Every word must use the center letter plus two or more of the other letters. No letter can be used more than once in a single word. There is one nine-letter seasonal word to find.

257. PICROSS

Shade in squares in the grid to reveal a picture. Numbers at the start of each row or column reveal, in order from left to right or top to bottom, the length of each consecutive run of shaded squares. There must be a gap of at least one empty square between each run of shaded squares in the same row or column.

Clue: Time for bed

Column clues (left to right, top to bottom):

			1											
			1			1	1	2	1		1	1		
		3	1	1	1	1	2	1	1		1	2	1	
	1	2	1	1	1	1	1	1	1	1	2	1	1	2
	1	1	1	2	1	1	1	1	1	1	1	1	1	1
10	10	2	2	2	2	2	2	2	2	2	2	2	8	8

Row clues (top to bottom):

5, 4
3, 1, 1
1, 1, 1
4, 4, 1
4
2
2, 2
3, 1, 4
4, 6, 2
2, 1, 2
15
2, 2
15
15
2, 2

258. WORD RECTANGLE

Can you find the 12-letter word hidden in this Word Rectangle? Find words by moving from letter to touching letter, including diagonally, and without revisiting a square in a single word. How many other words can you find?

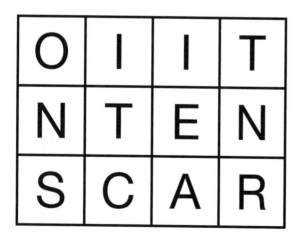

O	I	I	T
N	T	E	N
S	C	A	R

259. BRAIN CHAINS

Without using a calculator or making any written notes, solve these brain chains as quickly as you can. Write the solution in the "Result" box.

92	**41**
-75%	-33
+6	×1/2
×3	×17
+42	-34
÷3	+61
RESULT	RESULT

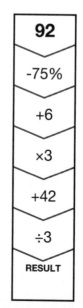

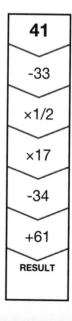

260. CROSSWORD

Solve the clues to complete the crossword grid.

Across

7 Fire-breathing beast (6)
8 Fantasy perfection (6)
9 On a single occasion (4)
10 School meeting (8)
11 Likely to be affected (11)
14 Pigeonholed (11)
18 System of computation (8)
19 Radio ham's "E" (4)
20 Frequent (6)
21 Get away (6)

Down

1 A word used to indicate someone (7)
2 Man-eating giant (4)
3 Build a temporary shelter (6)
4 Oat-based breakfast food (6)
5 Officially (8)
6 Hurriedly search (5)
12 Tunneled cemetery (8)
13 Possibly (7)
15 Judgment (6)
16 Without being asked (2,4)
17 Joyful-sounding key (5)
19 Corrode with acid (4)

261. DOMINOES

Draw solid lines to divide the grid to form a complete set of standard dominoes, with exactly one of each domino. A "0" represents a blank on a traditional domino.

Use the checkoff chart to help you keep track of which dominoes you've placed.

3	3	5	0	4	2	4	2
5	5	0	5	1	5	6	0
2	6	1	4	0	6	1	3
1	3	1	1	5	5	1	3
0	3	2	6	3	1	6	5
2	6	4	2	4	2	6	0
0	4	3	4	4	2	6	0

0	1	2	3	4	5	6	
							0
							1
							2
							3
							4
							5
							6

262. KILLER SUDOKU

Place the digits 1 to 9 once each into every row, column, and bold-lined 3 × 3 square.

Each dashed-line cage must contain digits that add up to the given number.

No digit can repeat within a dashed-line cage.

263. SNAKE

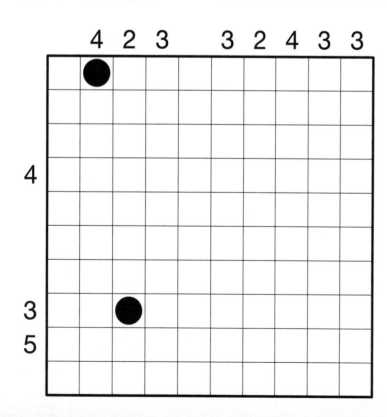

Shade some squares to form a snake that starts and ends at the given squares.

A snake is a single path of adjacent squares that does not branch or cross over itself.

The snake does not touch itself—not even diagonally.

Numbers outside the grid specify the number of squares in their row or column that contain part of the snake.

264. WORD SEARCH—BOUQUET FLOWERS

Can you find all of these words or phrases in the grid? They may be written in any direction, including diagonally.

DAFFODIL
DAISY
FREESIA
GLADIOLUS
IRIS
LILAC
LILY
ORCHID

PEONY
POPPY
ROSE
STOCK
SUNFLOWER
SWEET PEA
TULIP
WALLFLOWER

E	S	H	E	L	S	I	C	R	L	A	C	E	W	Y
S	O	E	S	O	R	K	A	R	P	R	U	W	A	R
D	L	I	S	D	C	A	L	S	W	U	R	T	E	L
F	D	D	S	T	W	L	I	P	T	E	I	W	W	T
P	A	A	S	S	H	R	L	S	W	O	O	P	R	S
S	F	P	E	S	O	L	L	O	E	L	C	R	L	U
L	F	T	T	P	A	U	L	L	F	E	H	K	R	L
L	O	L	S	Y	T	F	O	L	D	R	R	S	K	O
L	D	D	R	I	N	E	L	R	I	S	O	F	P	I
Y	I	W	L	U	T	A	E	S	C	L	D	P	R	D
N	L	U	S	U	W	W	S	W	C	H	Y	L	L	A
O	S	E	L	P	G	E	P	I	S	R	I	C	U	L
E	F	I	D	A	I	S	Y	C	R	W	I	D	A	G
P	P	U	L	Y	P	P	O	P	I	I	F	A	L	P
E	U	P	R	Y	L	F	F	Y	W	F	O	U	R	I

265. CIRCULAR MAZE

Can you find a route from the gap at the top to the gap at the bottom of this circular maze?

266. CODEWORD

A codeword is a coded crossword in which every letter has been replaced by a number, indicated by the small digits in the top left corner of each crossword square.

Work out which number represents each letter of the alphabet and use this information to complete the crossword grid.

Use the letters outside the grid, and the empty squares beneath the grid, to keep track of your deductions.

267. CHRISTMAS GIFT BOXES

Can you rearrange these gift boxes into their correct order? Once properly aligned they will spell out a word associated with Christmas.

268. KAKURO

Place a digit from 1 to 9 into each white square.

Each horizontal run of white squares adds up to the total above the diagonal line to the left of the run, and each vertical run of white squares adds up to the total below the diagonal line above the run.

No digit can be used more than once in any run.

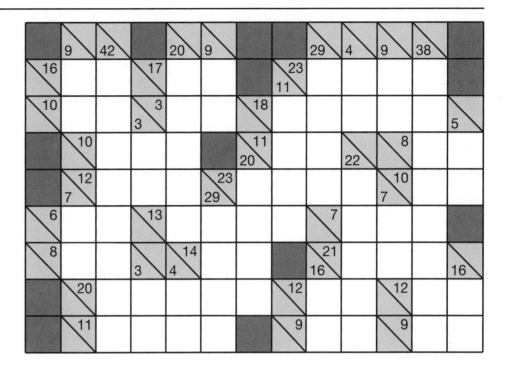

269. SLITHERLINK

Draw a single loop by connecting some dots with horizontal and vertical lines so that each numbered square has the specified number of adjacent line segments.

The loop cannot cross or touch itself.

270. RECTANGLES

Draw borders along some grid lines to divide the grid into a set of rectangles, such that each rectangle contains exactly one number.

All grid squares must be contained within exactly one rectangle.

The number inside each rectangle must be exactly equal to the number of grid squares that the rectangle contains, so for example a "4" could only be in a 1 × 4, 2 × 2, or 4 × 1 rectangle.

Note that the term "rectangle" also includes squares.

	4							2	
			6		2	2			
		9			6				
3								4	4
							4		
8				6		3			
				3					2
				6			10		4
	6		6						

271. CALCUDOKU

20×	9+		3÷		8+
		8+			
90×			5−		32×
	5÷		90×		
5+	1−			18×	
			20×		

Place the numbers 1 to 6 once each into every row and column of the grid, while obeying the region clues.

The value at the top left of each bold-lined region must be obtained when all of the numbers in that region have the given operation (+, -, ×, ÷) applied between them. For - and ÷ operations, begin with the largest number in the region and then subtract or divide by the other numbers in the region in any order.

272. SLANTED SUMS

Place 1 to 6 once each in every row and column.

Numbers outside the grid give the total of the indicated diagonals.

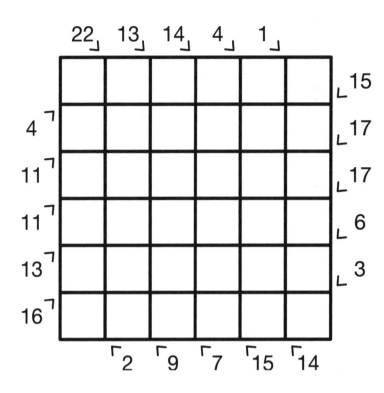

273. QUIZ

Test your knowledge of a specialist subject with this quiz.

Board Games

1. Which tile-placing board game, which involves building roads, cities, and fields, shares its name with a fortified town in the south of France?

2. Which best-selling multiplayer game, based around a hexagonal game board, was designed by Klaus Teuber?

3. What is the most expensive property on the *Monopoly* board?

4. Which board game is centered around the murder of Mr. Boddy?

5. How many white squares are there on a chessboard?

274. FUTOSHIKI

Place 1 to 7 once each into every row and column while obeying the inequality signs.

Greater than (>) signs between some squares indicate that the value in one square is greater than that in another as indicated by the sign. The sign always points toward the smaller number.

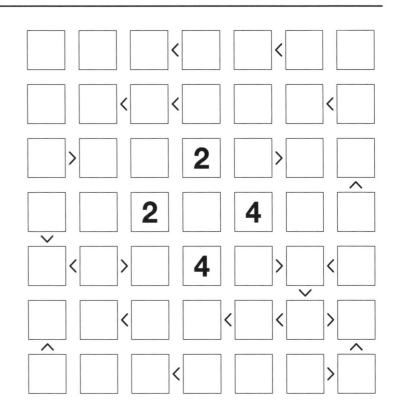

275. NUMBER LINK

1	2							3
		4		5			2	
6					7			
	8						5	
		9		1		7		
		10	11					12
		9	3		11	4		
		8			10			
			6			12		

Draw a series of separate paths, each connecting a pair of identical numbers.

No more than one path can enter any grid square, and paths can only travel horizontally or vertically, and never diagonally.

276. ARROWWORD

Complete this crossword where all of the clues are given within the grid.

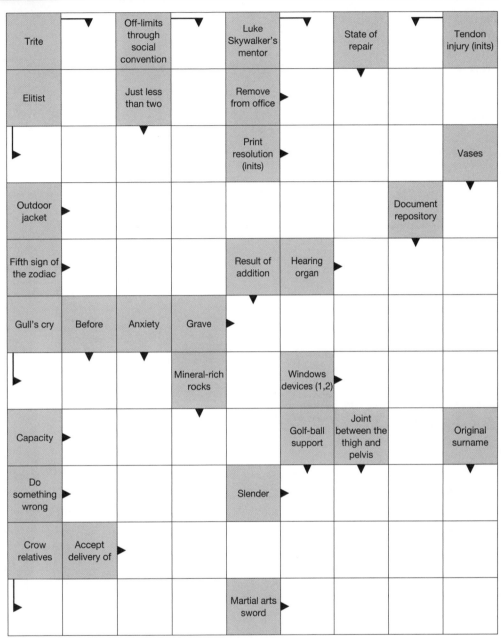

277. CHRISTMAS JUMBLE

Rearrange the following letters to reveal something associated with Christmas.

SECRET GRADING

278. JIGSAW LETTERS

Place A to H once each in every row, column, and bold-lined region.

279. SKYSCRAPERS

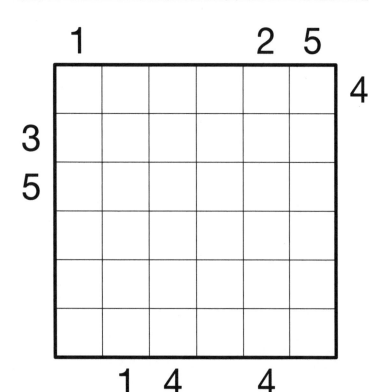

Place 1 to 6 once each into every row and column of the grid.

Place digits in the grid in such a way that each given clue number outside the grid represents the number of digits that are "visible" from that point, looking along that clue's row or column.

A digit is visible unless there is a higher digit preceding it, reading in order along that row or column. For example, if a row was "214356" then the 2, 4, 5, and 6 would be visible from the left end (giving a clue of "5" visible digits), since 1 is obscured by the preceding higher 2, and 3 is obscured by the preceding higher 4. A clue at the right-hand end of the same row would be "1," since only the 6 would be visible.

280. FITWORD

Place each of the following words into the empty squares, crossword-style.

3 Letters
Cup
Eon
Ski
Tar

4 Letters
Asap
Egos
Pyre
Stat

6 Letters
Ceased

Eraser
Graphs
Normal
Nuclei
Regret
Sonata
Stored

8 Letters
Genocide
Opponent
Randomly
Rhetoric

9 Letters
Advancing
Irritates
Presently
Reproduce
Unpopular
Viewpoint

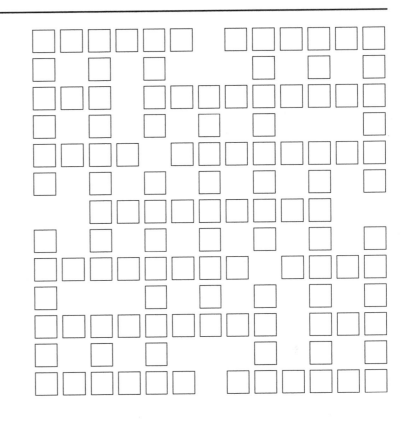

281. PATH HUNTER

Join dots with horizontal and vertical lines to form a single path which does not touch or cross itself at any point. The start and end of the path are given. Numbers outside the grid specify the number of dots in their row or column that are visited by the path.

282. TOUCHY

Place A to F once each in every row and column such that two identical letters never touch—not even diagonally.

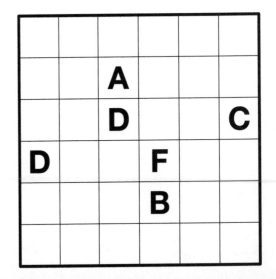

283. SUDOKU

Place 1 to 9 once each into every row, column, and bold-lined 3 × 3 square.

		5		1		8		
		3		5				
4		3				1		5
	6			7			5	
8			6	3	1			4
	9			4			8	
7		1				9		2
			4		7			
		8		9		4		

284. BRIDGES

Join circled numbers with horizontal or vertical lines. Each number must have as many lines connected to it as specified by its value.

No more than two lines may join any pair of numbers, and no lines may cross.

The finished layout must connect all numbers, so you can travel between any pair of numbers by following one or more lines.

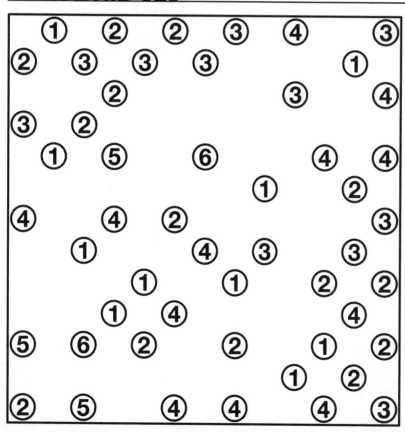

285. BRIDGE MAZE

Find a path from the entrance at the top of the maze to the exit at the bottom of the maze. The path may cross over or under itself by using the marked bridges.

286. WORD CHAIN

Can you complete this word chain, in order to convert the word at the top into the word at the bottom?

At each step you may change only one letter so as to form a new English word, and you may not rearrange any of the letters.

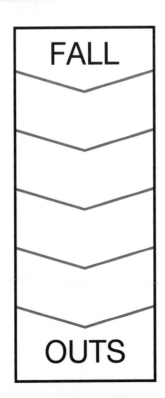

FALL

OUTS

287. LETTER CIRCLE

How many words can you find in this letter circle? Every word must use the center letter plus two or more of the other letters. No letter can be used more than once in a single word. There is one nine-letter seasonal word to find.

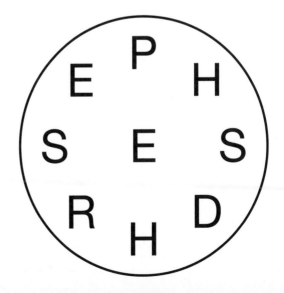

288. PICROSS

Shade in squares in the grid to reveal a picture. Numbers at the start of each row or column reveal, in order from left to right or top to bottom, the length of each consecutive run of shaded squares. There must be a gap of at least one empty square between each run of shaded squares in the same row or column.

Clue: Music-maker

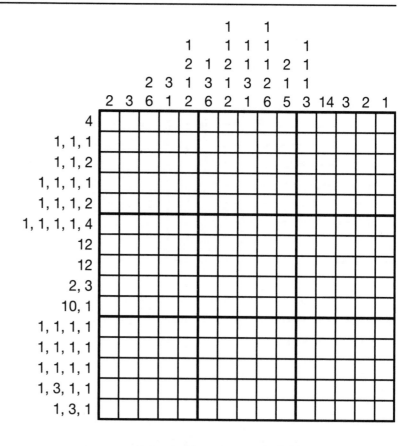

289. WORD RECTANGLE

Can you find the 12-letter word hidden in this Word Rectangle? Find words by moving from letter to touching letter, including diagonally, and without revisiting a square in a single word. How many other words can you find?

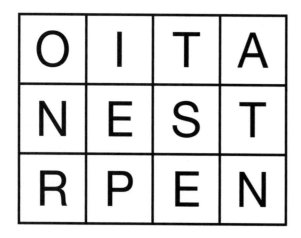

290. BRAIN CHAINS

Without using a calculator or making any written notes, solve these brain chains as quickly as you can. Write the solution in the "Result" box.

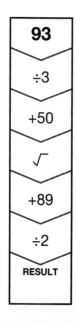

74
×1/2
+67
÷13
+25%
×15
RESULT

93
÷3
+50
√
+89
÷2
RESULT

291. CROSSWORD

Solve the clues to complete the crossword grid.

Across
- **1** Make changes (4)
- **4** Christmas animal (8)
- **8** Soak up (6)
- **9** Not familiar (6)
- **10** Wild guess (4)
- **11** Give the name of (8)
- **13** Offensive (13)
- **16** Electronic piano (8)
- **19** Recipe measure (abbr) (4)
- **20** Paths (6)
- **22** Used to stop a boat from moving (6)
- **23** Sencha or Longjing (5,3)
- **24** Has dinner (4)

Down
- **2** Open to question (9)
- **3** Aggravation (7)
- **4** Jewish teacher (5)
- **5** Before birth (2,5)
- **6** Distrust (5)
- **7** Woolly female (3)
- **12** Disappoint (4,5)
- **14** Public transport (7)
- **15** Item (7)
- **17** Immerse in liquid so as to clean (5)
- **18** Former Princess of Wales (5)
- **21** Prayer, ___ Father (3)

292. DOMINOES

Draw solid lines to divide the grid to form a complete set of standard dominoes, with exactly one of each domino. A "0" represents a blank on a traditional domino.

Use the checkoff chart to help you keep track of which dominoes you've placed.

6	5	2	1	2	4	0	4
2	0	5	5	1	4	4	3
5	5	0	6	0	0	3	3
0	2	3	2	4	3	5	4
0	1	4	6	6	5	2	6
3	6	2	6	0	1	2	3
1	1	1	6	5	1	4	3

0	1	2	3	4	5	6	
							0
							1
							2
							3
							4
							5
							6

293. KILLER SUDOKU

Place the digits 1 to 9 once each into every row, column, and bold-lined 3 × 3 square.

Each dashed-line cage must contain digits that add up to the given number.

No digit can repeat within a dashed-line cage.

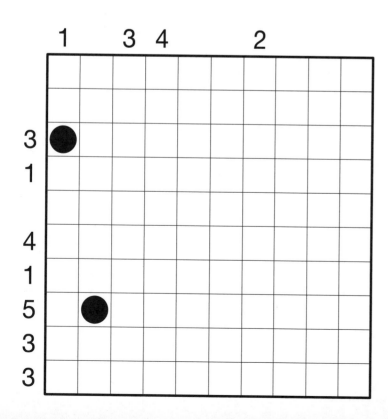

294. SNAKE

Shade some squares to form a snake that starts and ends at the given squares.

A snake is a single path of adjacent squares that does not branch or cross over itself.

The snake does not touch itself—not even diagonally.

Numbers outside the grid specify the number of squares in their row or column that contain part of the snake.

295. WORD SEARCH—FAMOUS COMPOSERS

Can you find all of these words or phrases in the grid? They may be written in any direction, including diagonally.

BACH
BEETHOVEN
BRAHMS
BRUCKNER
BYRD
DVORAK
GLUCK
GRIEG

HANDEL
HAYDN
MAHLER
PUCCINI
PURCELL
STRAUSS
TALLIS
WAGNER

T	S	I	R	L	N	R	T	L	B	D	M	A	M	R
A	M	K	N	G	R	E	R	A	H	B	T	R	A	R
R	H	K	A	I	L	N	V	I	L	N	A	S	H	E
E	A	A	E	P	C	B	A	O	G	L	E	L	L	L
L	R	R	S	R	C	C	A	H	H	L	I	H	E	Y
N	B	O	N	P	R	R	U	C	H	T	I	S	R	G
N	Y	V	B	E	P	H	E	P	H	E	E	K	E	E
D	B	D	R	S	A	U	A	N	G	L	E	E	N	I
Y	M	R	U	S	R	E	R	N	H	L	A	H	B	R
A	T	H	C	U	B	R	R	C	D	Y	U	P	T	G
H	R	C	K	A	H	A	L	E	E	E	A	C	C	M
K	N	C	N	R	U	B	R	N	N	L	L	H	K	S
E	R	W	E	T	K	B	R	H	R	G	L	O	N	I
C	A	E	R	S	T	B	Y	R	D	E	A	M	U	I
D	R	G	H	A	D	U	M	E	K	V	E	W	R	E

296. CIRCULAR MAZE

Can you find a route from the gap at the top to the gap at the bottom of this circular maze?

297. CODEWORD

A codeword is a coded crossword in which every letter has been replaced by a number, indicated by the small digits in the top left corner of each crossword square.

Work out which number represents each letter of the alphabet and use this information to complete the crossword grid.

Use the letters outside the grid, and the empty squares beneath the grid, to keep track of your deductions.

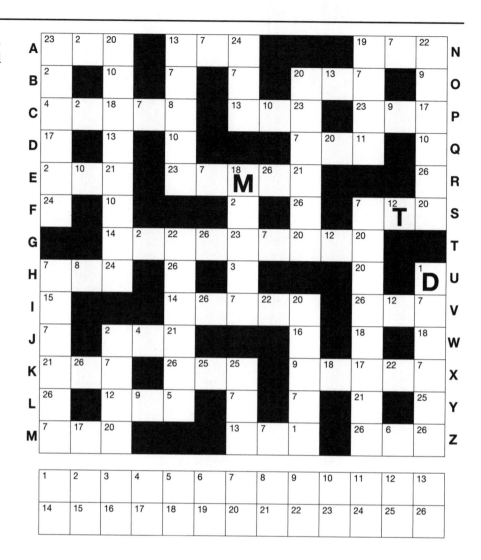

298. CHRISTMAS GIFT BOXES

Can you rearrange these gift boxes into their correct order? Once properly aligned they will spell out a word associated with Christmas.

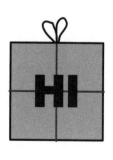

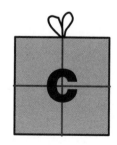

299. KAKURO

Place a digit from 1 to 9 into each white square.

Each horizontal run of white squares adds up to the total above the diagonal line to the left of the run, and each vertical run of white squares adds up to the total below the diagonal line above the run.

No digit can be used more than once in any run.

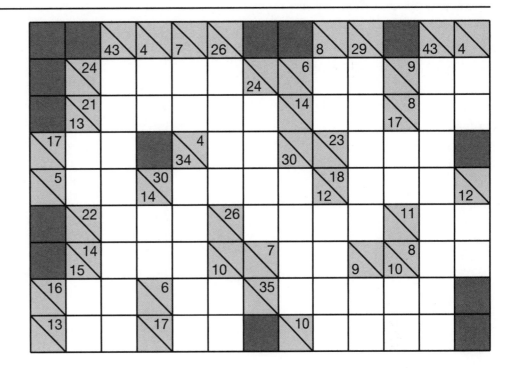

300. SLITHERLINK

Draw a single loop by connecting some dots with horizontal and vertical lines so that each numbered square has the specified number of adjacent line segments.

The loop cannot cross or touch itself.

```
.   .   .   .   .   .   .   .   .   .
          3       3  1
.   .   .   .   .   .   .   .   .   .
2     3     2     2  2     3
.   .   .   .   .   .   .   .   .   .
2  3     1     1
.   .   .   .   .   .   .   .   .   .
        1  1     3     3
.   .   .   .   .   .   .   .   .   .
  3     3  2  1           1
.   .   .   .   .   .   .   .   .   .
3        2  2  2     3
.   .   .   .   .   .   .   .   .   .
  1     2     3  1
.   .   .   .   .   .   .   .   .   .
           2     1     3  1
.   .   .   .   .   .   .   .   .   .
1     2  2     2     2     3
.   .   .   .   .   .   .   .   .   .
  3  3     3
```

301. RECTANGLES

Draw borders along some grid lines to divide the grid into a set of rectangles, such that each rectangle contains exactly one number.

All grid squares must be contained within exactly one rectangle.

The number inside each rectangle must be exactly equal to the number of grid squares that the rectangle contains, so for example a "4" could only be in a 1 × 4, 2 × 2, or 4 × 1 rectangle.

Note that the term "rectangle" also includes squares.

		4						8	
	2			9			4		
10		6	6						
					4				
				8		8			
						4		16	
	7	4							

302. CALCUDOKU

12+	10×	3×	11+		2-
			2×		
	15+	1-		2-	
		1-			30×
3+	5+		3-	9+	
	24×				

Place the numbers 1 to 6 once each into every row and column of the grid, while obeying the region clues.

The value at the top left of each bold-lined region must be obtained when all of the numbers in that region have the given operation (+, -, ×, ÷) applied between them. For - and ÷ operations, begin with the largest number in the region and then subtract or divide by the other numbers in the region in any order.

303. SLANTED SUMS

Place 1 to 6 once each in every row and column.

Numbers outside the grid give the total of the indicated diagonals.

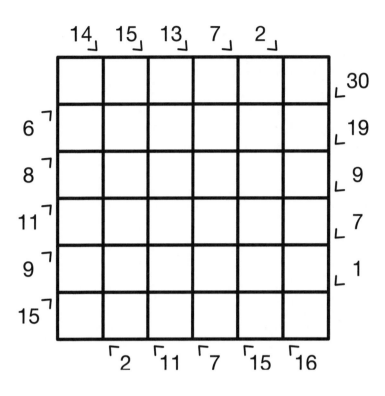

304. QUIZ

Test your knowledge of a specialist subject with this quiz.

Movie Magic

1. Which animation company did Apple cofounder Steve Jobs also cofound?

2. What is the name of the special effects company founded by George Lucas?

3. What is the name of the software, originally developed for *Lord of the Rings*, that creates animated on-screen fights between huge armies?

4. In movies, what do the initials "CGI" stand for?

5. Which New Zealand effects house was cofounded by Peter Jackson?

305. FUTOSHIKI

Place 1 to 7 once each into every row and column while obeying the inequality signs.

Greater than (>) signs between some squares indicate that the value in one square is greater than that in another as indicated by the sign. The sign always points toward the smaller number.

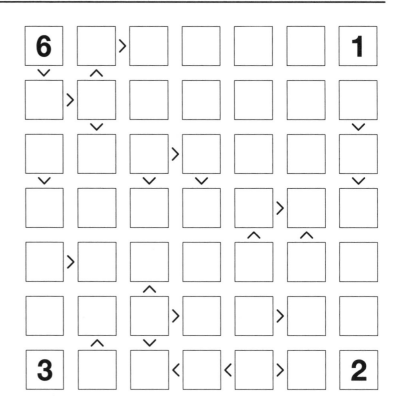

306. NUMBER LINK

Draw a series of separate paths, each connecting a pair of identical numbers.

No more than one path can enter any grid square, and paths can only travel horizontally or vertically, and never diagonally.

1								
2			2				3	4
							5	
	6			6	4		3	
							1	
							7	
	8					8		
								9
10	11			11	9		7	5	
				10				

307. ARROWWORD

Complete this crossword where all of the clues are given within the grid.

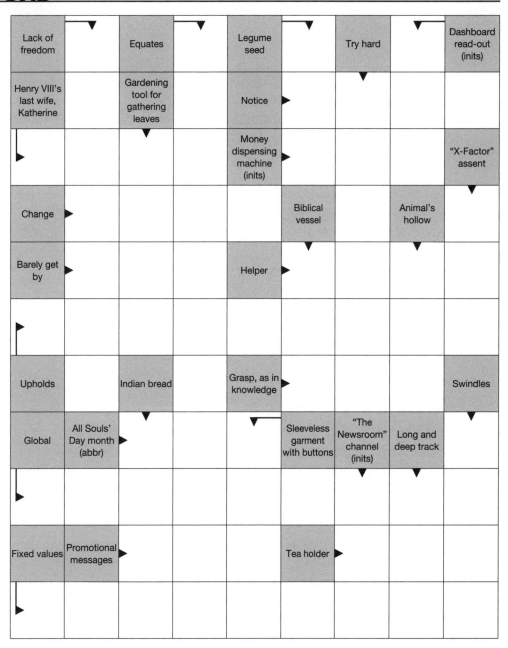

308. CHRISTMAS JUMBLE

Rearrange the following letters to reveal something associated with Christmas.

IGNORING CLASS

309. JIGSAW LETTERS

Place A to H once each in every row, column, and bold-lined region.

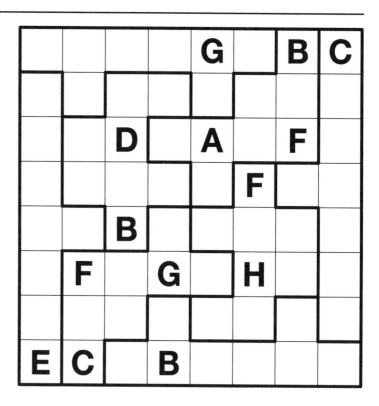

310. SKYSCRAPERS

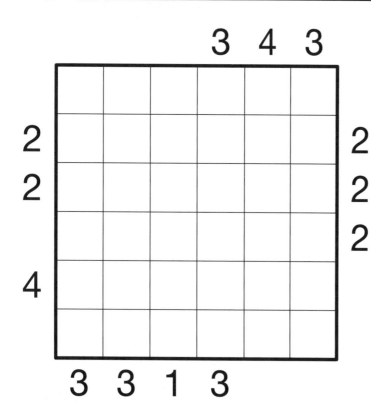

Place 1 to 6 once each into every row and column of the grid.

Place digits in the grid in such a way that each given clue number outside the grid represents the number of digits that are "visible" from that point, looking along that clue's row or column.

A digit is visible unless there is a higher digit preceding it, reading in order along that row or column. For example, if a row was "214356" then the 2, 4, 5, and 6 would be visible from the left end (giving a clue of "5" visible digits), since 1 is obscured by the preceding higher 2, and 3 is obscured by the preceding higher 4. A clue at the right-hand end of the same row would be "1," since only the 6 would be visible.

311. FITWORD

Place each of the following words into the empty squares, crossword-style.

3 Letters
Elm
Use

4 Letters
Clef
Onus

5 Letters
Beset
Ditch
Needs
Other

6 Letters
Beasts
Denied
Handed
Intake
Neural
Untrue

7 Letters
Shampoo
Whisper

8 Letters
Features
Updating

9 Letters
Creatures
Maintains
Witnesses

13 Letters
Enlightenment
Manufacturers

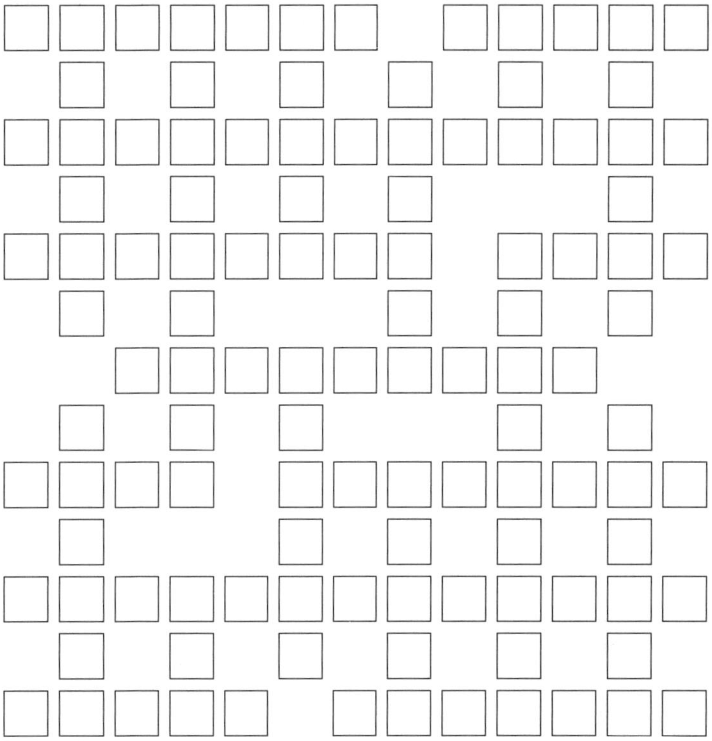

312. PATH HUNTER

Join dots with horizontal and vertical lines to form a single path which does not touch or cross itself at any point. The start and end of the path are given. Numbers outside the grid specify the number of dots in their row or column that are visited by the path.

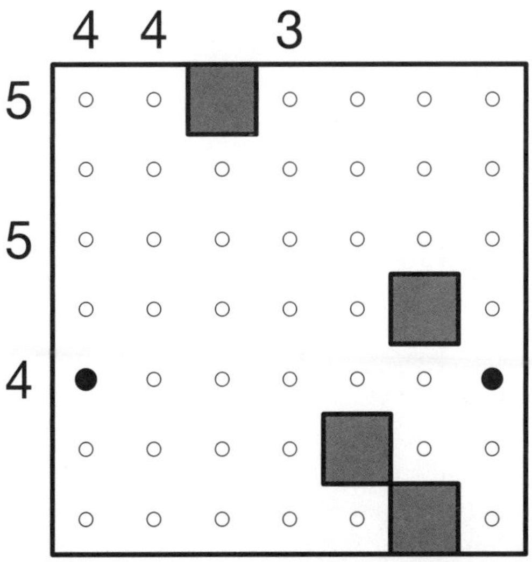

313. TOUCHY

Place A to F once each in every row and column such that two identical letters never touch—not even diagonally.

314. SUDOKU

Place 1 to 9 once each into every row, column, and bold-lined 3 × 3 square.

4		5	6		1	8		7
	9		5		8		3	
8								5
7	4		1		2		5	8
6	8		3		4		2	1
3								9
	7		2		6		8	
1		8	9		7	4		2

315. BRIDGES

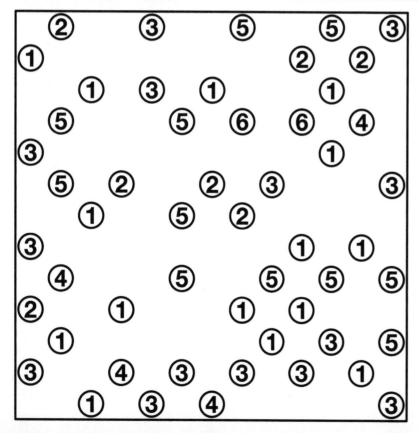

Join circled numbers with horizontal or vertical lines. Each number must have as many lines connected to it as specified by its value.

No more than two lines may join any pair of numbers, and no lines may cross.

The finished layout must connect all numbers, so you can travel between any pair of numbers by following one or more lines.

316. BRIDGE MAZE

Find a path from the entrance at the top of the maze to the exit at the bottom of the maze. The path may cross over or under itself by using the marked bridges.

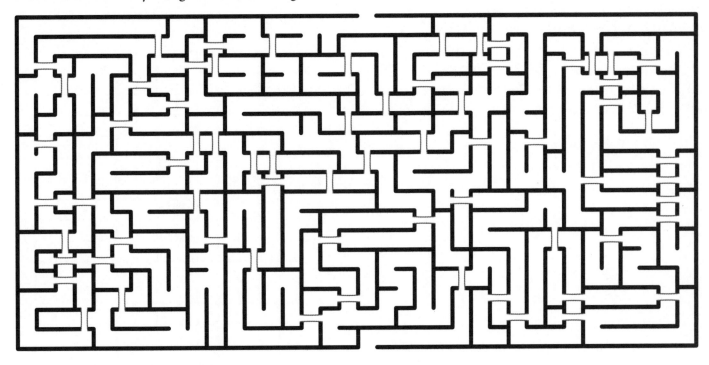

317. WORD CHAIN

Can you complete this word chain, in order to convert the word at the top into the word at the bottom?

At each step you may change only one letter so as to form a new English word, and you may not rearrange any of the letters.

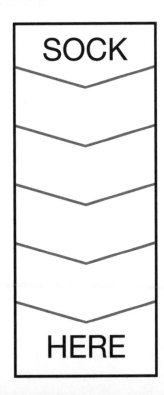

SOCK

HERE

318. LETTER CIRCLE

How many words can you find in this letter circle? Every word must use the center letter plus two or more of the other letters. No letter can be used more than once in a single word. There is one nine-letter seasonal word to find.

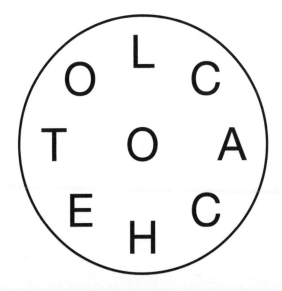

319. PICROSS

Shade in squares in the grid to reveal a picture. Numbers at the start of each row or column reveal, in order from left to right or top to bottom, the length of each consecutive run of shaded squares. There must be a gap of at least one empty square between each run of shaded squares in the same row or column.

Clue: Seasonal weather

Column clues (left to right, each read top to bottom):

4	3 2 2 2 2	2 2	2 2 2 2	2 1 1	3 2 2	2 2 3 1	1 2 1 1 1	2 1 2 1 1	1 2 1 1	2 2 2 4	1 1 1 1 1	2 2 2 1 2	2 1 1 1 2	4 1 3 1

Row clues (top to bottom):

2, 4, 3
7, 3, 2
2, 3, 2
1, 1
2, 4, 1
2, 4, 3
2, 3
1, 4, 1, 1
1, 5
1, 3, 3
1, 1, 2, 1
1, 11
1, 1
1, 1, 1, 2
1, 3, 5

320. WORD RECTANGLE

Can you find the 12-letter word hidden in this Word Rectangle? Find words by moving from letter to touching letter, including diagonally, and without revisiting a square in a single word. How many other words can you find?

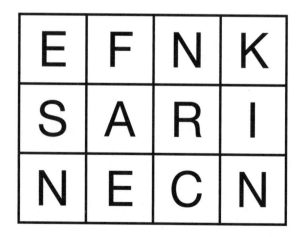

E	F	N	K
S	A	R	I
N	E	C	N

321. BRAIN CHAINS

Without using a calculator or making any written notes, solve these brain chains as quickly as you can. Write the solution in the "Result" box.

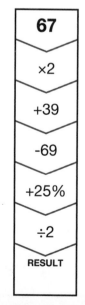

67
×2
+39
-69
+25%
÷2
RESULT

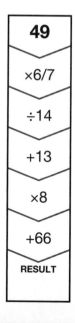

49
×6/7
÷14
+13
×8
+66
RESULT

322. CROSSWORD

Solve the clues to complete the crossword grid.

Across
1 A, B, or C (6)
4 European measurement system (6)
9 Acquire (3)
10 Acted a part (9)
11 Unpleasant sound (5)
12 Conducts oneself (7)
14 Crumbly white cheese of English origin (11)
17 Pendulous ornamental shrub (7)
18 *Tosca*, eg (5)
20 Financial aspects (9)
22 Bother (3)
23 Depressing (6)
24 Me (6)

Down
1 Fable (6)
2 As one, in music (5)
3 Fast trains (9)
5 Self-importance (3)
6 Separation (7)
7 Secret languages (5)
8 Dubious (11)
13 In an extremely ugly way (9)
15 Shut in (7)
16 Return on a bet (6)
17 Released (5)
19 Elude (5)
21 Rowing requirement (3)

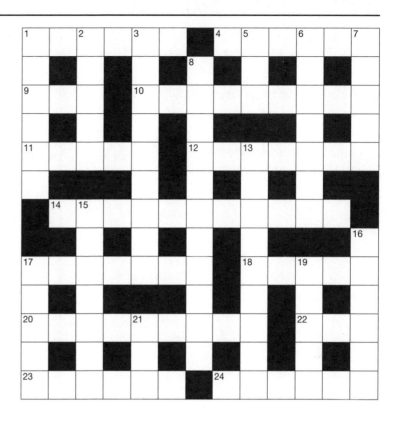

323. DOMINOES

Draw solid lines to divide the grid to form a complete set of standard dominoes, with exactly one of each domino. A "0" represents a blank on a traditional domino.

Use the checkoff chart to help you keep track of which dominoes you've placed.

5	2	0	4	4	1	1	3
3	5	2	0	1	3	6	3
2	6	4	2	6	6	2	6
4	1	3	0	1	2	0	4
1	6	3	5	0	5	2	2
5	0	6	4	4	3	1	6
5	5	0	0	3	5	4	1

0	1	2	3	4	5	6	
							0
							1
							2
							3
							4
							5
							6

324. KILLER SUDOKU

Place the digits 1 to 9 once each into every row, column, and bold-lined 3 × 3 square.

Each dashed-line cage must contain digits that add up to the given number.

No digit can repeat within a dashed-line cage.

325. SNAKE

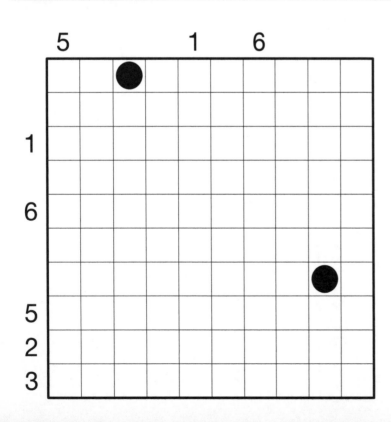

Shade some squares to form a snake that starts and ends at the given squares.

A snake is a single path of adjacent squares that does not branch or cross over itself.

The snake does not touch itself—not even diagonally.

Numbers outside the grid specify the number of squares in their row or column that contain part of the snake.

326. WORD SEARCH—PETS

Can you find all of these words or phrases in the grid? They may be written in any direction, including diagonally.

CAT
CHINCHILLA
DOG
DUCK
FROG
GERBIL
GOAT
GOLDFISH

GUINEA PIG
HAMSTER
HORSE
MOUSE
PARROT
PONY
RABBIT
TURTLE

G	G	I	H	S	I	F	D	L	O	G	D	U	C	K
O	I	T	D	L	I	A	S	E	E	D	I	I	L	R
A	T	A	D	C	O	I	I	G	B	G	B	O	H	N
T	T	O	D	M	A	L	L	I	H	C	N	I	H	C
O	G	N	R	G	A	R	U	G	E	N	D	S	O	L
S	O	G	L	R	S	H	C	Y	P	S	L	H	H	L
O	G	E	D	R	A	I	A	C	N	G	U	E	E	I
T	G	R	F	T	E	P	H	M	U	O	S	O	G	B
D	E	B	I	U	O	N	S	I	S	R	P	N	M	I
T	I	I	T	R	G	G	N	H	O	T	L	N	A	C
A	T	L	S	A	O	E	B	H	A	R	E	F	E	G
C	O	A	T	R	A	H	A	R	Y	R	L	R	C	P
M	L	O	F	P	I	L	A	G	C	I	H	H	O	E
F	S	I	I	T	U	R	T	L	E	D	T	R	E	R
S	L	G	D	G	L	T	R	A	B	B	I	T	E	I

327. CIRCULAR MAZE

Can you find a route from the gap at the top to the gap at the bottom of this circular maze?

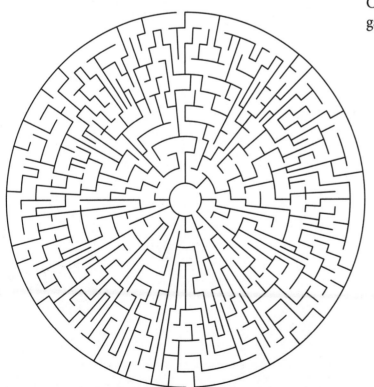

328. CODEWORD

A codeword is a coded crossword in which every letter has been replaced by a number, indicated by the small digits in the top left corner of each crossword square.

Work out which number represents each letter of the alphabet and use this information to complete the crossword grid.

Use the letters outside the grid, and the empty squares beneath the grid, to keep track of your deductions.

A	7	■	7	16	15	■	18 **L**	■	24	■	6	■	11	**N**
B	17	14	17	■	14	4	16	13	20	■	14	7	20	**O**
C	16	■	2	■	3	■	2	■	11	■	11	■	2	**P**
D	1	2	12	14	7	16	4	24	■	7	22	20	5	**Q**
E	13	■	19	■	18	■	■	■	4	■	25	■	■	**R**
F	7	16	7	■	2	18	23	■	9	14	16	22	■	**S**
G	■	13	■	20	■	■	2	■	3	■	20	■	■	**T**
H	■	12	26	10	15	■	7	2	5	■	20	18	11	**U**
I	■	17	■	13	■	■	■	21	■	■	21	■	14	**V**
J	24	8	11	7	■	9	14	10	15	13	20	15	7	**W**
K	14	■	10	■	13 **T**	■	15 **R**	■	14	■	4	■	18	**X**
L	8	20	22	■	5	10	24	2	4	■	18	20	16	**Y**
M	7	■	7	■	2	■	20	■	7	2	8	■	4	**Z**

1	2	3	4	5	6	7	8	9	10	11	12	13
14	15	16	17	18	19	20	21	22	23	24	25	26

329. CHRISTMAS GIFT BOXES

Can you rearrange these gift boxes into their correct order? Once properly aligned they will spell out a word associated with Christmas.

330. KAKURO

Place a digit from 1 to 9 into each white square.

Each horizontal run of white squares adds up to the total above the diagonal line to the left of the run, and each vertical run of white squares adds up to the total below the diagonal line above the run.

No digit can be used more than once in any run.

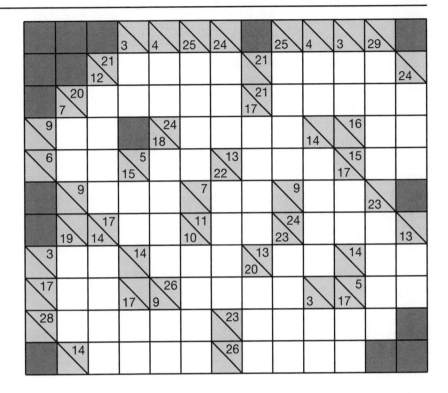

331. SLITHERLINK

Draw a single loop by connecting some dots with horizontal and vertical lines so that each numbered square has the specified number of adjacent line segments.

The loop cannot cross or touch itself.

```
 1   3   2   2   1
   3 1   2   3     1
           3   2     1
 3   3   1   2
       1 2 3   1   0
 1   1   2 0 1
         3   2   1   0
     3   2   1
   1     3   2   3 1
   3   3   3   1   2
```

332. RECTANGLES

Draw borders along some grid lines to divide the grid into a set of rectangles, such that each rectangle contains exactly one number.

All grid squares must be contained within exactly one rectangle.

The number inside each rectangle must be exactly equal to the number of grid squares that the rectangle contains, so for example a "4" could only be in a 1 × 4, 2 × 2, or 4 × 1 rectangle.

Note that the term "rectangle" also includes squares.

333. CALCUDOKU

Place the numbers 1 to 6 once each into every row and column of the grid, while obeying the region clues.

The value at the top left of each bold-lined region must be obtained when all of the numbers in that region have the given operation (+, -, ×, ÷) applied between them. For - and ÷ operations, begin with the largest number in the region and then subtract or divide by the other numbers in the region in any order.

334. SLANTED SUMS

Place 1 to 6 once each in every row and column.

Numbers outside the grid give the total of the indicated diagonals.

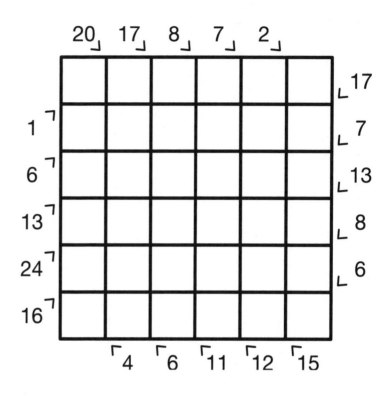

335. QUIZ

Test your knowledge of a specialist subject with this quiz.

The Periodic Table

1. Which element has an atomic weight of 2?

2. What type of element is in the first column of the Periodic Table?

3. What is the chemical symbol for gold?

4. What is the atomic weight of carbon?

5. Which element has the chemical symbol Xe?

336. FUTOSHIKI

Place 1 to 7 once each into every row and column while obeying the inequality signs.

Greater than (>) signs between some squares indicate that the value in one square is greater than that in another as indicated by the sign. The sign always points toward the smaller number.

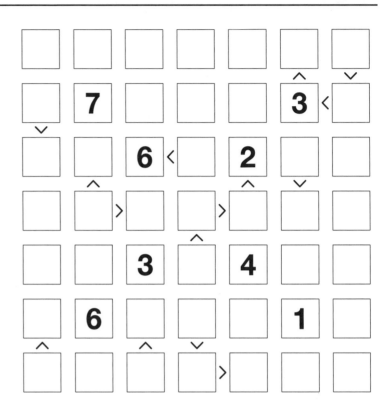

337. NUMBER LINK

Draw a series of separate paths, each connecting a pair of identical numbers.

No more than one path can enter any grid square, and paths can only travel horizontally or vertically, and never diagonally.

1		2	3				
4					3	5	
				5			
	6		7				
						8	9
		8		2			
							10
7		6			9		
			4		1	10	

338. ARROWWORD

Complete this crossword where all of the clues are given within the grid.

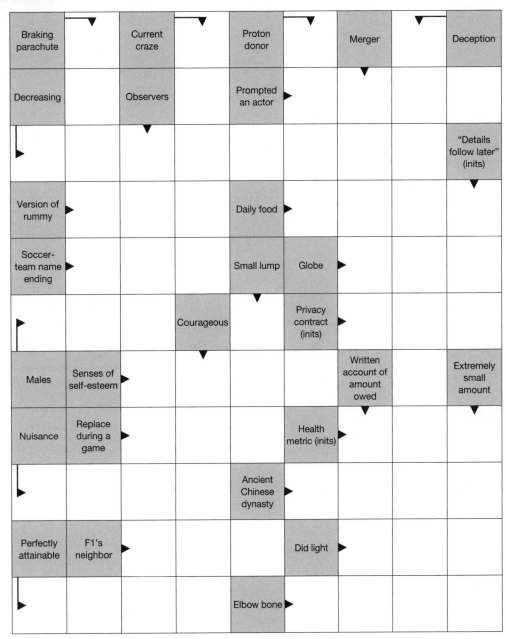

339. CHRISTMAS JUMBLE

Rearrange the following letters to reveal something associated with Christmas.

SOUNDING NEW LIMB

340. JIGSAW LETTERS

Place A to H once each in every row, column, and bold-lined region.

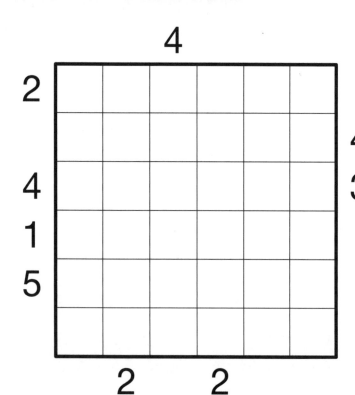

341. SKYSCRAPERS

Place 1 to 6 once each into every row and column of the grid.

Place digits in the grid in such a way that each given clue number outside the grid represents the number of digits that are "visible" from that point, looking along that clue's row or column.

A digit is visible unless there is a higher digit preceding it, reading in order along that row or column. For example, if a row was "214356" then the 2, 4, 5, and 6 would be visible from the left end (giving a clue of "5" visible digits), since 1 is obscured by the preceding higher 2, and 3 is obscured by the preceding higher 4. A clue at the right-hand end of the same row would be "1," since only the 6 would be visible.

342. FITWORD

Place each of the following words into the empty squares, crossword-style.

4 Letters
Eels
Envy
Rent
Unit

5 Letters
Merry
Stuns

6 Letters
Cinema
Errors
Invest

Locate
Nuncio
Oboist
Plasma
Safari

7 Letters
Enclose
Kidneys

8 Letters
Assuming
Aversion

Schmaltz
Teaspoon

11 Letters
Dynamically
Recognizing

343. PATH HUNTER

Join dots with horizontal and vertical lines to form a single path which does not touch or cross itself at any point. The start and end of the path are given. Numbers outside the grid specify the number of dots in their row or column that are visited by the path.

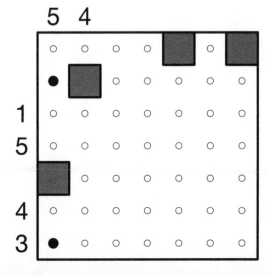

344. TOUCHY

Place A to F once each in every row and column such that two identical letters never touch—not even diagonally.

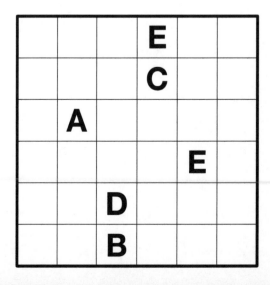

345. SUDOKU

Place 1 to 9 once each into every row, column, and bold-lined 3 × 3 square.

6								1
	3					6		
	9		2	5	6		7	
	8			2		7		
	6	1			4	5		
	7			6		2		
	7		9	8	1		4	
	9					1		
3								5

346. BRIDGES

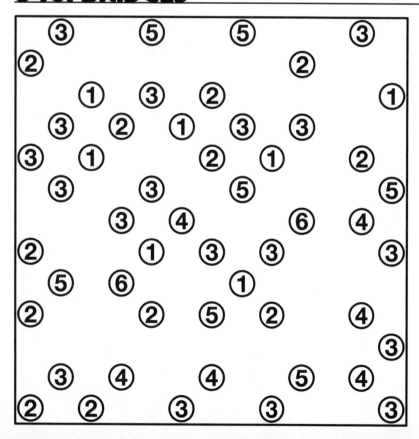

Join circled numbers with horizontal or vertical lines. Each number must have as many lines connected to it as specified by its value.

No more than two lines may join any pair of numbers, and no lines may cross.

The finished layout must connect all numbers, so you can travel between any pair of numbers by following one or more lines.

347. BRIDGE MAZE

Find a path from the entrance at the top of the maze to the exit at the bottom of the maze. The path may cross over or under itself by using the marked bridges.

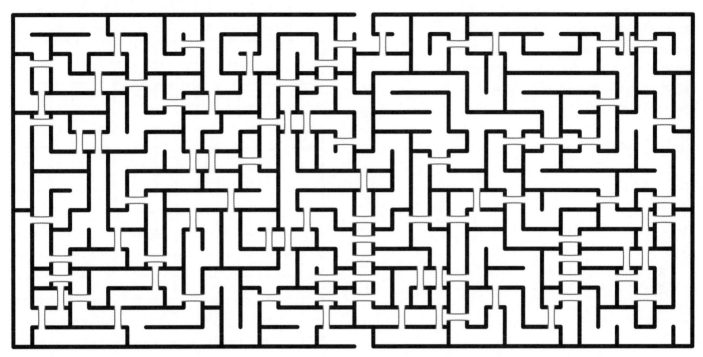

348. WORD CHAIN

Can you complete this word chain, in order to convert the word at the top into the word at the bottom?

At each step you may change only one letter so as to form a new English word, and you may not rearrange any of the letters.

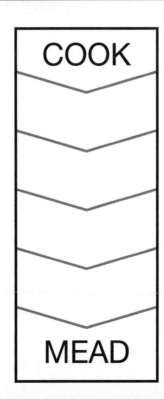

COOK

MEAD

349. LETTER CIRCLE

How many words can you find in this letter circle? Every word must use the center letter plus two or more of the other letters. No letter can be used more than once in a single word. There is one nine-letter seasonal word to find.

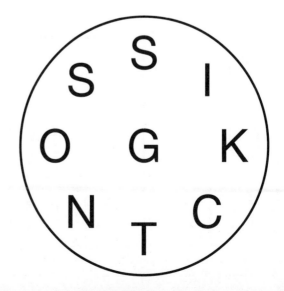

350. PICROSS

Shade in squares in the grid to reveal a picture. Numbers at the start of each row or column reveal, in order from left to right or top to bottom, the length of each consecutive run of shaded squares. There must be a gap of at least one empty square between each run of shaded squares in the same row or column.

Clue: Christmas treat

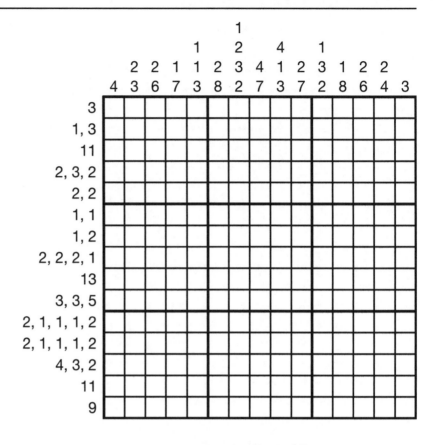

351. WORD RECTANGLE

Can you find the 12-letter word hidden in this Word Rectangle? Find words by moving from letter to touching letter, including diagonally, and without revisiting a square in a single word. How many other words can you find?

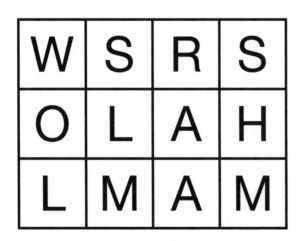

W	S	R	S
O	L	A	H
L	M	A	M

352. BRAIN CHAINS

Without using a calculator or making any written notes, solve these brain chains as quickly as you can. Write the solution in the "Result" box.

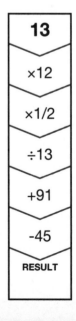

34	13
×1/2	×12
+22	×1/2
×2/3	÷13
-50%	+91
+86	-45
RESULT	RESULT

353. CROSSWORD

Solve the clues to complete the crossword grid.

Across
1 Bitter, yellow fruit (5)
4 Adjudicated (6)
10 Norms (9)
11 Was in charge (3)
12 Better-trained (5)
13 Small (6)
14 Basic (11)
18 Load (6)
20 VIP (5)
23 Payment promise (inits) (3)
24 Sorts (9)
25 Widen (6)
26 Medications (5)

Down
2 A digital letter (5)
3 Sent away for (7)
5 Make someone unhappy (5)
6 Large, African ape (7)
7 Wet and musty (4)
8 Everyday (5)
9 Preparatory (11)
15 Abnormal (7)
16 Fusion power type (7)
17 Vast chasm (5)
19 Quilt (5)
21 In a horizontal position (5)
22 Care about something (4)

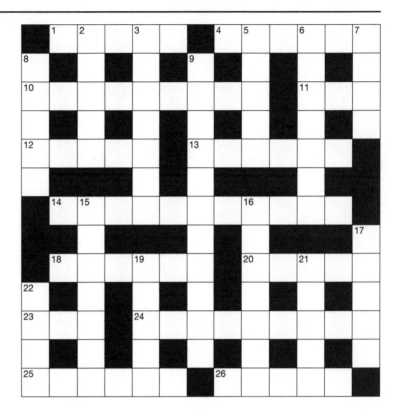

354. DOMINOES

Draw solid lines to divide the grid to form a complete set of standard dominoes, with exactly one of each domino. A "0" represents a blank on a traditional domino.

Use the checkoff chart to help you keep track of which dominoes you've placed.

3	1	5	2	2	4	2	5
1	6	6	1	6	3	6	6
3	0	2	0	4	2	1	2
3	0	0	5	1	6	1	3
1	5	4	4	5	5	1	3
4	4	4	2	6	2	5	4
3	5	0	0	6	0	3	0

0	1	2	3	4	5	6	
							0
							1
							2
							3
							4
							5
							6

355. KILLER SUDOKU

Place the digits 1 to 9 once each into every row, column, and bold-lined 3 × 3 square.

Each dashed-line cage must contain digits that add up to the given number.

No digit can repeat within a dashed-line cage.

356. SNAKE

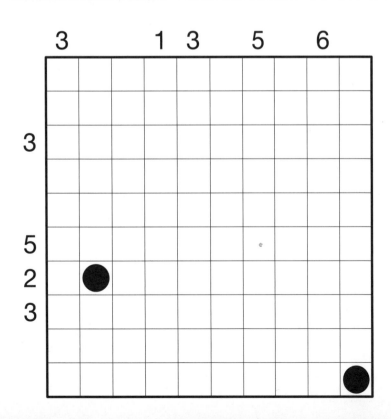

Shade some squares to form a snake that starts and ends at the given squares.

A snake is a single path of adjacent squares that does not branch or cross over itself.

The snake does not touch itself—not even diagonally.

Numbers outside the grid specify the number of squares in their row or column that contain part of the snake.

357. WORD SEARCH—SHAPES

Can you find all of these words or phrases in the grid? They may be written in any direction, including diagonally.

CONE
CYLINDER
DIAMOND
ELLIPSE
HEART
HEXAGON
OVAL
PENTAGON

POLYGON
PYRAMID
RECTANGLE
RHOMBUS
SPHERE
SQUARE
STAR
TRIANGLE

```
M Q E O L O G L A E T D O A P
E R I E P R N A E E N A R E N
L T R A E H S L R O L O R R I
E S P I L L E C G I S A C E E
A L T E N H Q A L U P O N L E
A L C T M T T A B O E A S O L
N R Y N E N V M L U N P O T G
I N L M E O O Y E P H V I R N
R A I P A H G R Y E D G T A A
L E N I R O A R R C E H D T T
S A D O N U A E P M P N L S C
O O E R Q M T R I A N G L E E
L G R S I E H U D E L N E E R
R I E D N O G A X E H Y E A Q
R D I A M O N D V Y N P X A M
```

358. CIRCULAR MAZE

Can you find a route from the gap at the top to the gap at the bottom of this circular maze?

359. CODEWORD

A codeword is a coded crossword in which every letter has been replaced by a number, indicated by the small digits in the top left corner of each crossword square.

Work out which number represents each letter of the alphabet and use this information to complete the crossword grid.

Use the letters outside the grid, and the empty squares beneath the grid, to keep track of your deductions.

Grid (rows A–M, with letters N–Z marked down the right side):

	1	2	3	4	5	6	7	8	9	10	11
A	■	1	9	2	■	18	2	1	■	21	■
B	■	24	■	26	25	16 **S**	11	■	11	4	11	22
C	12	7	22	1	■	13	11	22 **R**	■	7	■
D	■	25	■	22	11	21	17	■	5	2	16	1
E	1	23	25	21	■	11	■	1	■	1	22	1
F	12	■	■	2	7	22	■	11	15	2	■	9
G	20	25	12	14	■	2	25	12	■	23	22	2	23
H	■	10	■	1	3	3	■	12	1	10	■	2
I	25 **I**	21	6	■	2	■	2	■	25	3	1	8
J	■	18	2	7	22	■	16	13	7	14	■	11
K	■	17	■	22	18	2	■	25	5	10	2
L	■	23	1	16	2	■	2	6	1	19	■	1
M	■	16	■	13	1	10	■	1	2	5	■

1	2	3	4	5	6	7	8	9	10	11	12	13

14	15	16	17	18	19	20	21	22	23	24	25	26

360. CHRISTMAS GIFT BOXES

Can you rearrange these gift boxes into their correct order? Once properly aligned they will spell out a word associated with Christmas.

361. KAKURO

Place a digit from 1 to 9 into each white square.

Each horizontal run of white squares adds up to the total above the diagonal line to the left of the run, and each vertical run of white squares adds up to the total below the diagonal line above the run.

No digit can be used more than once in any run.

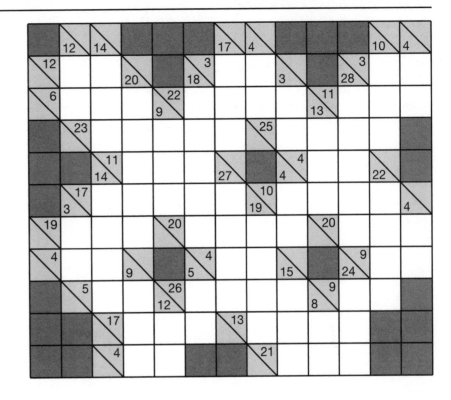

362. SLITHERLINK

Draw a single loop by connecting some dots with horizontal and vertical lines so that each numbered square has the specified number of adjacent line segments.

The loop cannot cross or touch itself.

363. RECTANGLES

Draw borders along some grid lines to divide the grid into a set of rectangles, such that each rectangle contains exactly one number.

All grid squares must be contained within exactly one rectangle.

The number inside each rectangle must be exactly equal to the number of grid squares that the rectangle contains, so for example a "4" could only be in a 1 × 4, 2 × 2, or 4 × 1 rectangle.

Note that the term "rectangle" also includes squares.

						6	4	
6					3			
	2	8			3			
3		6		10				
	4	6			6	3	14	
						3		
3			4				6	

364. CALCUDOKU

Place the numbers 1 to 6 once each into every row and column of the grid, while obeying the region clues.

The value at the top left of each bold-lined region must be obtained when all of the numbers in that region have the given operation (+, -, ×, ÷) applied between them. For - and ÷ operations, begin with the largest number in the region and then subtract or divide by the other numbers in the region in any order.

7+		1−		6×	
7+	2−		8×		5×
	120×		17+		
1−					6+
	5−		2−		
2−		2×		8+	

365. SLANTED SUMS

Place 1 to 6 once each in every row and column.

Numbers outside the grid give the total of the indicated diagonals.

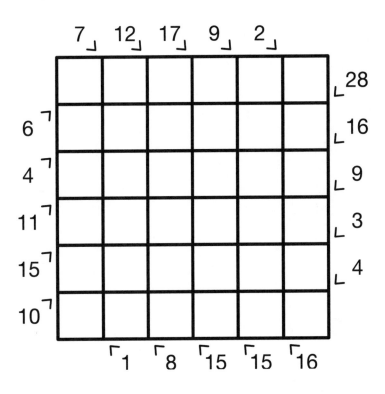

366. QUIZ

Test your knowledge of a specialist subject with this quiz.

Biology

1. How is deoxyribonucleic acid better known?

2. What is the basic structural, functional, and biological unit of a living organism?

3. Which classification is immediately above "phylum" in taxonomic rank?

4. What green pigment plays a key part in plant photosynthesis?

5. How many bones are there in the adult human body?

367. FUTOSHIKI

Place 1 to 7 once each into every row and
column while obeying the inequality signs.

Greater than (>) signs between some
squares indicate that the value in one square
is greater than that in another as indicated
by the sign. The sign always points toward
the smaller number.

1	4				5	6
5						7
				>		
			>			
	>		<			
6						4
3	7		>		6	2

368. NUMBER LINK

Draw a series of separate paths, each
connecting a pair of identical numbers.

No more than one path can enter any grid
square, and paths can only travel horizontally
or vertically, and never diagonally.

					1		
1			2	3		4	
	5						
	6	2	7				
5		4					
			3				
7	8						
6	8						

369. ARROWWORD

Complete this crossword where all of the clues are given within the grid.

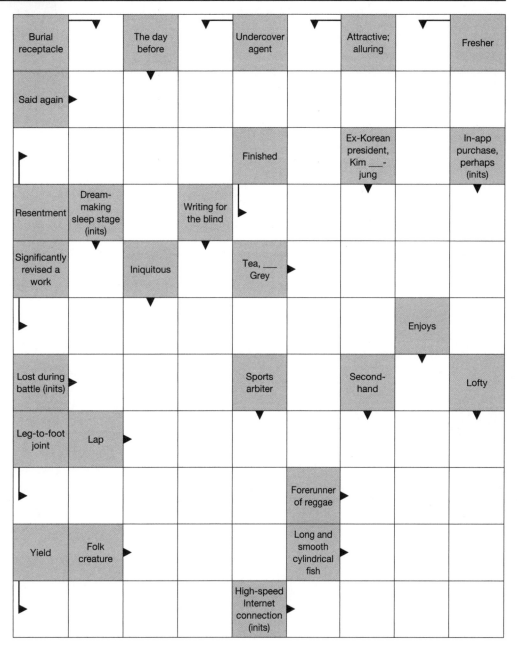

370. CHRISTMAS JUMBLE

Rearrange the following letters to reveal something associated with Christmas.

GANGLAND SHARING

371. JIGSAW LETTERS

Place A to H once each in every row, column, and bold-lined region.

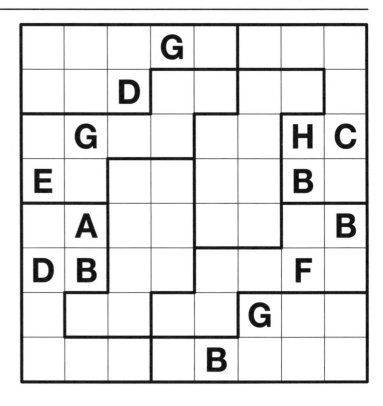

372. SKYSCRAPERS

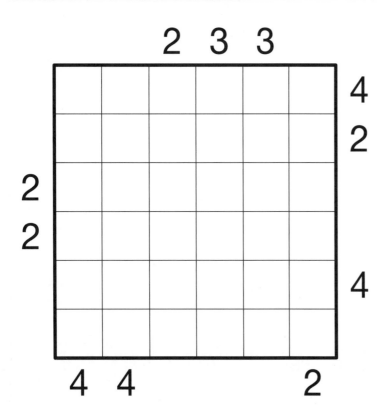

Place 1 to 6 once each into every row and column of the grid.

Place digits in the grid in such a way that each given clue number outside the grid represents the number of digits that are "visible" from that point, looking along that clue's row or column.

A digit is visible unless there is a higher digit preceding it, reading in order along that row or column. For example, if a row was "214356" then the 2, 4, 5, and 6 would be visible from the left end (giving a clue of "5" visible digits), since 1 is obscured by the preceding higher 2, and 3 is obscured by the preceding higher 4. A clue at the right-hand end of the same row would be "1," since only the 6 would be visible.

373. FITWORD

Place each of the following words into the empty squares, crossword-style.

3 Letters
Pie

4 Letters
Numb
Peso
Pity
Taro

5 Letters
Anima
Corgi
Email
Extra

Gaffe
Optic
Rabbi
Stick

6 Letters
Dahlia
Tattoo

7 Letters
Adverse
Faculty
Include
Patient

Periods
Surplus

8 Letters
Mischief
Travesty

12 Letters
Differential
Disappointed

374. PATH HUNTER

Join dots with horizontal and vertical lines to form a single path which does not touch or cross itself at any point. The start and end of the path are given. Numbers outside the grid specify the number of dots in their row or column that are visited by the path.

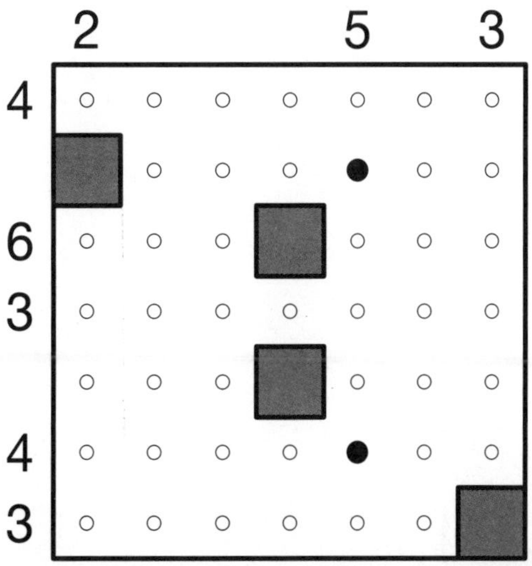

375. TOUCHY

Place A to F once each in every row and column such that two identical letters never touch—not even diagonally.

376. SUDOKU

Place 1 to 9 once each into every row, column, and bold-lined 3 × 3 square.

	1		3		5		4	
2			9		7			6
		5		2		1		
5	2						6	1
		4				5		
7	3						9	4
		3		6		2		
9			5		2			7
	7		4		8		3	

377. BRIDGES

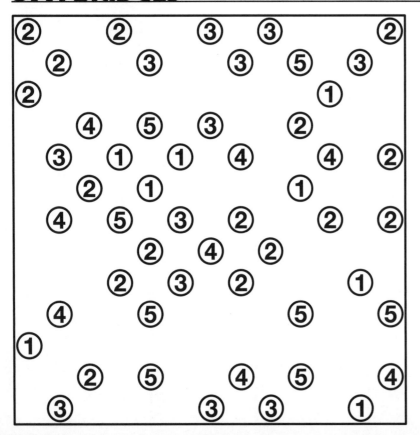

Join circled numbers with horizontal or vertical lines. Each number must have as many lines connected to it as specified by its value.

No more than two lines may join any pair of numbers, and no lines may cross.

The finished layout must connect all numbers, so you can travel between any pair of numbers by following one or more lines.

378. BRIDGE MAZE

Find a path from the entrance at the top of the maze to the exit at the bottom of the maze. The path may cross over or under itself by using the marked bridges.

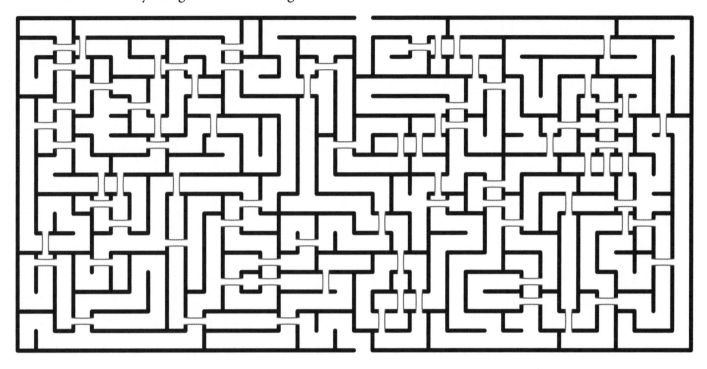

379. WORD CHAIN

Can you complete this word chain, in order to convert the word at the top into the word at the bottom?

At each step you may change only one letter so as to form a new English word, and you may not rearrange any of the letters.

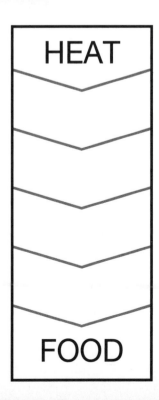

HEAT

FOOD

380. LETTER CIRCLE

How many words can you find in this letter circle? Every word must use the center letter plus two or more of the other letters. No letter can be used more than once in a single word. There is one nine-letter seasonal word to find.

381. PICROSS

Shade in squares in the grid to reveal a picture. Numbers at the start of each row or column reveal, in order from left to right or top to bottom, the length of each consecutive run of shaded squares. There must be a gap of at least one empty square between each run of shaded squares in the same row or column.

Clue: Waste management

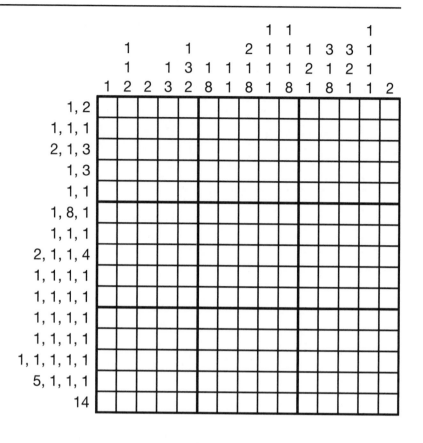

382. WORD RECTANGLE

Can you find the 12-letter word hidden in this Word Rectangle? Find words by moving from letter to touching letter, including diagonally, and without revisiting a square in a single word. How many other words can you find?

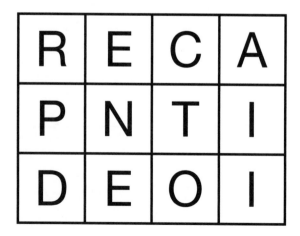

383. BRAIN CHAINS

Without using a calculator or making any written notes, solve these brain chains as quickly as you can. Write the solution in the "Result" box.

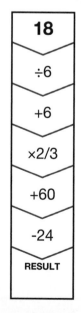

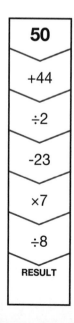

384. CROSSWORD

Solve the clues to complete the crossword grid.

Across
1 Stay attached (6)
4 Type of classical music form (6)
9 Fail (2,5)
10 Track (5)
11 Periods of time before events (4)
12 Relating to a circular path (7)
14 Religious dissent (6)
16 Jail (6)
19 Island in the Mediterranean (7)
21 Candle string (4)
23 Go over with a pen (3,2)
24 Very near (5,2)
25 Chows down (6)
26 Muddles (6)

Down
1 Pond organism (4)
2 In any case (7)
3 Genealogy (5)
5 Halloween month (7)
6 Separated by distance (5)
7 Continually (3,5)
8 House made of ice (5)
13 Protagonist (8)
15 Weird (7)
17 Electricity outlets (7)
18 Fire starter (5)
20 Wisecracks (5)
21 Entire (5)
22 Large creative work (4)

385. DOMINOES

Draw solid lines to divide the grid to form a complete set of standard dominoes, with exactly one of each domino. A "0" represents a blank on a traditional domino.

Use the checkoff chart to help you keep track of which dominoes you've placed.

3	4	0	2	5	1	0	0
3	4	0	3	1	4	4	4
3	1	0	6	1	0	3	1
2	3	2	6	0	4	0	3
5	5	1	6	5	6	6	1
6	2	5	6	5	2	5	4
2	6	4	1	3	2	5	2

0	1	2	3	4	5	6	
							0
							1
							2
							3
							4
							5
							6

386. KILLER SUDOKU

Place the digits 1 to 9 once each into every row, column, and bold-lined 3 × 3 square.

Each dashed-line cage must contain digits that add up to the given number.

No digit can repeat within a dashed-line cage.

387. SNAKE

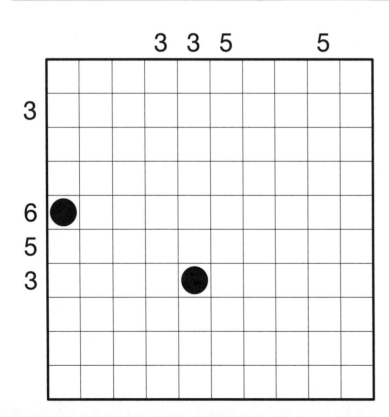

Shade some squares to form a snake that starts and ends at the given squares.

A snake is a single path of adjacent squares that does not branch or cross over itself.

The snake does not touch itself—not even diagonally.

Numbers outside the grid specify the number of squares in their row or column that contain part of the snake.

388. WORD SEARCH—VEGETABLES

Can you find all of these words or phrases in the grid? They may be written in any direction, including diagonally.

BROCCOLI
CABBAGE
CAULIFLOWER
CORN
CUCUMBER
DAIKON
EGGPLANT
ENDIVE

LETTUCE
ONION
PARSNIP
PEA
SHALLOT
SQUASH
WATER CHESTNUT
ZUCCHINI

```
R C U C U M B E R L E C C C I
L B N P A R S N I P S E H R N
R N W P L S K S E Z E U T T R
C P B A S T H O T V E R N N S
H L E T T U C E N G I A C H E
E I N Z A E U R A I L D A U A
T B E U E I R B Z P O L N H B
P W E C C L B C G N L N E E A
F E Q C P A G G H O C A Q U R
P A A H C E E I T E S O C O O
L P S I P O S Q U A S H R Q G
F U G N E E Q H U L A T Z N C
U N L I C E D A I K O N N Q C
R E W O L F I L U A C A R U R
A C E P I L O C C O R B G A T
```

389. CIRCULAR MAZE

Can you find a route from the gap at the top to the gap at the bottom of this circular maze?

390. CODEWORD

A codeword is a coded crossword in which every letter has been replaced by a number, indicated by the small digits in the top left corner of each crossword square.

Work out which number represents each letter of the alphabet and use this information to complete the crossword grid.

Use the letters outside the grid, and the empty squares beneath the grid, to keep track of your deductions.

391. CHRISTMAS GIFT BOXES

Can you rearrange these gift boxes into their correct order? Once properly aligned they will spell out a word associated with Christmas.

392. KAKURO

Place a digit from 1 to 9 into each white square.

Each horizontal run of white squares adds up to the total above the diagonal line to the left of the run, and each vertical run of white squares adds up to the total below the diagonal line above the run.

No digit can be used more than once in any run.

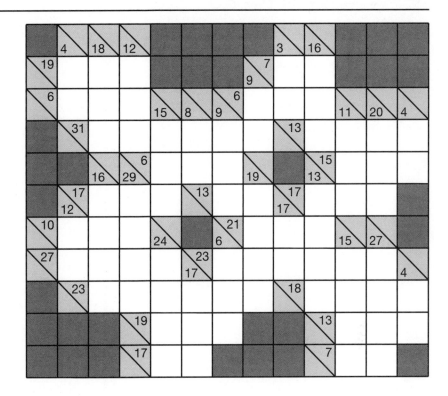

393. SLITHERLINK

Draw a single loop by connecting some dots with horizontal and vertical lines so that each numbered square has the specified number of adjacent line segments.

The loop cannot cross or touch itself.

394. RECTANGLES

Draw borders along some grid lines to divide the grid into a set of rectangles, such that each rectangle contains exactly one number.

All grid squares must be contained within exactly one rectangle.

The number inside each rectangle must be exactly equal to the number of grid squares that the rectangle contains, so for example a "4" could only be in a 1 × 4, 2 × 2, or 4 × 1 rectangle.

Note that the term "rectangle" also includes squares.

						3			
	8		8	9					
5								4	
									5
	4							2	
	3		4	4			2	2	
3								2	
			10						
						6		6	
	3			7					

395. CALCUDOKU

10×			18×	12×	20×
4−	12×				
	7+		9+		
48×			6+		3−
1−	8+	3÷	4×		
			8+		

Place the numbers 1 to 6 once each into every row and column of the grid, while obeying the region clues.

The value at the top left of each bold-lined region must be obtained when all of the numbers in that region have the given operation (+, -, ×, ÷) applied between them. For - and ÷ operations, begin with the largest number in the region and then subtract or divide by the other numbers in the region in any order.

396. SLANTED SUMS

Place 1 to 6 once each in every row and column.

Numbers outside the grid give the total of the indicated diagonals.

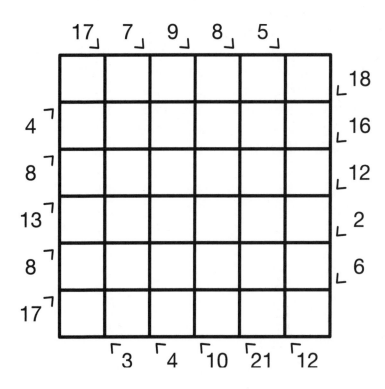

397. QUIZ

Test your knowledge of a specialist subject with this quiz.

Musicals

1. Which musical features the song *Memory*?

2. In what decade is *Hairspray* set?

3. Which musical is about a man-eating plant?

4. Which Lloyd Webber/Rice musical is set in Argentina?

5. Which musical did Schönberg and Boublil write as their follow-up after *Miss Saigon*?

398. FUTOSHIKI

Place 1 to 7 once each into every row and column while obeying the inequality signs.

Greater than (>) signs between some squares indicate that the value in one square is greater than that in another as indicated by the sign. The sign always points toward the smaller number.

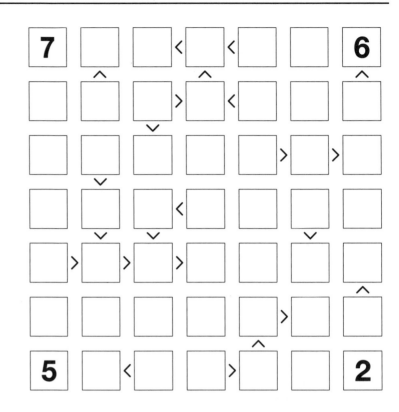

399. NUMBER LINK

Draw a series of separate paths, each connecting a pair of identical numbers.

No more than one path can enter any grid square, and paths can only travel horizontally or vertically, and never diagonally.

400. ARROWWORD

Complete this crossword where all of the clues are given within the grid.

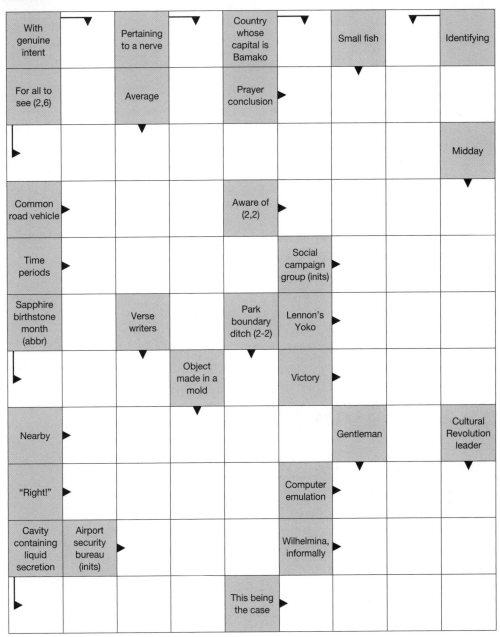

401. CHRISTMAS JUMBLE

Rearrange the following letters to reveal something associated with Christmas.

SYNC A DANCE

402. JIGSAW LETTERS

Place A to H once each in every row, column, and bold-lined region.

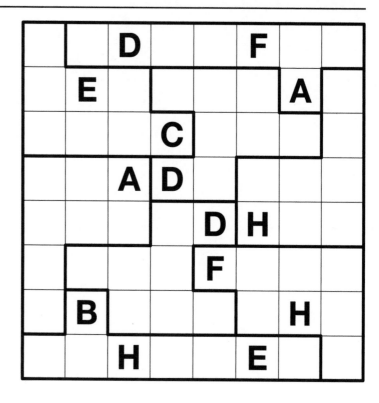

403. SKYSCRAPERS

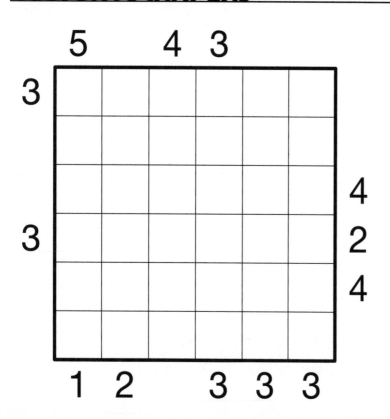

Place 1 to 6 once each into every row and column of the grid.

Place digits in the grid in such a way that each given clue number outside the grid represents the number of digits that are "visible" from that point, looking along that clue's row or column.

A digit is visible unless there is a higher digit preceding it, reading in order along that row or column. For example, if a row was "214356" then the 2, 4, 5, and 6 would be visible from the left end (giving a clue of "5" visible digits), since 1 is obscured by the preceding higher 2, and 3 is obscured by the preceding higher 4. A clue at the right-hand end of the same row would be "1," since only the 6 would be visible.

404. FITWORD

Place each of the following words into the empty squares, crossword-style.

3 Letters
Roe
Ute

4 Letters
Aura
Lion
Oral
Urns

5 Letters
Nylon
Rarer

Smart
Tense

6 Letters
Offset
Prefer
Resist
Routes
Severe
Silent

7 Letters
Fiddles
Fragile

Strange
Unusual

8 Letters
Graduate
Inviting
Particle
Uniquely

9 Letters
Realistic
Varieties

405. PATH HUNTER

Join dots with horizontal and vertical lines to form a single path which does not touch or cross itself at any point. The start and end of the path are given. Numbers outside the grid specify the number of dots in their row or column that are visited by the path.

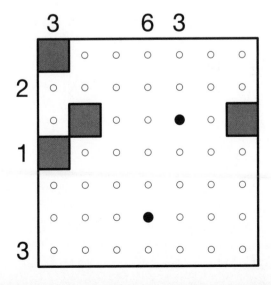

406. TOUCHY

Place A to F once each in every row and column such that two identical letters never touch—not even diagonally.

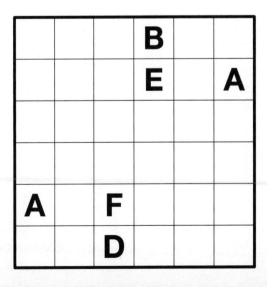

407. SUDOKU

Place 1 to 9 once each into every row, column, and bold-lined 3 × 3 square.

		3	8		5	4		
		6		2		5		
1	8			4			7	2
3								7
	4	8				3	5	
6								9
8	6			7			2	5
		1		5		8		
		4	9		1	7		

408. BRIDGES

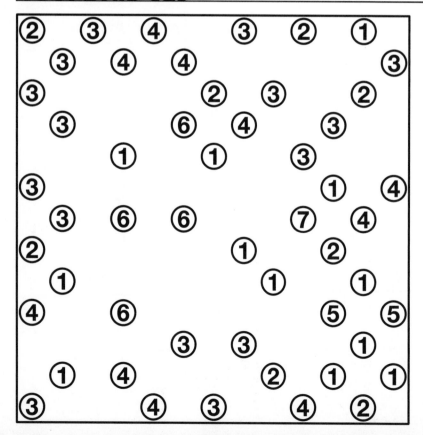

Join circled numbers with horizontal or vertical lines. Each number must have as many lines connected to it as specified by its value.

No more than two lines may join any pair of numbers, and no lines may cross.

The finished layout must connect all numbers, so you can travel between any pair of numbers by following one or more lines.

409. BRIDGE MAZE

Find a path from the entrance at the top of the maze to the exit at the bottom of the maze. The path may cross over or under itself by using the marked bridges.

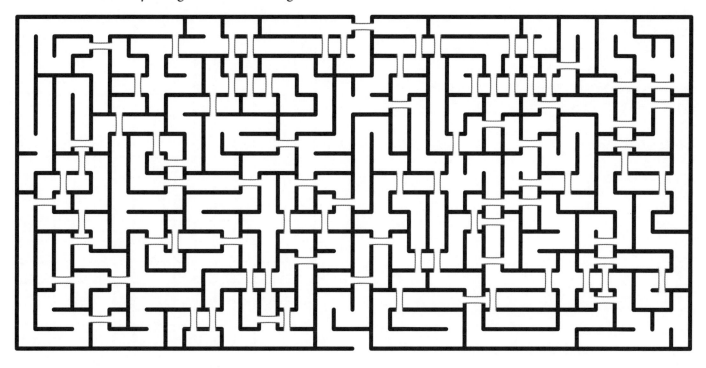

410. WORD CHAIN

Can you complete this word chain, in order to convert the word at the top into the word at the bottom?

At each step you may change only one letter so as to form a new English word, and you may not rearrange any of the letters.

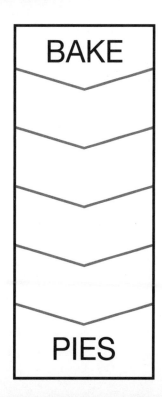

BAKE

PIES

411. LETTER CIRCLE

How many words can you find in this letter circle? Every word must use the center letter plus two or more of the other letters. No letter can be used more than once in a single word. There is one nine-letter seasonal word to find.

412. PICROSS

Shade in squares in the grid to reveal a picture. Numbers at the start of each row or column reveal, in order from left to right or top to bottom, the length of each consecutive run of shaded squares. There must be a gap of at least one empty square between each run of shaded squares in the same row or column.

Clue: Coffee time

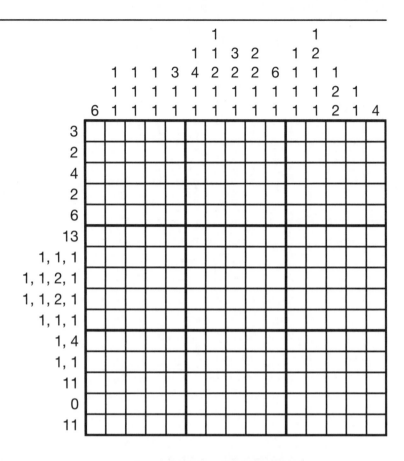

413. WORD RECTANGLE

Can you find the 12-letter word hidden in this Word Rectangle? Find words by moving from letter to touching letter, including diagonally, and without revisiting a square in a single word. How many other words can you find?

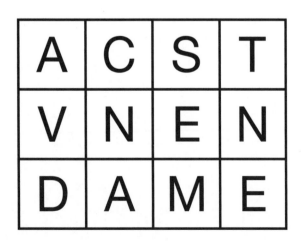

414. BRAIN CHAINS

Without using a calculator or making any written notes, solve these brain chains as quickly as you can. Write the solution in the "Result" box.

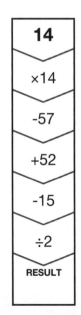

14
×14
-57
+52
-15
÷2
RESULT

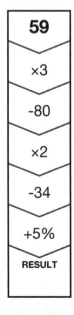

59
×3
-80
×2
-34
+5%
RESULT

415. CROSSWORD

Solve the clues to complete the crossword grid.

Across
1 Husband or wife (6)
5 Offend (6)
8 Yokel (4)
9 Hard candy on a stick (8)
10 Positions (8)
11 Secure with a rope (4)
12 Allege (6)
14 Deplete (6)
16 Used to identify a specific item (4)
18 Common to a country (8)
20 Second personality (5,3)
21 Musical movement (4)
22 Group of six (6)
23 Lackey (6)

Down
2 North Star (7)
3 Shadow (5)
4 Open-mindedness (13)
5 Examples (13)
6 Adept (7)
7 Visages (5)
13 Simplest (7)
15 Covering (7)
17 Split in two (5)
19 Exceed (5)

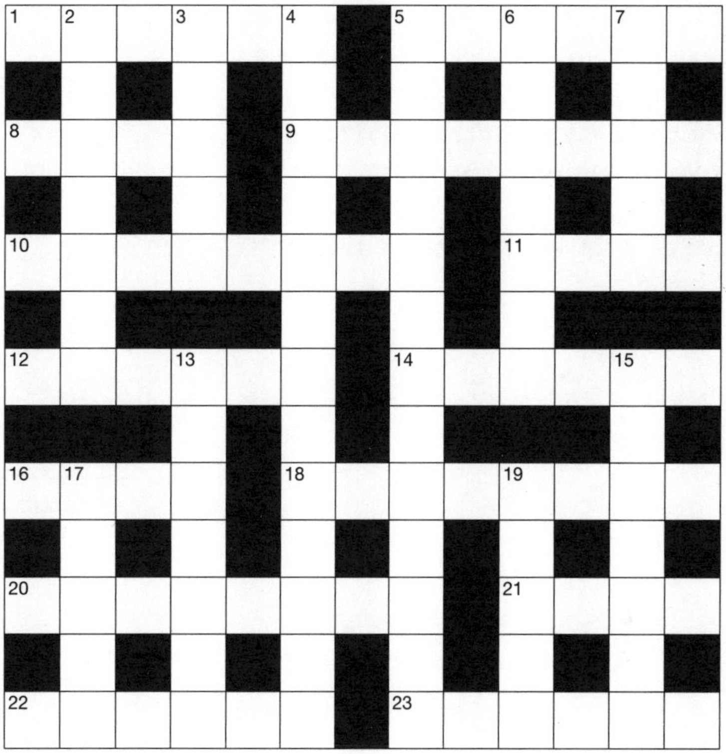

416. DOMINOES

Draw solid lines to divide the grid to form a complete set of standard dominoes, with exactly one of each domino. A "0" represents a blank on a traditional domino.

Use the checkoff chart to help you keep track of which dominoes you've placed.

1	5	2	6	0	5	1	6
4	2	1	6	6	6	3	5
3	0	5	0	4	4	4	4
0	3	2	6	0	1	4	2
4	5	3	1	6	5	0	0
6	5	3	0	2	3	2	3
2	5	1	4	1	1	2	3

0	1	2	3	4	5	6	
							0
							1
							2
							3
							4
							5
							6

417. KILLER SUDOKU

Place the digits 1 to 9 once each into every row, column, and bold-lined 3 × 3 square.

Each dashed-line cage must contain digits that add up to the given number.

No digit can repeat within a dashed-line cage.

418. SNAKE

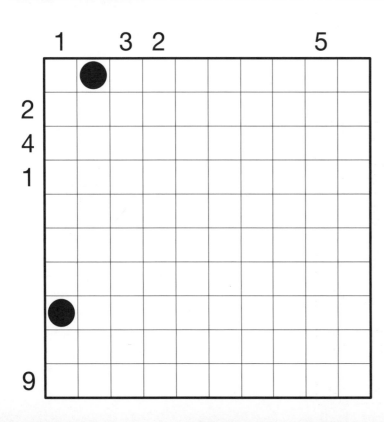

Shade some squares to form a snake that starts and ends at the given squares.

A snake is a single path of adjacent squares that does not branch or cross over itself.

The snake does not touch itself—not even diagonally.

Numbers outside the grid specify the number of squares in their row or column that contain part of the snake.

419. WORD SEARCH—WEATHER

Can you find all of these words or phrases in the grid? They may be written in any direction, including diagonally.

BREEZE
CALM
CLOUDS
CYCLONE
DEW
DROUGHT
FOG
FROST

HEAT WAVE
ICE
LIGHTNING
SLEET
SLUSH
SNOW
SUN
WIND

W	W	N	W	A	W	H	A	L	N	H	A	A	E	W
O	D	A	T	H	D	R	O	U	G	H	T	H	S	T
N	I	I	M	E	D	H	H	S	U	L	S	L	M	R
Y	H	E	U	G	N	I	N	T	H	G	I	L	N	U
R	G	O	H	I	T	F	O	G	D	H	T	L	L	N
O	N	D	T	N	M	S	U	S	E	U	E	C	S	W
E	N	L	E	H	D	W	O	A	T	C	D	C	E	L
L	H	A	T	U	I	C	T	R	E	H	E	C	S	T
T	U	B	R	N	C	W	L	N	F	T	S	W	F	O
I	W	R	D	R	A	R	O	T	S	N	U	D	E	S
I	W	E	B	V	L	L	C	L	O	U	D	S	L	D
Z	L	E	E	L	C	C	N	W	C	O	H	E	U	T
O	S	Z	N	Y	A	I	A	A	C	L	E	T	D	N
S	R	E	C	S	E	C	L	L	E	T	H	G	G	R
B	I	T	W	N	H	E	U	L	M	O	U	E	U	S

420. CIRCULAR MAZE

Can you find a route from the gap at the top to the gap at the bottom of this circular maze?

421. CODEWORD

A codeword is a coded crossword in which every letter has been replaced by a number, indicated by the small digits in the top left corner of each crossword square.

Work out which number represents each letter of the alphabet and use this information to complete the crossword grid.

Use the letters outside the grid, and the empty squares beneath the grid, to keep track of your deductions.

1	2	3	4	5	6	7	8	9	10	11	12	13
14	15	16	17	18	19	20	21	22	23	24	25	26

422. CHRISTMAS GIFT BOXES

Can you rearrange these gift boxes into their correct order? Once properly aligned they will spell out a word associated with Christmas.

423. KAKURO

Place a digit from 1 to 9 into each white square.

Each horizontal run of white squares adds up to the total above the diagonal line to the left of the run, and each vertical run of white squares adds up to the total below the diagonal line above the run.

No digit can be used more than once in any run.

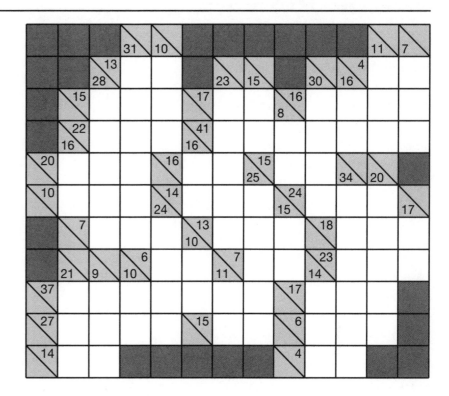

424. SLITHERLINK

Draw a single loop by connecting some dots with horizontal and vertical lines so that each numbered square has the specified number of adjacent line segments.

The loop cannot cross or touch itself.

425. RECTANGLES

Draw borders along some grid lines to divide the grid into a set of rectangles, such that each rectangle contains exactly one number.

All grid squares must be contained within exactly one rectangle.

The number inside each rectangle must be exactly equal to the number of grid squares that the rectangle contains, so for example a "4" could only be in a 1 × 4, 2 × 2, or 4 × 1 rectangle.

Note that the term "rectangle" also includes squares.

5					18			
								4
						6		
				18				
		3		12		3		
4	3					4		
							6	3
	2							
2					7			

426. CALCUDOKU

10×		13+		5+	10×
12×	8+		13+		
		2÷		30×	
3÷					2−
	1−		1−		
				12×	

Place the numbers 1 to 6 once each into every row and column of the grid, while obeying the region clues.

The value at the top left of each bold-lined region must be obtained when all of the numbers in that region have the given operation (+, -, ×, ÷) applied between them. For - and ÷ operations, begin with the largest number in the region and then subtract or divide by the other numbers in the region in any order.

427. SLANTED SUMS

Place 1 to 6 once each in every row and column.

Numbers outside the grid give the total of the indicated diagonals.

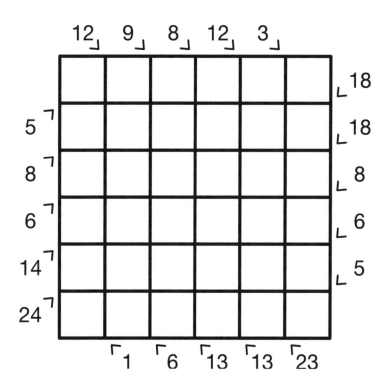

428. QUIZ

Test your knowledge of a specialist subject with this quiz.

The Internet

1. What was the name of the world's first internet web browser?

2. Which web browser had a letter "N" as its logo?

3. What does the "http" at the start of an Internet URL address stand for?

4. What country uses the top-level domain name ".tv"?

5. What is Apple's default web browser called?

429. FUTOSHIKI

Place 1 to 7 once each into every row and column while obeying the inequality signs.

Greater than (>) signs between some squares indicate that the value in one square is greater than that in another as indicated by the sign. The sign always points toward the smaller number.

Futoshiki grid (7×7), given clues:

Row 2: col3 = 5, col5 = 2
Row 3: col2 = 2, col4 = 5, col6 = 1
Row 4: col3 = 3, col4 = 1, col5 = 5
Row 5: col2 = 1, col4 = 6, col6 = 2
Row 6: col3 = 2, col5 = 1

Inequalities:
- Row 1: col3 > col4; col6 > col7
- Row 2: col3 (5) > col4
- Row 4: col1 < col2; col5 < col6
- Row 7: col4 < col5; col6 < col7 (wait, col5 < col6)
- Vertical: col4 row2 > row1 (^); col1 row3 > row2 (^); col7 row3 > row2 (^); col7 row5 > row6 (v); col1 row7 > row6 (v); col7 row7 > row6 (v)

430. NUMBER LINK

Draw a series of separate paths, each connecting a pair of identical numbers.

No more than one path can enter any grid square, and paths can only travel horizontally or vertically, and never diagonally.

1	2		3	4			3	5
						5		
	6					7		
						8		
6		9				7		
		2	4		8			
1	10		11					
10		12				12		
9	11							

431. ARROWWORD

Complete this crossword where all of the clues are given within the grid.

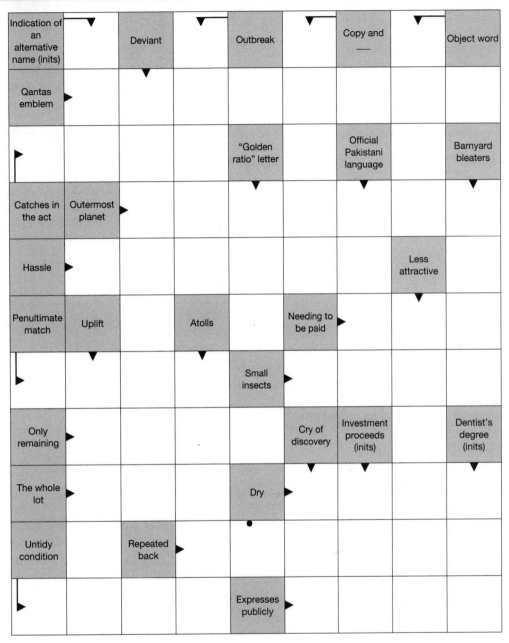

432. CHRISTMAS JUMBLE

Rearrange the following letters to reveal something associated with Christmas.

SERPENT IN SPONGE

433. JIGSAW LETTERS

Place A to H once each in every row, column, and bold-lined region.

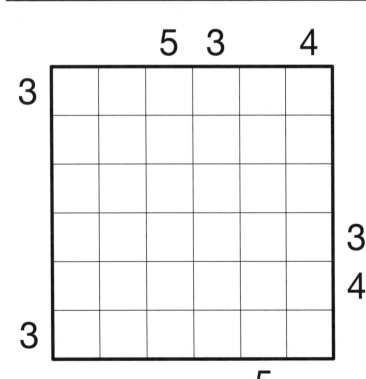

434. SKYSCRAPERS

Place 1 to 6 once each into every row and column of the grid.

Place digits in the grid in such a way that each given clue number outside the grid represents the number of digits that are "visible" from that point, looking along that clue's row or column.

A digit is visible unless there is a higher digit preceding it, reading in order along that row or column. For example, if a row was "214356" then the 2, 4, 5, and 6 would be visible from the left end (giving a clue of "5" visible digits), since 1 is obscured by the preceding higher 2, and 3 is obscured by the preceding higher 4. A clue at the right-hand end of the same row would be "1," since only the 6 would be visible.

435. FITWORD

Place each of the following words into the empty squares, crossword-style.

3 Letters
Led
Lei

4 Letters
Plod
Tidy

5 Letters
Edits
Mount
Noise
Noose
Onset

Sushi
Tones
Tutti
Typed
Usage

6 Letters
Assist
Degree
Things
Tunnel

7 Letters
Amusing

Illegal
Nesting
Utterly

9 Letters
Disasters
Observing

11 Letters
Dangerously
Featureless

436. PATH HUNTER

Join dots with horizontal and vertical lines to form a single path which does not touch or cross itself at any point. The start and end of the path are given. Numbers outside the grid specify the number of dots in their row or column that are visited by the path.

437. TOUCHY

Place A to F once each in every row and column such that two identical letters never touch—not even diagonally.

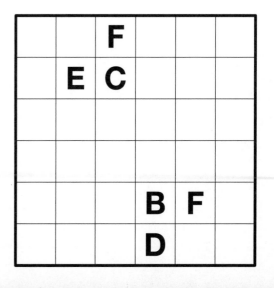

438. SUDOKU

Place 1 to 9 once each into every row, column, and bold-lined 3 × 3 square.

					5			
	1		3		6		7	
		2	9	7	4	3		
	7	9				5	2	
2		8				9		1
	6	5				8	4	
		7	8	6	5	1		
	5		7		2		3	
				9				

439. BRIDGES

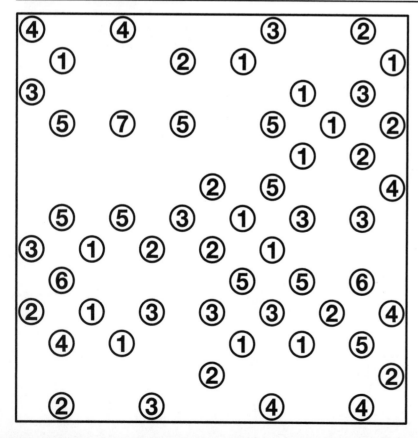

Join circled numbers with horizontal or vertical lines. Each number must have as many lines connected to it as specified by its value.

No more than two lines may join any pair of numbers, and no lines may cross.

The finished layout must connect all numbers, so you can travel between any pair of numbers by following one or more lines.

440. BRIDGE MAZE

Find a path from the entrance at the top of the maze to the exit at the bottom of the maze. The path may cross over or under itself by using the marked bridges.

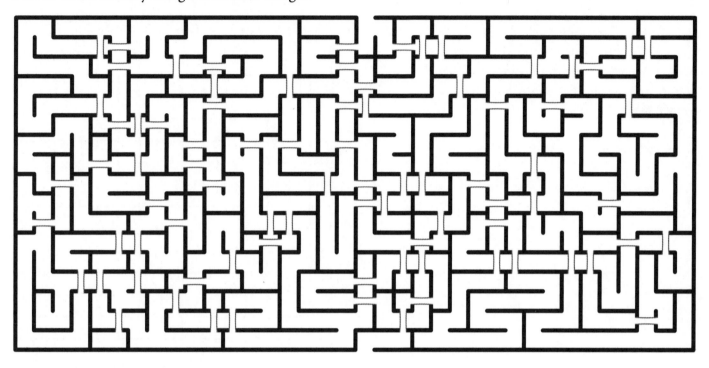

441. WORD CHAIN

Can you complete this word chain, in order to convert the word at the top into the word at the bottom?

At each step you may change only one letter so as to form a new English word, and you may not rearrange any of the letters.

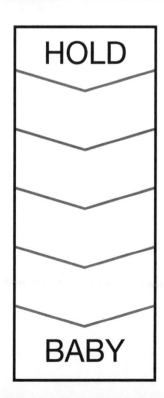

HOLD

BABY

442. LETTER CIRCLE

How many words can you find in this letter circle? Every word must use the center letter plus two or more of the other letters. No letter can be used more than once in a single word. There is one nine-letter seasonal word to find.

443. PICROSS

Shade in squares in the grid to reveal a picture. Numbers at the start of each row or column reveal, in order from left to right or top to bottom, the length of each consecutive run of shaded squares. There must be a gap of at least one empty square between each run of shaded squares in the same row or column.

Clue: Muddy marks

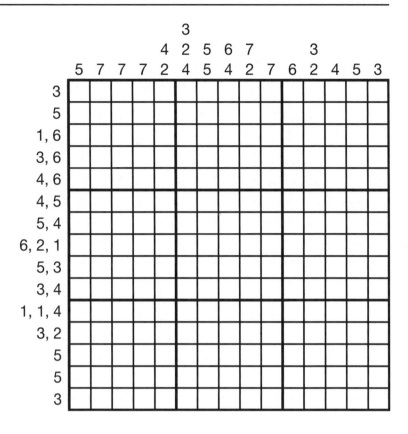

444. WORD RECTANGLE

Can you find the 12-letter word hidden in this Word Rectangle? Find words by moving from letter to touching letter, including diagonally, and without revisiting a square in a single word. How many other words can you find?

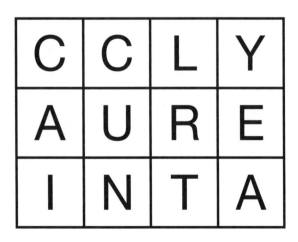

445. BRAIN CHAINS

Without using a calculator or making any written notes, solve these brain chains as quickly as you can. Write the solution in the "Result" box.

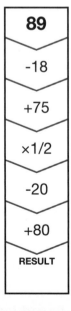

61	89
+99	-18
×1/4	+75
-4	×1/2
+69	-20
-50	+80
RESULT	**RESULT**

446. CROSSWORD

Solve the clues to complete the crossword grid.

Across
1 Workout exercises (3-3)
4 Materialize (6)
9 Largest native Australian bird (3)
10 Having a strong desire to succeed (9)
11 Accepted, as in money (5)
12 Visitor (7)
14 Guesses (11)
17 Advantage (7)
18 Alternative (5)
20 Modify (9)
22 Mitt Romney's wife (3)
23 Method (6)
24 Of hidden meaning (6)

Down
1 Bed covers (6)
2 An elephant's nose (5)
3 Someone who brings a legal action (9)
5 Household companion (3)
6 Natural wearing-away (7)
7 Return to zero (5)
8 Simplifying metaphor (11)
13 Equally (9)
15 Strapped shoes (7)
16 Wry (6)
17 Groups of eight binary digits (5)
19 Your body's most important muscle (5)
21 Realize (3)

447. DOMINOES

Draw solid lines to divide the grid to form a complete set of standard dominoes, with exactly one of each domino. A "0" represents a blank on a traditional domino.

Use the checkoff chart to help you keep track of which dominoes you've placed.

3	6	4	6	0	0	3	6
6	2	5	4	1	5	2	0
1	2	6	3	4	4	1	0
3	2	2	1	3	3	1	0
3	5	5	5	6	6	4	0
1	2	4	3	1	5	5	0
2	6	0	2	4	5	1	4

0	1	2	3	4	5	6	
							0
							1
							2
							3
							4
							5
							6

448. KILLER SUDOKU

Place the digits 1 to 9 once each into every row, column, and bold-lined 3 × 3 square.

Each dashed-line cage must contain digits that add up to the given number.

No digit can repeat within a dashed-line cage.

449. SNAKE

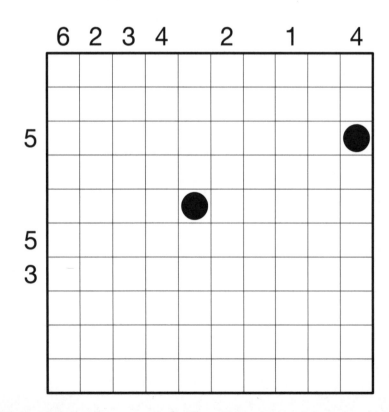

Shade some squares to form a snake that starts and ends at the given squares.

A snake is a single path of adjacent squares that does not branch or cross over itself.

The snake does not touch itself—not even diagonally.

Numbers outside the grid specify the number of squares in their row or column that contain part of the snake.

450. WORD SEARCH—CASINO NIGHT

Can you find all of these words or phrases in the grid? They may be written in any direction, including diagonally.

BACCARAT
BAIZE
BANK
BET
BLACKJACK
CARDS
CHIP
CRAPS

CROUPIER
DEALER
DECK
DICE
MONEY
POKER
ROULETTE
WHEEL

A	A	R	B	T	Z	R	E	K	O	P	N	O	E	E
R	R	E	L	A	B	J	A	Y	B	B	M	A	C	E
I	E	E	P	E	I	B	E	A	E	I	O	T	S	E
A	I	B	O	K	P	Z	C	T	E	K	N	A	P	A
D	R	E	L	W	U	C	E	A	D	E	E	K	D	K
I	E	W	H	A	A	E	S	L	D	R	Y	C	O	A
R	E	E	I	R	C	O	E	P	E	I	A	E	H	K
A	E	R	A	S	E	K	L	K	A	E	T	D	O	C
L	E	T	C	C	A	T	J	A	E	R	O	A	H	N
W	D	E	A	L	E	R	T	A	S	K	C	I	E	N
E	R	K	C	I	K	R	C	E	C	L	P	A	A	R
C	W	N	R	B	I	O	E	K	L	K	A	I	D	C
I	J	A	T	C	A	R	D	S	E	U	C	R	E	N
D	L	B	A	L	P	A	I	C	K	T	O	N	R	E
C	R	O	U	P	I	E	R	R	T	A	E	R	K	A

451. CIRCULAR MAZE

Can you find a route from the gap at the top to the gap at the bottom of this circular maze?

452. CODEWORD

A codeword is a coded crossword in which every letter has been replaced by a number, indicated by the small digits in the top left corner of each crossword square.

Work out which number represents each letter of the alphabet and use this information to complete the crossword grid.

Use the letters outside the grid, and the empty squares beneath the grid, to keep track of your deductions.

The codeword grid (letters N–Z run down the right-hand side, A–M down the left):

	1	2	3	4	5	6	7	8	9	10	11	12	13	
A	■	23	■	13	■	20	■	13 M	2	■	15			N
B	23	12	15 T	4	12	8	■	26	6	4	2	4		O
C	■	17	■	15	■	17	12	24	■	14	■	14		P
D	17	26	6	6	4	17	■	26	20	20	12	14		Q
E	12	■	■	4	■	■	15	■	12	■	17	■		R
F	17	7 I	10	4	17	2	■	12	9	15	7	25		S
G	4	■	7	■	■	5	26	21	■	■	14	■	2	T
H	■	19	12	20	4	17	■	7	15	12	14	7	25	U
I	■	12	■	4	■	22	■	■	■	17	■	■	12	V
J	20	17	26	16	4	■	■	11	4	15	4	25	15	W
K	7	■	1	■	6	4	11	■	11	■	13	■		X
L	2	25	17	8	6	■	8	9	7	3	8	4		Y
M	18	■	12	■	2	■	26	■	15	■	2			Z

1	2	3	4	5	6	7	8	9	10	11	12	13
14	15	16	17	18	19	20	21	22	23	24	25	26

453. CHRISTMAS GIFT BOXES

Can you rearrange these gift boxes into their correct order? Once properly aligned they will spell out a word associated with Christmas.

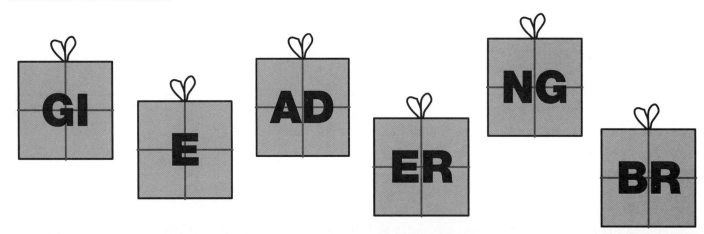

GI   E   AD   NG   ER   BR

454. KAKURO

Place a digit from 1 to 9 into each white square.

Each horizontal run of white squares adds up to the total above the diagonal line to the left of the run, and each vertical run of white squares adds up to the total below the diagonal line above the run.

No digit can be used more than once in any run.

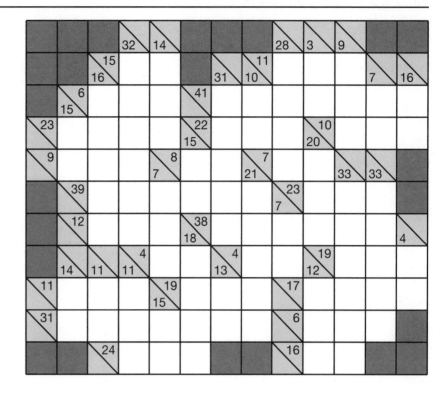

455. SLITHERLINK

Draw a single loop by connecting some dots with horizontal and vertical lines so that each numbered square has the specified number of adjacent line segments.

The loop cannot cross or touch itself.

456. RECTANGLES

Draw borders along some grid lines to divide the grid into a set of rectangles, such that each rectangle contains exactly one number.

All grid squares must be contained within exactly one rectangle.

The number inside each rectangle must be exactly equal to the number of grid squares that the rectangle contains, so for example a "4" could only be in a 1 × 4, 2 × 2, or 4 × 1 rectangle.

Note that the term "rectangle" also includes squares.

457. CALCUDOKU

Place the numbers 1 to 6 once each into every row and column of the grid, while obeying the region clues.

The value at the top left of each bold-lined region must be obtained when all of the numbers in that region have the given operation (+, -, ×, ÷) applied between them. For - and ÷ operations, begin with the largest number in the region and then subtract or divide by the other numbers in the region in any order.

458. SLANTED SUMS

Place 1 to 6 once each in every row
and column.

Numbers outside the grid give the
total of the indicated diagonals.

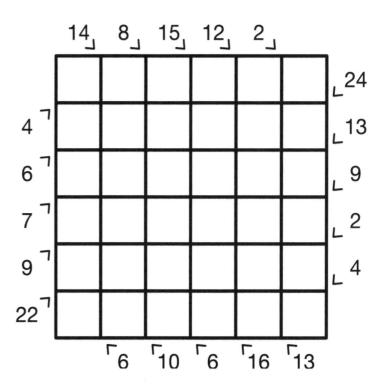

459. QUIZ

Test your knowledge of a specialist subject with this quiz.

Tennis

1. Which former number one female tennis player failed a drugs test at the 2016 Australian Open?

2. Which Swiss tennis player held the world number one position for 237 consecutive weeks?

3. Which Spanish player is nicknamed "The King of Clay"?

4. Which female tennis player and then world number one was stabbed in the back while waiting on court during a match in 1993?

5. Which Swedish former number one player won the US Open in 1991?

460. FUTOSHIKI

Place 1 to 7 once each into every row and column while obeying the inequality signs.

Greater than (>) signs between some squares indicate that the value in one square is greater than that in another as indicated by the sign. The sign always points toward the smaller number.

6	5		<		3	2
5						6
				>		
		>				
4			>		>	3
3	2				5	4

461. NUMBER LINK

Draw a series of separate paths, each connecting a pair of identical numbers.

No more than one path can enter any grid square, and paths can only travel horizontally or vertically, and never diagonally.

					1			
	2		3	4				1
		5						
					6		7	
4	2							
	8							3
	9		5					
				10		11		
	9	8	11	6		10		
							7	

462. ARROWWORD

Complete this crossword where all of the clues are given within the grid.

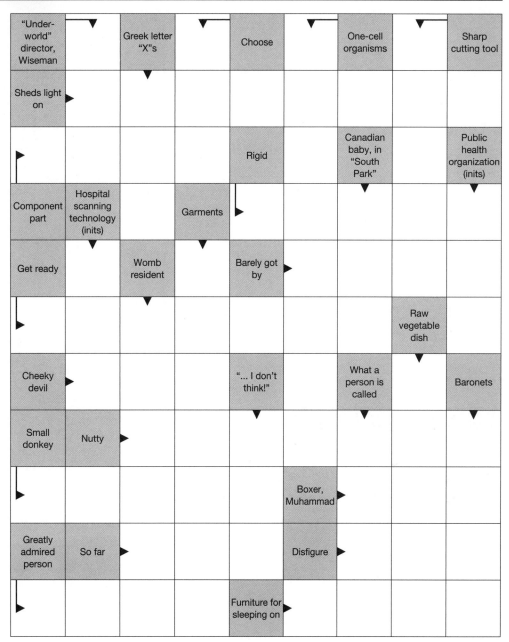

463. CHRISTMAS JUMBLE

Rearrange the following letters to reveal something associated with Christmas.

SING IF TV GIG

464. JIGSAW LETTERS

Place A to H once each in every row, column, and bold-lined region.

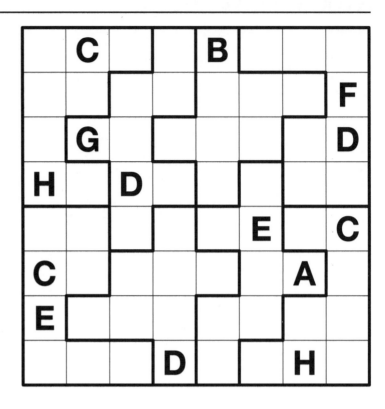

465. SKYSCRAPERS

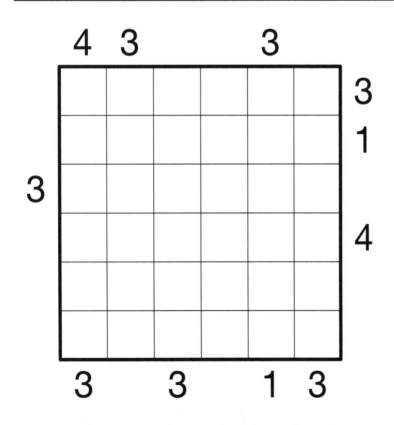

Place 1 to 6 once each into every row and column of the grid.

Place digits in the grid in such a way that each given clue number outside the grid represents the number of digits that are "visible" from that point, looking along that clue's row or column.

A digit is visible unless there is a higher digit preceding it, reading in order along that row or column. For example, if a row was "214356" then the 2, 4, 5, and 6 would be visible from the left end (giving a clue of "5" visible digits), since 1 is obscured by the preceding higher 2, and 3 is obscured by the preceding higher 4. A clue at the right-hand end of the same row would be "1," since only the 6 would be visible.

466. FITWORD

Place each of the following words into the empty squares, crossword-style.

3 Letters
End
Uke

4 Letters
Crew
Epic
Sash
Swat

5 Letters
Clear
Cramp

Islet
Issue

6 Letters
Global
Shelve
Stands
Superb

7 Letters
Fashion
Tickets
Tobacco
Trouble

8 Letters
Broccoli
Infected
Retrieve
Tailpipe

9 Letters
Preserves
Wallpaper

13 Letters
Opportunities

467. PATH HUNTER

Join dots with horizontal and vertical lines to form a single path which does not touch or cross itself at any point. The start and end of the path are given. Numbers outside the grid specify the number of dots in their row or column that are visited by the path.

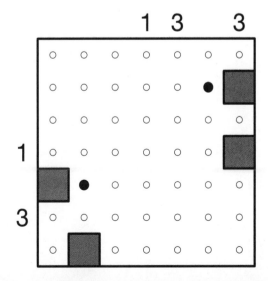

468. TOUCHY

Place A to F once each in every row and column such that two identical letters never touch—not even diagonally.

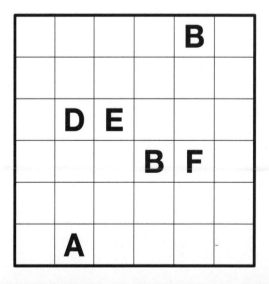

469. SUDOKU

Place 1 to 9 once each into every row, column, and bold-lined 3 × 3 square.

	1						4	
7			1		9			8
		5	6	3	4	7		
	4	2				3	5	
		9		1		4		
	6	1				9	8	
		8	4	9	6	2		
2			8		5			4
	9						6	

470. BRIDGES

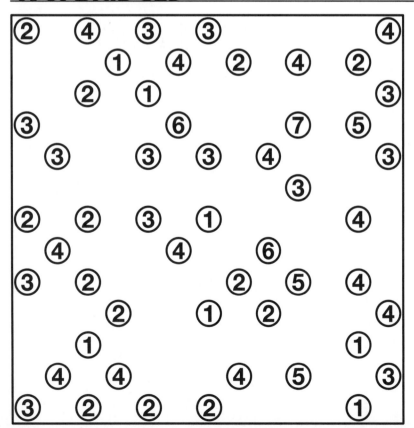

Join circled numbers with horizontal or vertical lines. Each number must have as many lines connected to it as specified by its value.

No more than two lines may join any pair of numbers, and no lines may cross.

The finished layout must connect all numbers, so you can travel between any pair of numbers by following one or more lines.

471. BRIDGE MAZE

Find a path from the entrance at the top of the maze to the exit at the bottom of the maze. The path may cross over or under itself by using the marked bridges.

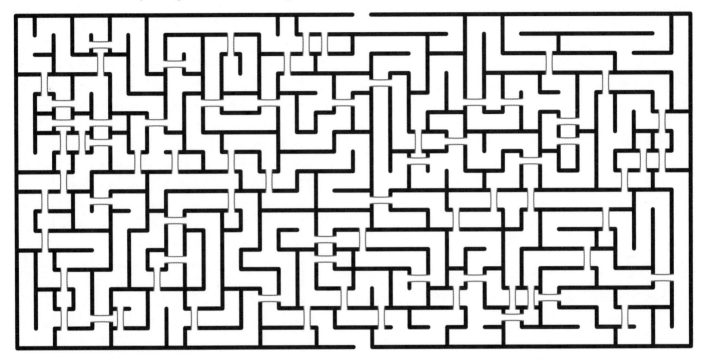

472. WORD CHAIN

Can you complete this word chain, in order to convert the word at the top into the word at the bottom?

At each step you may change only one letter so as to form a new English word, and you may not rearrange any of the letters.

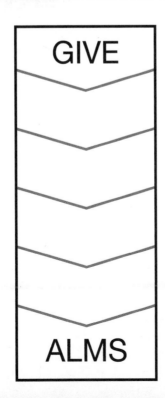

GIVE

ALMS

473. LETTER CIRCLE

How many words can you find in this letter circle? Every word must use the center letter plus two or more of the other letters. No letter can be used more than once in a single word. There is one nine-letter seasonal word to find.

474. PICROSS

Shade in squares in the grid to reveal a picture. Numbers at the start of each row or column reveal, in order from left to right or top to bottom, the length of each consecutive run of shaded squares. There must be a gap of at least one empty square between each run of shaded squares in the same row or column.

Clue: Breakfast time

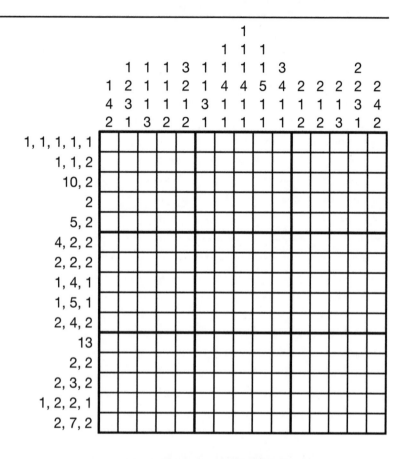

Row clues (top to bottom): 1, 1, 1, 1, 1 / 1, 1, 2 / 10, 2 / 2 / 5, 2 / 4, 2, 2 / 2, 2, 2 / 1, 4, 1 / 1, 5, 1 / 2, 4, 2 / 13 / 2, 2 / 2, 3, 2 / 1, 2, 2, 1 / 2, 7, 2

475. WORD RECTANGLE

Can you find the 12-letter word hidden in this Word Rectangle? Find words by moving from letter to touching letter, including diagonally, and without revisiting a square in a single word. How many other words can you find?

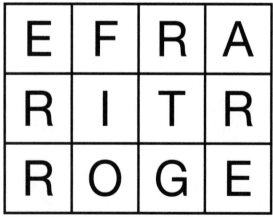

E	F	R	A
R	I	T	R
R	O	G	E

476. BRAIN CHAINS

Without using a calculator or making any written notes, solve these brain chains as quickly as you can. Write the solution in the "Result" box.

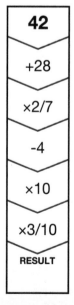

42
+28
×2/7
−4
×10
×3/10
RESULT

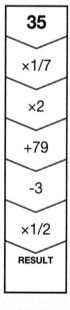

35
×1/7
×2
+79
−3
×1/2
RESULT

477. CROSSWORD

Solve the clues to complete the crossword grid.

Across
- **1** Subsequent part (6)
- **4** Amended (6)
- **8** Seventh Greek letter (3)
- **9** Helper (9)
- **11** Elegant (4)
- **12** Buffs (8)
- **15** Exactly the same (9)
- **18** Window covers (8)
- **19** Musical instrument (4)
- **21** Cutthroat (3-3-3)
- **23** Decorative pond fish (3)
- **24** Stops (6)
- **25** Rarely (6)

Down
- **1** Rough design (6)
- **2** Pretournament event (9)
- **3** Enthusiasm (4)
- **5** Different from one another (8)
- **6** Hot or iced drink (3)
- **7** Abhor (6)
- **10** Truncated (9)
- **13** Crazy (4-5)
- **14** Divided (8)
- **16** Opposite of alkaline (6)
- **17** Floating-balloon gas (6)
- **20** Fever (4)
- **22** India's smallest state (3)

478. DOMINOES

Draw solid lines to divide the grid to form a complete set of standard dominoes, with exactly one of each domino. A "0" represents a blank on a traditional domino.

Use the checkoff chart to help you keep track of which dominoes you've placed.

1	3	2	2	6	0	5	1
4	1	5	0	6	6	2	1
5	1	5	1	2	4	4	3
0	3	3	2	4	2	0	3
4	6	4	0	6	5	0	3
6	6	1	5	2	3	0	5
0	2	4	4	5	3	6	1

0	1	2	3	4	5	6	
							0
							1
							2
							3
							4
							5
							6

479. KILLER SUDOKU

Place the digits 1 to 9 once each into every row, column, and bold-lined 3 × 3 square.

Each dashed-line cage must contain digits that add up to the given number.

No digit can repeat within a dashed-line cage.

480. SNAKE

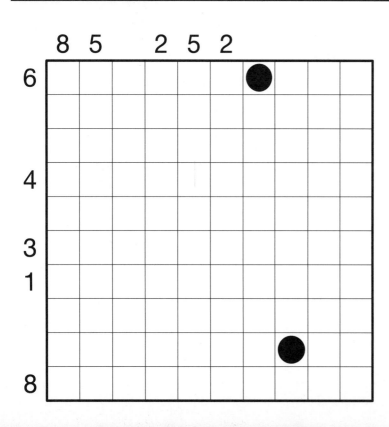

Shade some squares to form a snake that starts and ends at the given squares.

A snake is a single path of adjacent squares that does not branch or cross over itself.

The snake does not touch itself—not even diagonally.

Numbers outside the grid specify the number of squares in their row or column that contain part of the snake.

481. WORD SEARCH—DINOSAURS

Can you find all of these words or phrases in the grid? They may be written in any direction, including diagonally.

ALLOSAURUS
ARCHAEOPTERYX
BRACHIOSAURUS
BRONTOSAURUS
CERATOSAURUS
CORYTHOSAURUS
DILOPHOSAURUS
DIPLODOCUS

GALLIMIMUS
GIGANTOSAURUS
IGUANODON
ORNITHOMIMUS
PTERODACTYL
STEGOSAURUS
TRICERATOPS
VELOCIRAPTOR

```
O R G A L L I M I M U S C G S
T L Y T C A D O R E T P I C U
O S S U E L A T R E S G Y S C
O A U B S S I R G N A E R G O
O S U R U A S O T N O R B N D
I S U R U A S O T A R E C L O
U A R C H A E O P T E R Y X L
S S U R U A S O L L A C O I P
T S U R U A S O I H C A R B I
R S U R U A S O H P O L I D D
A S T R I C E R A T O P S I Y
I G U A N O D O N L Y P A H R
C S U M I M O H T I N R O O E
T I V E L O C I R A P T O R D
L P A U R R A O C Y H I U C D
```

482. CIRCULAR MAZE

Can you find a route from the gap at the top to the gap at the bottom of this circular maze?

483. CODEWORD

A codeword is a coded crossword in which every letter has been replaced by a number, indicated by the small digits in the top left corner of each crossword square.

Work out which number represents each letter of the alphabet and use this information to complete the crossword grid.

Use the letters outside the grid, and the empty squares beneath the grid, to keep track of your deductions.

484. CHRISTMAS GIFT BOXES

Can you rearrange these gift boxes into their correct order? Once properly aligned they will spell out a word associated with Christmas.

485. KAKURO

Place a digit from 1 to 9 into each white square.

Each horizontal run of white squares adds up to the total above the diagonal line to the left of the run, and each vertical run of white squares adds up to the total below the diagonal line above the run.

No digit can be used more than once in any run.

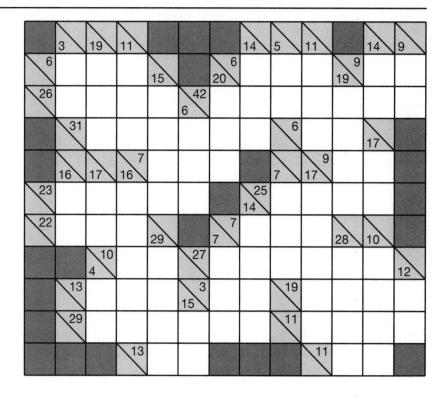

486. SLITHERLINK

Draw a single loop by connecting some dots with horizontal and vertical lines so that each numbered square has the specified number of adjacent line segments.

The loop cannot cross or touch itself.

487. RECTANGLES

Draw borders along some grid lines to divide the grid into a set of rectangles, such that each rectangle contains exactly one number.

All grid squares must be contained within exactly one rectangle.

The number inside each rectangle must be exactly equal to the number of grid squares that the rectangle contains, so for example a "4" could only be in a 1 × 4, 2 × 2, or 4 × 1 rectangle.

Note that the term "rectangle" also includes squares.

488. CALCUDOKU

Place the numbers 1 to 6 once each into every row and column of the grid, while obeying the region clues.

The value at the top left of each bold-lined region must be obtained when all of the numbers in that region have the given operation (+, -, ×, ÷) applied between them. For - and ÷ operations, begin with the largest number in the region and then subtract or divide by the other numbers in the region in any order.

489. SLANTED SUMS

Place 1 to 6 once each in every row and column.

Numbers outside the grid give the total of the indicated diagonals.

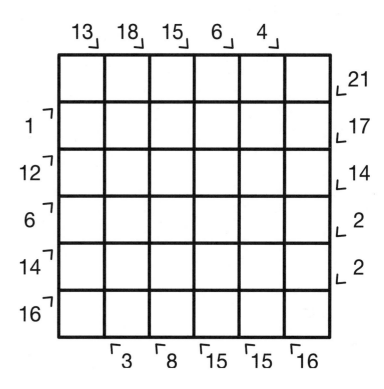

490. QUIZ

Test your knowledge of a specialist subject with this quiz.

Classical Music

1. What do the J and the S in J. S. Bach stand for?

2. During which century did the Baroque period begin?

3. Which celebrated Finnish composer, who lived from 1865 to 1957, produced no major works in his final thirty years?

4. Which well-known Russian composer had the first names Pyotr and Ilyich?

5. Who composed the opera *The Magic Flute*?

491. FUTOSHIKI

Place 1 to 7 once each into every row and column while obeying the inequality signs.

Greater than (>) signs between some squares indicate that the value in one square is greater than that in another as indicated by the sign. The sign always points toward the smaller number.

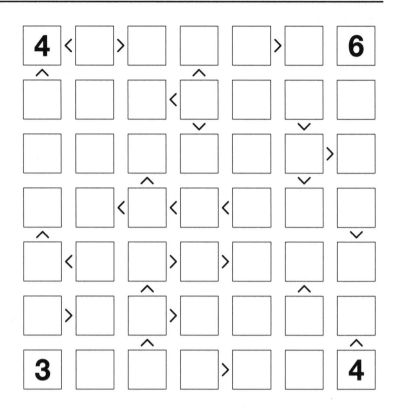

492. NUMBER LINK

Draw a series of separate paths, each connecting a pair of identical numbers.

No more than one path can enter any grid square, and paths can only travel horizontally or vertically, and never diagonally.

1								
2							3	
4						5		
	6	7		4		1		
		8				9	3	
		10	7			5		
	8		11		12			13
						9		
	10	11						
	6	2			12	13		

493. ARROWWORD

Complete this crossword where all of the clues are given within the grid.

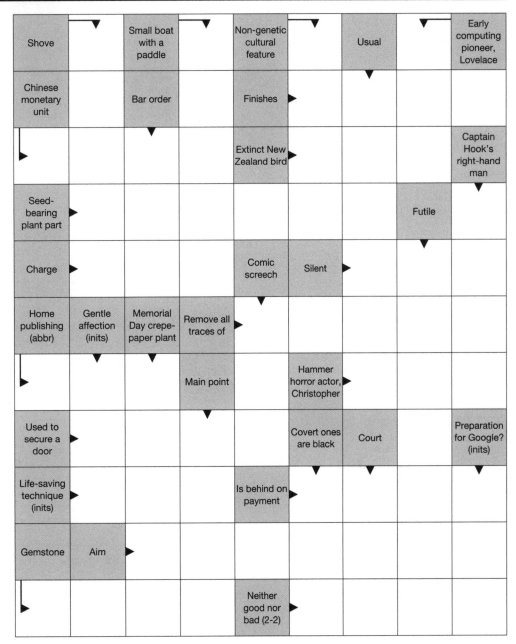

Shove		Small boat with a paddle		Non-genetic cultural feature		Usual			Early computing pioneer, Lovelace
Chinese monetary unit		Bar order		Finishes					
				Extinct New Zealand bird					Captain Hook's right-hand man
Seed-bearing plant part							Futile		
Charge				Comic screech	Silent				
Home publishing (abbr)	Gentle affection (inits)	Memorial Day crepe-paper plant	Remove all traces of						
			Main point		Hammer horror actor, Christopher				
Used to secure a door					Covert ones are black	Court			Preparation for Google? (inits)
Life-saving technique (inits)				Is behind on payment					
Gemstone	Aim								
				Neither good nor bad (2-2)					

494. CHRISTMAS JUMBLE

Rearrange the following letters to reveal something associated with Christmas.

LENGTH WITH FT

495. JIGSAW LETTERS

Place A to H once each in every row, column, and bold-lined region.

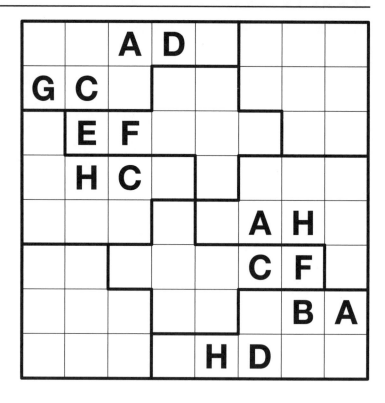

496. SKYSCRAPERS

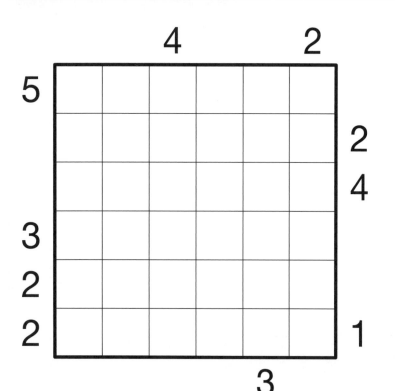

Place 1 to 6 once each into every row and column of the grid.

Place digits in the grid in such a way that each given clue number outside the grid represents the number of digits that are "visible" from that point, looking along that clue's row or column.

A digit is visible unless there is a higher digit preceding it, reading in order along that row or column. For example, if a row was "214356" then the 2, 4, 5, and 6 would be visible from the left end (giving a clue of "5" visible digits), since 1 is obscured by the preceding higher 2, and 3 is obscured by the preceding higher 4. A clue at the right-hand end of the same row would be "1," since only the 6 would be visible.

497. FITWORD

Place each of the following words into the empty squares, crossword-style.

3 Letters
Elf
Out

4 Letters
Iota
Menu
Nets
That

5 Letters
Admit
Depth
Gusto

Gypsy
Pinch
Wound

6 Letters
Closet
Uneven

8 Letters
Dwelling
Flabbily
Insulted
Sunbathe

9 Letters
Shortened
Spaghetti

11 Letters
Adjustments
Needfulness

13 Letters
Conversations
Differentiate

498. PATH HUNTER

Join dots with horizontal and vertical lines to form a single path which does not touch or cross itself at any point. The start and end of the path are given. Numbers outside the grid specify the number of dots in their row or column that are visited by the path.

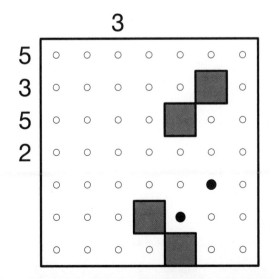

499. TOUCHY

Place A to F once each in every row and column such that two identical letters never touch—not even diagonally.

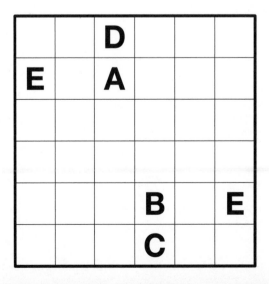

500. SUDOKU

Place 1 to 9 once each into every row, column, and bold-lined 3 × 3 square.

		1		3		5		
	5	1		4	8			
3	6						9	2
	2		7		3		5	
9								6
	1		5		9		8	
5	8						1	9
	9	2			6	4		
	6			8		3		

501. BRIDGES

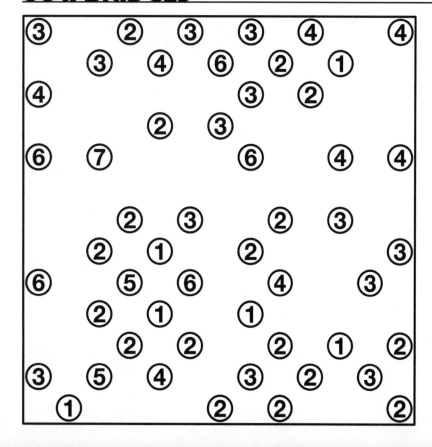

Join circled numbers with horizontal or vertical lines. Each number must have as many lines connected to it as specified by its value.

No more than two lines may join any pair of numbers, and no lines may cross.

The finished layout must connect all numbers, so you can travel between any pair of numbers by following one or more lines.

502. BRIDGE MAZE

Find a path from the entrance at the top of the maze to the exit at the bottom of the maze. The path may cross over or under itself by using the marked bridges.

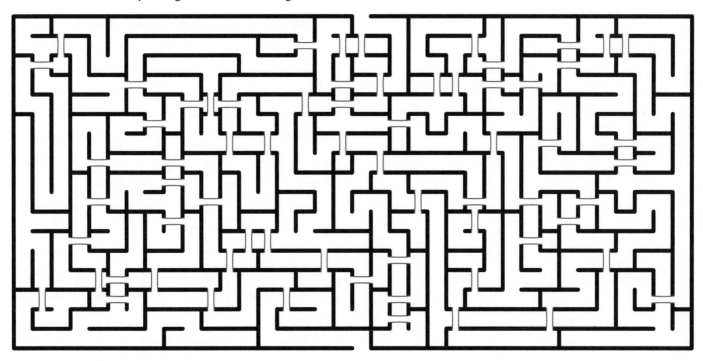

503. WORD CHAIN

Can you complete this word chain, in order to convert the word at the top into the word at the bottom?

At each step you may change only one letter so as to form a new English word, and you may not rearrange any of the letters.

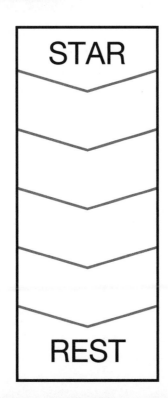

STAR

REST

504. LETTER CIRCLE

How many words can you find in this letter circle? Every word must use the center letter plus two or more of the other letters. No letter can be used more than once in a single word. There is one nine-letter seasonal word to find.

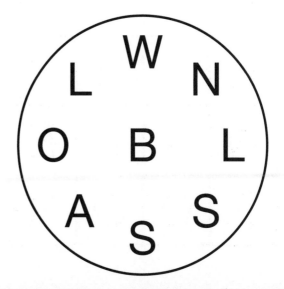

505. PICROSS

Shade in squares in the grid to reveal a picture. Numbers at the start of each row or column reveal, in order from left to right or top to bottom, the length of each consecutive run of shaded squares. There must be a gap of at least one empty square between each run of shaded squares in the same row or column.

Clue: Zooming in

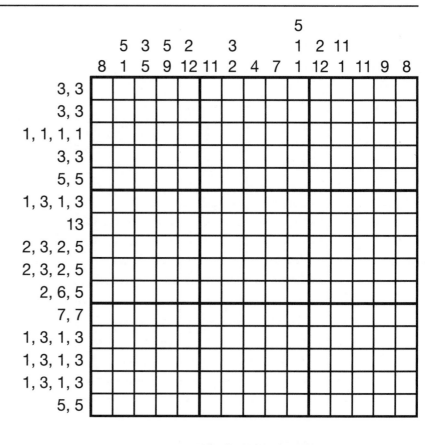

506. WORD RECTANGLE

Can you find the 12-letter word hidden in this Word Rectangle? Find words by moving from letter to touching letter, including diagonally, and without revisiting a square in a single word. How many other words can you find?

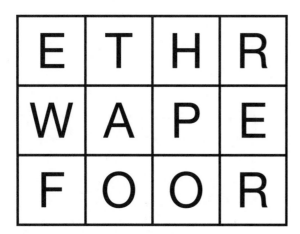

507. BRAIN CHAINS

Without using a calculator or making any written notes, solve these brain chains as quickly as you can. Write the solution in the "Result" box.

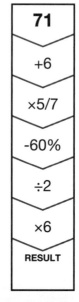

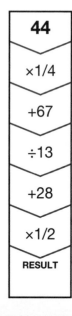

508. CROSSWORD

Solve the clues to complete the crossword grid.

Across
- **7** Factual yearbook (7)
- **9** Easily frightened (5)
- **10** Former senator, Kennedy (3)
- **11** February 14th card (9)
- **12** Come to maturity (5)
- **14** Diagonally moving pieces (7)
- **16** Eighth sign of the zodiac (7)
- **18** Visitors to a website (5)
- **19** Wins over (9)
- **20** Arabian peninsula country (inits) (3)
- **21** ___ fatale (5)
- **22** Remove ice from something (7)

Down
- **1** Templates (8)
- **2** Among (4)
- **3** Not uniform (6)
- **4** Gets up (6)
- **5** Plant and meat eater (8)
- **6** Rim (4)
- **8** Hard-hearted (4-7)
- **13** TV shows (8)
- **15** Possibly guilty people (8)
- **17** Flowed out (6)
- **18** Risky (6)
- **19** Burst of breath (4)
- **20** Thereon (4)

509. DOMINOES

Draw solid lines to divide the grid to form a complete set of standard dominoes, with exactly one of each domino. A "0" represents a blank on a traditional domino.

Use the checkoff chart to help you keep track of which dominoes you've placed.

5	0	6	0	4	2	1	0
5	0	5	1	5	3	3	4
4	2	1	5	5	2	6	0
2	6	3	6	6	6	1	3
2	6	1	0	5	3	0	2
3	2	1	3	1	4	2	0
4	4	6	1	3	4	4	5

0	1	2	3	4	5	6	
							0
							1
							2
							3
							4
							5
							6

510. KILLER SUDOKU

Place the digits 1 to 9 once each into every row, column, and bold-lined 3 × 3 square.

Each dashed-line cage must contain digits that add up to the given number.

No digit can repeat within a dashed-line cage.

511. SNAKE

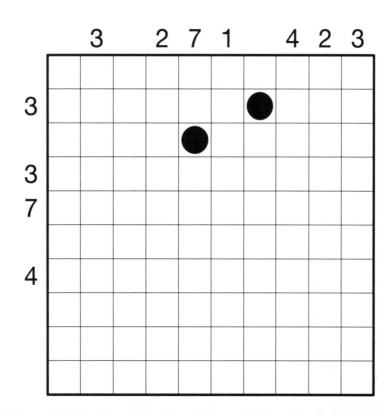

Shade some squares to form a snake that starts and ends at the given squares.

A snake is a single path of adjacent squares that does not branch or cross over itself.

The snake does not touch itself—not even diagonally.

Numbers outside the grid specify the number of squares in their row or column that contain part of the snake.

512. WORD SEARCH—CLOTHING MATERIALS

Can you find all of these words or phrases in the grid? They may be written in any direction, including diagonally.

ARTIFICIAL FIBER
BLEND
DAMASK
FUR
KNITTED
LEATHER
LINEN
NYLON
POLYESTER
PRINTED
STRETCH
SUEDE
SYNTHETIC
WATERPROOF
WOOL
WOVEN

U	A	E	D	E	T	N	I	R	P	S	F	A	Y	T
R	E	B	I	F	L	A	I	C	I	F	I	T	R	A
T	O	W	S	Y	B	O	E	N	R	E	R	O	E	D
S	S	F	T	C	K	N	T	U	U	N	W	E	C	C
U	S	T	O	R	O	O	F	O	R	F	O	W	D	E
E	S	K	R	O	R	R	E	T	S	E	Y	L	O	P
D	Y	F	H	E	R	T	D	L	E	A	T	H	E	R
E	N	C	N	R	T	P	F	E	V	W	D	Y	E	E
T	T	T	R	O	I	C	R	Y	T	W	O	A	R	R
E	H	D	S	U	L	O	H	E	A	T	H	O	C	A
L	E	O	K	N	B	Y	C	L	T	Y	I	S	L	T
I	T	T	L	W	E	L	N	F	C	A	W	N	S	R
I	I	D	H	T	E	V	E	O	C	L	W	A	K	I
T	C	L	D	R	T	T	O	N	D	A	M	A	S	K
S	N	E	N	I	L	S	I	W	D	O	U	C	E	O

513. CIRCULAR MAZE

Can you find a route from the gap at the top to the gap at the bottom of this circular maze?

514. CODEWORD

A codeword is a coded crossword in which every letter has been replaced by a number, indicated by the small digits in the top left corner of each crossword square.

Work out which number represents each letter of the alphabet and use this information to complete the crossword grid.

Use the letters outside the grid, and the empty squares beneath the grid, to keep track of your deductions.

	1	2	3	4	5	6	7	8	9	10	11	12	13	
A	2	20	7 (U)	10	2	16	■	10	1	1	10	23	15	**N**
B	25	■	15	■	10	■	■	■	8	■	16	■	24	**O**
C	3	10	8	■	3	24	6	15	23	22	10	15	1	**P**
D	7	■	25	■	2	■	25	■	19	■	■	■	10	**Q**
E	5	24	19	25	■	25	15	6	23	15	25	25	5	**R**
F	25	■	3	■	23	■	25	■	6	■	4	■	21	**S**
G	■	■	24	8	15	25	5	2	16	23 (I)	26	■	■	**T**
H	2	■	9	■	3	■	10	■	1	■	19	■	2	**U**
I	7	2	25	12	7	19	19	21	■	21	24	17	25	**V**
J	18	■	■	■	5	■	19	■	23	■	2	■	19	**W**
K	18	25	2	1	5	24	21	25	18	■	23	3	25	**X**
L	25	■	7	■	25	■	■	■	19	■	11	■	3	**Y**
M	15	24	14	24	18	21	■	5	25	13	25	3	1 (T)	**Z**

1	2	3	4	5	6	7	8	9	10	11	12	13
14	15	16	17	18	19	20	21	22	23	24	25	26

515. CHRISTMAS GIFT BOXES

Can you rearrange these gift boxes into their correct order? Once properly aligned they will spell out a word associated with Christmas.

516. KAKURO

Place a digit from 1 to 9 into each white square.

Each horizontal run of white squares adds up to the total above the diagonal line to the left of the run, and each vertical run of white squares adds up to the total below the diagonal line above the run.

No digit can be used more than once in any run.

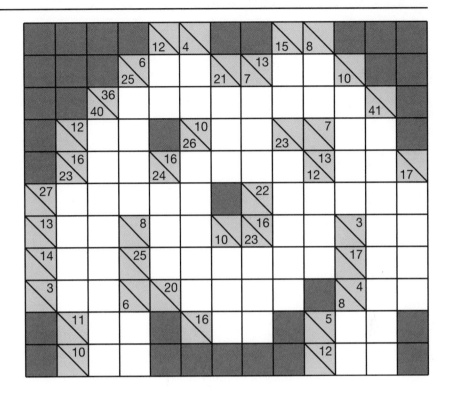

517. SLITHERLINK

Draw a single loop by connecting some dots with horizontal and vertical lines so that each numbered square has the specified number of adjacent line segments.

The loop cannot cross or touch itself.

```
  0     3       2     3
     1           1     1
     1     2     1  2  0  2
  0     3     3     2  3     2
        3                 1
     2              3
  2     3  2     1     3     0
  2  2  1  3     3     2
     2     2           0
     2     3        1     0
```

518. RECTANGLES

Draw borders along some grid lines to divide the grid into a set of rectangles, such that each rectangle contains exactly one number.

All grid squares must be contained within exactly one rectangle.

The number inside each rectangle must be exactly equal to the number of grid squares that the rectangle contains, so for example a "4" could only be in a 1 × 4, 2 × 2, or 4 × 1 rectangle.

Note that the term "rectangle" also includes squares.

519. CALCUDOKU

Place the numbers 1 to 6 once each into every row and column of the grid, while obeying the region clues.

The value at the top left of each bold-lined region must be obtained when all of the numbers in that region have the given operation (+, -, ×, ÷) applied between them. For - and ÷ operations, begin with the largest number in the region and then subtract or divide by the other numbers in the region in any order.

520. SLANTED SUMS

Place 1 to 6 once each in every row and column.

Numbers outside the grid give the total of the indicated diagonals.

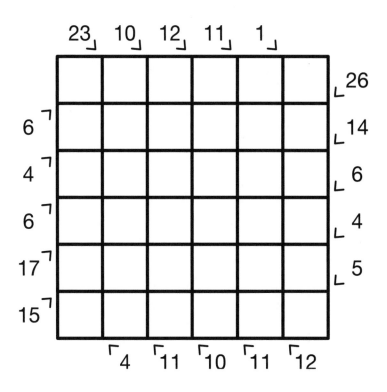

521. SKYSCRAPERS

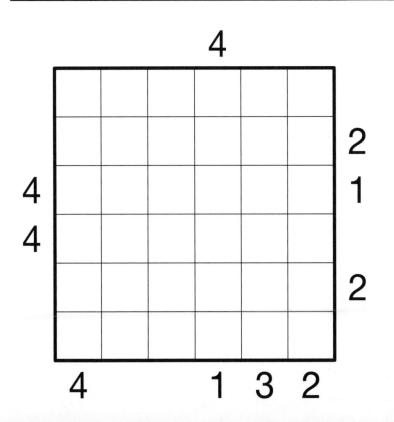

Place 1 to 6 once each into every row and column of the grid.

Place digits in the grid in such a way that each given clue number outside the grid represents the number of digits that are "visible" from that point, looking along that clue's row or column.

A digit is visible unless there is a higher digit preceding it, reading in order along that row or column. For example, if a row was "214356" then the 2, 4, 5, and 6 would be visible from the left end (giving a clue of "5" visible digits), since 1 is obscured by the preceding higher 2, and 3 is obscured by the preceding higher 4. A clue at the right-hand end of the same row would be "1," since only the 6 would be visible.

522. FUTOSHIKI

Place 1 to 7 once each into every row and column while obeying the inequality signs.

Greater than (>) signs between some squares indicate that the value in one square is greater than that in another as indicated by the sign. The sign always points toward the smaller number.

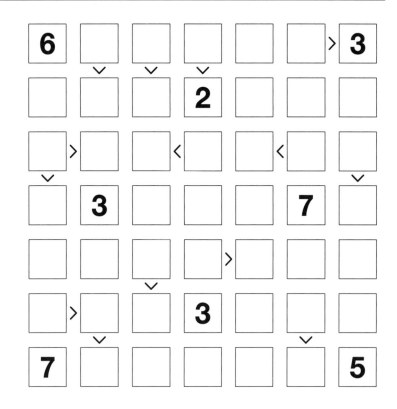

523. NUMBER LINK

Draw a series of separate paths, each connecting a pair of identical numbers.

No more than one path can enter any grid square, and paths can only travel horizontally or vertically, and never diagonally.

	1		2				2
	3		1	4		5	
5							
			6				
	7			7	8		4
	9	10			6		3
	11		11				
					9	10	8

SOLUTION 1

G	L	O	B	E			B	I	S	H	O	P	S
	O		A		B		L		E		R		
E	V	E	N	T	U	A	L			A	N	O	N
	E				A		R		U		R		
O	R	A	N	G	E			M	E	T	R	O	
		A			A		I		U				
O	F	F	S		U	R	N			A	C	N	E
		O					C		A		L		
U	T	T	E	R		T	O	G	G	L	E		
N			I		A		I		E		E		
I	D	E	A		T	R	O	U	B	L	E	S	
	E		R		I		N		R		R		
A	D	V	A	N	C	E		R	A	I	S	E	

SOLUTION 2

SOLUTION 3

C	B	F	D	A	E
D	A	E	C	B	F
B	F	D	A	E	C
E	C	B	F	D	A
F	D	A	E	C	B
A	E	C	B	F	D

SOLUTION 4

6	9	5	7	2	8	1	3	4
7	3	2	5	1	4	6	8	9
8	1	4	6	9	3	5	2	7
1	7	3	8	6	9	4	5	2
5	8	6	2	4	7	9	1	3
4	2	9	1	3	5	8	7	6
3	5	7	9	8	6	2	4	1
9	4	1	3	5	2	7	6	8
2	6	8	4	7	1	3	9	5

SOLUTION 5

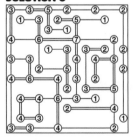

SOLUTION 6

SOLUTION 7

| SING |
| SINK |
| SILK |
| SILL |
| BILL |
| BELL |

SOLUTION 8

FAMILIES

There are around 40 words in total

SOLUTION 9

SOLUTION 10

COMPLEXITIES

There are around 25 words in total

SOLUTION 11

26		73
13		144
169		112
112		8
32		14
16		88

SOLUTION 12

P	R	A	I	S	E		I	M	P	O	S	E
O		L		C		T		I		W		M
P	R	O	M	O	T	I	O	N		N	A	B
A		N			O	T		D		G		A
R	Y	E		T	O	A	D	S	T	O	O	L
T			E		N				A			M
	M	E	T	R	O		A	P	P	L	E	
S		U			N		A			P		P
T	E	R	R	O	R	I	S	T		S	N	L
R		A		D		N		H		E		A
I	D	S		I	N	T	H	E	M	A	I	N
C		I		U		H		N		R		E
T	R	A	U	M	A		S	T	A	T	U	S

SOLUTION 13

0	6	5	5	2	2	6	3
5	1	6	1	6	4	4	2
5	2	3	4	1	3	0	4
0	3	3	3	4	1	0	4
1	1	0	5	5	3	5	2
1	4	0	6	6	6	6	2
1	0	5	4	3	2	0	2

SOLUTION 14

3	9	5	7	6	1	4	2	8
1	4	8	2	9	3	5	6	7
6	7	2	8	4	5	3	9	1
2	8	4	5	7	6	9	1	3
9	3	6	1	2	4	8	7	5
5	1	7	3	8	9	2	4	6
8	6	9	4	5	2	1	3	7
4	2	1	6	3	8	7	5	9
7	5	3	9	1	2	6	8	4

SOLUTION 15

SOLUTION 16

SOLUTION 17

SOLUTION 18

F	O	P		V		R			S	N	U	B
O		H		O	B	E	Y		I			I
C	H	I	L	I		I		W	A	L	T	Z
U			L			K		O				A
S	O	C	I	A	L	I	S	M		J	A	R
	W			E			A		O			R
B	E	T		C	A	B	I	N		B	Y	E
A		A		L		L			E			E
R	I	P		E	X	P	L	O	D	I	N	G
O			R			R		R				U
Q	U	A	C	K		O		A	M	A	Z	E
U		L		E	X	I	T		D			S
E	K	E	D		Y		E		S	I	S	

SOLUTION 19

DECORATIONS

SOLUTION 20

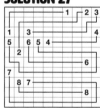

SOLUTION 21

SOLUTION 22

SOLUTION 23

4	5	6	1	2	3
3	6	1	2	5	4
5	1	2	3	4	6
6	2	3	4	1	5
1	4	5	6	3	2
2	3	4	5	6	1

SOLUTION 24

4	5	6	2	1	3
1	6	2	3	5	4
6	2	3	1	4	5
3	1	4	5	2	6
2	4	5	6	3	1
5	3	1	4	6	2

SOLUTION 25

1. Indian and Pacific
2. Fragrant gum resin
3. Kelly Clarkson
4. *Holiday Inn*
5. January 6

SOLUTION 26

1	7	5	3	4	2	6
5	2	3	7	6	1	4
2	4	6	1	3	7	5
3	6	1	2	5	4	7
4	1	2	6	7	5	3
7	3	4	5	1	6	2
6	5	7	4	2	3	1

SOLUTION 27

SOLUTION 28

K		B		Z		T		
E		A		E	R	R	S	
H	Y	S	T	E	R	I	A	
B	L	T		O	D	D	S	
O	Y	E	Z		D	I	E	
A		R		E	T	C		
E	R	A		L	N	I	T	
D	R	A	I	N		O		
S	O	L	O		A	N	Y	
	M	S	N		B	A	A	
C	I	A	O		H	E	L	M

SOLUTION 29

EGGNOG

SOLUTION 30

H	A	B	F	E	D	C	G
D	G	H	A	F	C	B	E
A	C	E	B	D	H	G	F
E	B	G	H	C	F	D	A
B	F	D	C	G	E	A	H
C	E	A	D	H	G	F	B
G	D	F	E	B	A	H	C
F	H	C	G	A	B	E	D

SOLUTION 31

6	3				
1	3	6	4	2	5
2	4	5	1	6	3
3	1	4	6	5	2	3
4	2	3	5	1	6	1
5	6	2	3	4	1	3
6	5	1	2	3	4	3

6 4

SOLUTION 32

```
E A V E   U N U S A B L E
  D C P N L I
S M I L E S   D R I V E S
  I   I   E   E B
D R O P   T E R M I N A L
  A S     A       G L
O B J E C T I O N A B L E
  L     R     R O
T E A C H I N G   R O W S
  A   N A   I A
S C A M P I   W A V I N G
  R E T K E C
S Y N O N Y M S   D Y E D
```

SOLUTION 33

1 1 4

6
4
1

SOLUTION 34

A	E	B	F	C	D
B	C	D	E	A	F
D	A	F	C	B	E
F	B	E	A	D	C
E	D	C	B	F	A
C	F	A	D	E	B

SOLUTION 35

5	9	8	1	2	3	6	7	4
6	1	3	7	9	4	8	5	2
4	7	2	8	5	6	9	3	1
9	3	1	4	7	2	5	8	6
2	4	5	6	3	8	7	1	9
7	8	6	9	1	5	4	2	3
8	5	9	3	4	1	2	6	7
3	6	4	2	8	7	1	9	5
1	2	7	5	6	9	3	4	8

SOLUTION 36

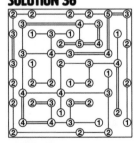

SOLUTION 37

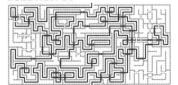

SOLUTION 38

LOVE
LORE
LORD
LARD
BARD
BIRD

SOLUTION 39
PRESENTS
There are around 65 words in total

SOLUTION 40

SOLUTION 41
EVANGELICALS
There are around 40 words in total

SOLUTION 42

70	12
13	108
65	164
11	68
77	34
22	51

SOLUTION 43

```
Y   P F     D E   S
O V E R L A P   R E N E W
U   S O A   Y   G   I
R I O   O B S E R V I N G
S   D   S   U N   N
E A R N S   T U N N E L S
L   E   H     E     A
F R A G I L E   C A R O B
S   S C   B   R     O
I N S T I T U T E   S E T
S   U   E   C   D   T   A
B U R N S   K N O W I N G
N   E   T     S   R   E
```

SOLUTION 44

1	2	4	5	0	2	1	0
3	3	6	5	1	1	5	2
6	6	2	6	0	0	3	3
3	1	4	6	5	4	3	2
3	2	2	2	6	5	0	1
5	4	4	1	3	0	6	5
0	0	4	6	4	5	1	4

SOLUTION 45

1	5	4	3	6	8	7	9	2
9	3	8	2	5	7	6	4	1
6	7	2	9	1	4	8	3	5
7	8	6	1	9	5	4	2	3
3	4	1	8	7	2	5	6	9
5	2	9	4	3	6	1	7	8
2	1	5	6	4	9	3	7	8
4	9	7	5	8	3	2	1	6
8	6	3	7	2	1	9	5	4

SOLUTION 46

4   2   6

6
3
5
6
4
3

SOLUTION 47

SOLUTION 48

SOLUTION 49

```
S   C D   E     A C E
P R O J E C T S     I   S
A   D S A     B A H T
  P A C K S   W O O   R
  E   O     A H A     I
M A S S I V E L Y   O A K
A   H     E G     R   E
I V Y   D I S A S T E R S
L   F U N     W   O   O
B   W E B   Q U O T E   N
O Y E Z   C   S   W   A
X   L     P O W E R I N G
  O L D     N   S   G   O
```

SOLUTION 50
SHOPPING

SOLUTION 51

SOLUTION 52

SOLUTION 53

16   2
5
3 4
5   8
3
8   2
3
6   8   12
3   12

SOLUTION 54

2-	72x	3-	2+	2+	
5	4	3	6	2	1
3	6	4	1	5	2
1	2	5	3	4	6
6	3	2	5	1	4
2	5	1	4	6	3
4	1	6	2	3	5

SOLUTION 55

29 5 8 6 5

| 1 | 6 | 2 | 4 | 3 | 5 | 12
|---|---|---|---|---|---|
| 4 | 5 | 6 | 1 | 2 | 3 | 11
| 6 | 3 | 4 | 5 | 1 | 2 | 11
| 2 | 4 | 5 | 3 | 6 | 1 | 11
| 5 | 1 | 3 | 2 | 4 | 6 | 4
| 3 | 2 | 1 | 6 | 5 | 4 |

3 7 4 19 19

SOLUTION 56
1. Nine
2. Athena
3. A coin
4. At the marketplace
5. Archimedes

SOLUTION 57

7	2	6	3	4	5	1
1	7	3	5	2	6	4
6	5	1	4	3	7	2
5	1	4	2	6	3	7
3	4	7	6	1	2	5
4	6	2	7	5	1	3
2	3	5	1	7	4	6

SOLUTION 58

SOLUTION 59

```
  O   D   E   P
  P   I   A N O N
A P P R O V A L
  O A T   E V I L
  S T Y   A T E
H E R   S   L I D
  O B I T   C
  N E T   H I S
I S I S   F I A T
  Z E N   D N A
W H E T   R E S T
```

SOLUTION 60
SANTA CLAUS

SOLUTION 61

C	F	A	D	B	E	H	G
B	G	H	E	F	A	D	C
G	A	E	C	H	D	B	F
H	D	C	G	A	F	E	B
E	H	D	F	C	B	G	A
F	E	B	A	D	G	C	H
D	C	F	B	G	H	A	E
A	B	G	H	E	C	F	D

SOLUTION 62

		3		3		3	
	1	5	6	2	4	3	
3	3	4	2	1	6	5	
5	2	3	4	5	1	6	
	6	2	1	3	5	4	3
3	4	1	5	6	3	2	3
	5	6	3	4	2	1	4
		1			4		

SOLUTION 63

		D		D		G		A		V		G	
T	O	M	A	T	O			N	E	E	D	L	E
		C		S		S		G		R		O	
I	T	C	H		S	N	O	B	B	E	R	Y	
		O				I		R		A		Y	
T	R	A	N	S	P	L	A	N	T	S			
		S		O				I		U			
			E	N	V	I	R	O	N	M	E	N	T
		O		S		O		X					L
F	R	I	E	N	D	L	Y		P	L	U	S	
		D		N		I		G		U		C	
L	E	S	S	E	N		E	U	R	E	K	A	
		R				E		E		N		E	Y

SOLUTION 64

SOLUTION 65

C	E	D	F	A	B
D	A	B	E	C	F
B	C	F	A	D	E
F	D	E	C	B	A
E	B	A	D	F	C
A	F	C	B	E	D

SOLUTION 66

8	7	9	2	4	1	6	5	3
5	2	1	3	6	8	9	4	7
4	6	3	7	9	5	8	2	1
3	1	4	9	5	2	7	6	8
6	9	8	1	7	4	2	3	5
2	5	7	6	8	3	4	1	9
7	4	6	5	1	9	3	8	2
9	3	5	8	2	6	1	7	4
1	8	2	4	3	7	5	9	6

SOLUTION 67

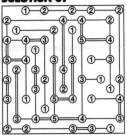

SOLUTION 68

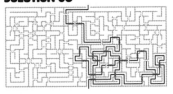

SOLUTION 69

CARE
CANE
LANE
LAND
LEND
TEND

SOLUTION 70

WRAPPING
There are around 25 words in total

SOLUTION 71

SOLUTION 72

REPRODUCIBLE
There are around 30 words in total

SOLUTION 73

50		21
25		14
5		49
8		7
4		77
44		36

SOLUTION 74

	S	T	E	E	R	E	D		E	M	I	T
C	E		N		U		I		E			
R	U	N	O	V	E	R		B	A	S	E	S
I		S		I		E		L		T		
C	L	E	A	R		K	R	A	K	E	N	
K			O		A		U		A			P
E	R	R	A	N	T		S	T	U	D	I	O
T		E		M		S		I				S
	A	F	F	E	C	T		F	A	D	E	S
E		O		N		R		U		W		E
M	E	R	I	T		I	L	L	N	E	S	S
U		M		K		L		L		S		
S	A	S	S		R	E	C	Y	C	L	E	

SOLUTION 75

0	1	1	5	2	1	6	1
4	6	6	1	5	0	3	0
4	3	3	3	6	0	0	6
2	6	2	2	1	5	2	5
5	4	0	2	3	6	4	5
2	0	4	4	3	6	4	1
2	3	4	5	3	1	5	0

SOLUTION 76

SOLUTION 77

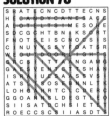

SOLUTION 78

SOLUTION 79

SOLUTION 80

W		W		E		Q		I		T	
C	H	O	R	A	L		U	D	D	E	R
I		E		K	O	I		E		E	
D	O	Z	E	N	S		T	R	A	D	E
O					H		A		R		
L	O	V	E	L	Y		E	N	J	O	Y
T		E		E	L	F		D		D	E
E	X	P	E	L		T	E	N	D	E	D
W		A			I		I				I
B	E	E	R	S		S	E	X	T	E	T
I	V		L	I	E		B		O		
A	M	I	G	O		E	M	B	R	Y	O
S		L		P		K		S		S	

SOLUTION 81

JOYFULNESS

SOLUTION 82

SOLUTION 83

SOLUTION 84

SOLUTION 85

1	6	3	4	2	5
2	5	4	3	1	6
3	4	1	5	6	2
5	1	6	2	4	3
4	2	5	6	3	1
6	3	2	1	5	4

SOLUTION 86

6	1	4	3	2	5
1	4	6	5	3	2
2	5	3	4	6	1
5	3	2	1	4	6
4	6	5	2	1	3
3	2	1	6	5	4

SOLUTION 87

1. Hawaii
2. Kettledrums
3. *Wicked*
4. *Bohemian Rhapsody*
5. Leonard Bernstein

SOLUTION 88

5	3	1	2	6	7	4
1	5	2	7	3	4	6
6	2	5	3	4	1	7
7	6	3	4	2	5	1
2	7	4	5	1	6	3
3	4	6	1	7	2	5
4	1	7	6	5	3	2

SOLUTION 89

SOLUTION 90

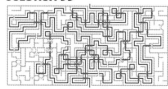

```
    G   H   V D
  O A   I C E S
S O L D I E R S
  D Y E   W I K I
  G N A W   M C
  R   N   L E G O
M I C   Z   S I N
  E L S E     V
F E A T U R E S
  A M A T E U R
G E N E   E X P O
```

SOLUTION 91
KRISS KRINGLE

SOLUTION 92

B	D	A	F	C	H	E	G
D	G	H	C	B	F	A	E
A	F	E	B	G	D	H	C
C	H	G	E	A	B	D	F
E	A	C	D	F	G	B	H
G	B	F	H	E	A	C	D
H	E	B	G	D	C	F	A
F	C	D	A	H	E	G	B

SOLUTION 93

```
      3   3       3
    3 5 2 1 4 6
    4 6 1 3 5 2
    6 4 5 2 3 1   4
  5 1 2 3 4 6 5
    5 1 4 6 2 3   2
  3 2 3 6 5 1 4   3
      3   2 3
```

SOLUTION 94

```
A N I M A L   M E S S E S
R   G   M   C   G   A   T
E E L   U N I F O R M L Y
N   O   S   T     P   L
A L O N E   I N D U L G E
S       M   Z I E
  U N N E C E S S A R Y
  E   N     C     R   R
R O T A T E S   O P E R A
E   W     H   U   V   I
P R O M O T I O N   A D S
E   R   I   P   T   D   E
L I K E L Y   A S C E N D
```

SOLUTION 95

SOLUTION 96

E	C	B	A	F	D
B	F	D	E	C	A
D	A	C	F	B	E
F	B	E	D	A	C
C	D	A	B	E	F
A	E	F	C	D	B

SOLUTION 97

3	6	8	5	7	4	9	1	2
5	7	9	6	1	2	3	8	4
4	1	2	3	9	8	6	5	7
2	4	1	9	8	3	7	6	5
9	5	7	4	6	1	8	2	3
8	3	6	7	2	5	1	4	9
1	9	4	8	5	7	2	3	6
7	2	3	1	4	6	5	9	8
6	8	5	2	3	9	4	7	1

SOLUTION 98

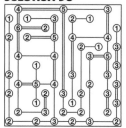
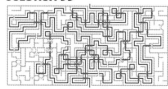

SOLUTION 99

(maze solution)

SOLUTION 100

```
PASS
PALS
PALE
TALE
TAME
TIME
```

SOLUTION 101
CAROLING
There are around 30 words in total

SOLUTION 102

SOLUTION 103
MANIPULATION
There are around 30 words in total

SOLUTION 104

42	62
138	31
69	124
46	155
119	93
72	38

SOLUTION 105

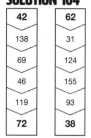

```
S O U N D S   F R E E Z E
P   T   I   I E M       A
R O T   S A N D P A P E R
A   E   A   D     E     L
Y A R D S   E L D E R L Y
S     S   T   P   E   O
  U N N E C E S S A R Y
  E         E   N   I   A
D R E S S E D   G A M E S
I     E     D   E   N   S
A L L O W A N C E   D O E
L   E   Y   T   R   I   S
S I S T E R   E S S A Y S
```

SOLUTION 106

0	3	4	5	1	0	5	6
0	0	1	6	1	3	0	2
4	0	6	6	3	3	1	5
2	6	1	6	2	5	4	5
3	3	1	3	2	2	4	0
2	0	4	1	5	5	2	4
1	5	6	3	2	4	6	4

SOLUTION 107

8	4	5	7	1	9	3	6	2
6	9	1	5	3	2	7	4	8
3	7	2	6	8	4	9	5	1
9	8	6	4	5	7	1	2	3
2	3	4	9	6	1	5	8	7
5	1	7	3	2	8	6	9	4
1	6	3	8	4	5	2	7	9
7	2	8	1	9	6	4	3	5
4	5	9	2	7	3	8	1	6

SOLUTION 108

SOLUTION 109

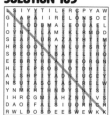

SOLUTION 110

SOLUTION 111

```
G O U T   S   C   O W E D
U   L   E Q U I P   O   U
Y A N G   U   N   T W I N
S   A U R A   E M U S   E
  P   R   R U M   B   R
M A N U R E   A Z A L E A
  S   E       O   J
S H E L V E   M O S A I C
  A   O   M O A   H   G
S   F O R E   S T A G   A
K E L P   R   S   M O B S
I   E   O G L E S   W   K
T A X I   E   S   O N U S
```

SOLUTION 112
BETHLEHEM

SOLUTION 113

SOLUTION 114

(loop puzzle solution)

SOLUTION 115

(grid solution)

SOLUTION 116

5	6	2	4	3	1
3	2	4	6	1	5
1	3	6	5	2	4
6	4	1	2	5	3
2	1	5	3	4	6
4	5	3	1	6	2

SOLUTION 117

3	1	2	5	6	4
2	6	1	4	5	3
5	4	3	1	2	6
1	3	5	6	4	2
4	2	5	6	3	1
6	3	4	2	1	5

SOLUTION 118
1. Dan Brown
2. Clive Staples
3. *Harry Potter and the Prisoner of Azkaban*
4. *Black Beauty*
5. *Go Set a Watchman*

SOLUTION 119

7	3	5	2	6	1	4
3	1	7	4	5	2	6
6	5	2	3	4	7	1
2	4	1	7	3	6	5
1	2	6	5	7	4	3
5	6	4	1	2	3	7
4	7	3	6	1	5	2

SOLUTION 120

SOLUTION 121

	E	T		T		T	
	P	O		O	A	R	S
F	I	R	M		S	P	A
T	E	A	C	H	I	N	G
A	P	T		E	S	L	
P	R	O	S		C	P	U
W	H	O		I		E	A
	D	E	L	I		L	M
P	U	R	E		E	N	T
C	O	N	M	O	T	O	
C	H	E	S	T		N	S	W

SOLUTION 122
CHRISTMAS TREE

SOLUTION 123

G	C	B	H	D	E	A	F
F	E	A	D	C	G	B	H
E	A	D	G	F	C	H	B
C	D	H	B	E	F	G	A
H	F	G	C	A	B	E	D
A	G	F	E	B	H	D	C
B	H	C	A	G	D	F	E
D	B	E	F	H	A	C	G

SOLUTION 124

		3		3	4		
	6	4	5	1	3	2	4
	4	5	6	2	1	3	2
2	3	1	2	6	4	5	2
2	2	6	4	3	5	1	
5	1	2	3	5	6	4	2
	5	3	1	4	2	6	
		4	3				

SOLUTION 125

	A	B	Y	S	S		A	P	A	T	H	Y
E		A		U		R		A		A		A
D	E	S	I	G	N	E	R	S		B	A	R
G		E		G		C		T		L		D
E	N	S	U	E		O	B	E	Y	E	D	
S			S			G				A		
	C	O	N	T	E	N	T	I	O	U	S	
	R			I		M				S		
A	B	S	E	N	T		P	I	L	O	T	
U		I		N		I		R		Y		A
S	E	T		E	C	O	N	O	M	I	C	S
E		A		M		N		V		N		H
D	E	L	A	Y	S		W	E	I	G	H

SOLUTION 126

SOLUTION 127

B	F	D	A	E	C
E	C	B	F	D	A
F	D	A	E	C	B
A	E	C	B	F	D
C	B	F	D	A	E
D	A	E	C	B	F

SOLUTION 128

1	2	8	3	9	6	5	4	7
9	4	5	8	7	2	3	6	1
3	6	7	4	5	1	9	2	8
4	7	9	2	3	5	8	1	6
5	3	6	1	8	7	2	9	4
8	1	2	6	4	9	7	5	3
7	5	1	9	6	3	4	8	2
2	9	4	7	1	8	6	3	5
6	8	3	5	2	4	1	7	9

SOLUTION 129

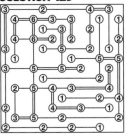

SOLUTION 130

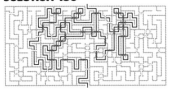

SOLUTION 131

| EVEN |
| EVES |
| EWES |
| OWES |
| ODES |
| ODDS |

SOLUTION 132
RELIGION
There are around 30 words in total

SOLUTION 133

SOLUTION 134
PRECIPITATED
There are around 50 words in total

SOLUTION 135

97	91
183	13
61	66
12	36
120	18
174	63

SOLUTION 136

	A		T	G	R	G	A		A	
S	P	O	O	K	Y		E	R	R	A	N	D
	P		Y		P	G	E		G			
L	E	S	S		S	U	I	T	A	B	L	Y
	A			U		O	T		E			
B	R	O	A	D	M	I	N	D	E	D		
	S	V				S	A			A		
		T	E	M	P	E	R	A	T	U	R	E
	R	R		A			E				R	
N	O	N	S	E	N	S	E		I	R	I	S
	W		I		C		T	V				
	M	A	R	O	O	N		H	A	C	K	E	R
	N		N		I		O	H		D		

SOLUTION 137

6	6	2	0	5	5	1	5
0	0	2	4	3	2	1	0
2	6	4	0	5	0	6	0
5	1	1	6	4	3	1	3
5	1	5	3	2	4	4	6
3	3	1	6	5	3	4	2
6	4	2	3	2	1	4	0

SOLUTION 138

5	4	9	7	2	3	1	8	6
2	6	3	4	8	1	5	9	7
7	8	1	9	6	5	3	4	2
3	5	2	6	4	8	7	1	9
8	9	6	1	5	7	2	3	4
4	1	7	2	3	9	6	5	8
9	3	8	5	7	2	4	6	1
1	2	4	3	9	6	8	7	5
6	7	5	8	1	4	9	2	3

SOLUTION 139

SOLUTION 140

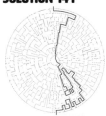

SOLUTION 141

SOLUTION 142

	S		S	B		G	R		P	
P	A	N	I	N	I		E	Q	U	A	L	S
	F		N		N	E	T		G		A	
J	A	G	G	E	D		U		S	A	S	S
	R			I	M	P			M		
D	I	S	C	O		O		T	O	P	A	Z
	K		F	L	U	S	H		E		
C	O	A	S	T		T		E	X	A	L	T
	P				W	H	Y		E		
S	P	U	R		A		V	I	A		L	
U	S	A	B	L	E		R	O	D	E	N	T
	E		S		D		S		E		S	

SOLUTION 143
REINDEER

SOLUTION 144

9	3	1		7	6	5	8	9	
5	1	2	2	4	7	3	6	8	1
	5	3	9	8		8	9	4	6
2	3	1	5	1		1	2		
6	4	2	8	9	3	7	9	5	3
8	5		7	8	1		8	3	1
	1	2	3	4		9	1	5	3	2
	4	1	3		3	9	7	

SOLUTION 145

SOLUTION 146

SOLUTION 147

4	6	5	1	3	2
6	3	4	5	2	1
5	4	2	3	1	6
1	2	3	6	4	5
2	5	1	4	6	3
3	1	6	2	5	4

SOLUTION 148

2	4	6	5	3	1
4	5	1	2	6	3
5	6	3	1	2	4
1	3	4	6	5	2
3	2	5	4	1	6
6	1	2	3	4	5

SOLUTION 149

1. Nonagon
2. A number equal to the sum of its factors
3. Pi
4. Yes
5. 40%

SOLUTION 150

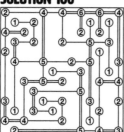

SOLUTION 151

SOLUTION 152

SOLUTION 153

FALLING SNOW

SOLUTION 154

D	H	E	B	C	G	F	A
A	G	C	D	F	E	B	H
E	F	A	H	D	B	G	C
C	B	H	A	G	F	E	D
G	D	B	E	H	A	C	F
B	E	F	C	A	H	D	G
F	A	D	G	B	C	H	E
H	C	G	F	E	D	A	B

SOLUTION 155

SOLUTION 156

UTPTCPG
SCHERZO AROMA
I O I R M U R
NERVE CLEARED
G O S R E
SUBTERRANEAN
S G Y N S
ACHIEVEMENTS
T S F I I
CHOOSES FIRED
H G A I O E E
EARLY GORILLA
L E S N T Y L

SOLUTION 157

SOLUTION 158

A	B	C	E	F	D
F	E	A	D	B	C
B	D	F	C	E	A
E	C	B	A	D	F
D	A	E	F	C	B
C	F	D	B	A	E

SOLUTION 159

8	3	1	4	6	7	9	2	5
4	9	6	2	5	8	3	7	1
2	7	5	1	3	9	6	4	8
7	5	9	6	2	1	4	8	3
1	4	2	7	8	3	5	6	9
6	8	3	9	4	5	2	1	7
9	6	8	3	1	4	7	5	2
3	1	4	5	7	2	8	9	6
5	2	7	8	9	6	1	3	4

SOLUTION 160

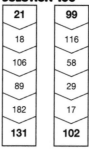

SOLUTION 161

SOLUTION 162

| CALL |
| CELL |
| WELL |
| WELD |
| WEED |
| WEEK |

SOLUTION 163

GARLANDS
There are around 50 words in total

SOLUTION 164

SOLUTION 165

REPUBLISHING
There are around 70 words in total

SOLUTION 166

21	99
18	116
106	58
89	29
182	17
131	102

SOLUTION 167

SOLUTION 168

0	0	0	2	4	6	5	4
3	2	5	3	4	1	3	2
4	5	2	3	6	6	2	4
5	6	2	1	3	3	6	0
1	6	1	1	1	2	0	3
0	0	5	1	4	3	6	5
2	4	1	5	4	0	6	5

SOLUTION 169

8	2	5	4	6	7	3	1	9
9	7	6	3	1	8	4	2	5
4	3	1	5	2	9	6	7	8
2	6	9	8	3	1	5	4	7
5	4	8	7	9	2	1	6	3
3	5	2	1	8	6	7	9	4
1	8	7	9	5	4	2	3	6
6	9	4	7	3	8	5	1	?

SOLUTION 170

SOLUTION 171

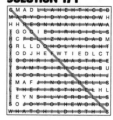

SOLUTION 172

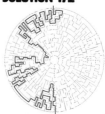

SOLUTION 173

SOLUTION 174

ORNAMENTS

SOLUTION 175

SOLUTION 176

SOLUTION 177

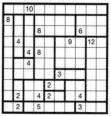

SOLUTION 178

4	5	1	2	6	3
3	4	6	1	2	5
2	3	4	5	1	6
1	6	3	4	5	2
5	1	2	6	3	4
6	2	5	3	4	1

SOLUTION 179

4	2	1	6	5	3
5	3	2	1	4	6
1	4	5	3	6	2
3	1	6	4	2	5
6	5	4	2	3	1
2	6	3	5	1	4

SOLUTION 180

1. IBM
2. United Kingdom
3. Android
4. 2
5. Amazon

SOLUTION 181

5	3	1	6	2	4	7
2	6	3	1	5	7	4
1	7	6	5	4	2	3
4	5	2	7	3	6	1
6	2	4	3	7	1	5
7	4	5	2	1	3	6
3	1	7	4	6	5	2

SOLUTION 182

SOLUTION 183

SOLUTION 184

WINTER WEATHER

SOLUTION 185

D	G	A	C	H	B	F	E
F	B	H	G	A	E	C	D
A	H	C	D	E	F	G	B
E	C	G	F	B	D	H	A
G	A	D	B	F	C	E	H
H	D	B	E	C	G	A	F
C	E	F	A	D	H	B	G
B	F	E	H	G	A	D	C

SOLUTION 186

4	6	1	5	2	3	3
6	5	4	3	1	2	5
5	3	2	6	4	1	
1	4	3	2	5	6	
2	1	5	6	3	4	2
3	2	6	1	4	5	2

SOLUTION 187

SOLUTION 188

SOLUTION 189

D	F	A	C	E	B
E	C	D	B	F	A
F	B	E	A	C	D
C	A	F	D	B	E
B	D	C	E	A	F
A	E	B	F	D	C

SOLUTION 190

6	9	3	4	7	5	8	2	1
4	8	5	1	9	2	3	6	7
7	1	2	6	3	8	4	5	9
3	5	7	8	1	6	2	9	4
2	4	8	3	5	9	7	1	6
9	6	1	7	2	4	5	8	3
8	3	9	5	4	1	6	7	2
1	7	6	2	8	3	9	4	5
5	2	4	9	6	7	1	3	8

SOLUTION 191

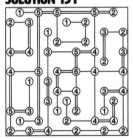

SOLUTION 192

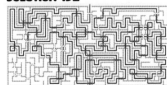

SOLUTION 193

GOES
DOES
DOTS
DOTE
DATE
LATE

SOLUTION 194

NATIVITY
There are around 15 words in total

SOLUTION 195

SOLUTION 196

PROVOCATIONS
There are around 35 words in total

SOLUTION 197

63	39
9	103
6	40
3	80
24	100
42	84

SOLUTION 198

S	T	A	T	E		A	D	V	E	R	S	E
I		R		B	E		N		U			
A	T	T	I	T	U	D	E		T	U	F	T
L		N		R			S		E		F	
B	E	S	I	D	E		C	O	R	G	I	
	T			A		A				A		
D	E	N	Y		U	R	L		A	R	E	A
C		C			A			C	A			
	L	A	T	E	R		T	O	G	G	L	E
I		O			A				A			I
A	P	E	X		T	R	O	U	B	L	E	S
	I		N			N				I		
P	E	A	C	O	C	K		F	A	I	N	T

SOLUTION 199

2	4	2	4	6	6	4	1
2	5	6	4	0	1	5	6
1	5	0	3	6	4	0	3
1	5	1	2	2	3	0	3
1	2	4	4	2	3	5	6
3	0	5	0	6	1	5	4
0	6	1	0	6	2	3	3

SOLUTION 200

3	4	6	9	2	8	5	7
9	2	8	5	7	4	6	1	3
5	6	7	3	1	8	2	9	4
2	1	4	7	6	5	3	8	9
8	5	6	9	4	3	1	7	2
7	9	3	8	2	1	4	6	5
1	3	5	2	8	9	7	4	6
4	7	2	1	5	6	9	3	8

SOLUTION 201

SOLUTION 202

R	L	O	Y	N	I	A	R	G	E	N	T	I	N	A
A	M	I	S	R	A	E	L	A	I	D	N	I		D
L	K	A	N	N	A	R	O	M	A	N	I	A		D
A	D	L	I	S	I	E	G	I	L	S	H	V		A
T	A	S	T	D	I	A	N	T	L	N	R	T		E
E	G	T	O	E	D	E	A	N	K	E	I	O		E
L	C	H	H	T	E	I	N	A	A	E		L		L
A	G	N	N	A	I	O	V	M	I	A	A	H		A
R	M	Y	H	N	I	E	I		I	A	A			N
T	E	N	S	T	R	E	G	G	A	R	E	O		
S	A	R	N	S	E	T	A	A	A	P	E	O		
U	J	O	E	Y	I	G	I	T	T	O	I	A		
A	M	V	R	A	N	I	G	N	T	Y	S			
R	E	I	H	D	A	M	S	A	D	N	A	I	Y	S
N	K	E	N	I	H	L	E	U	P	O	P	T	R	A

SOLUTION 203

SOLUTION 204

I		B	I	O		E		O	P		G
S	K	I		V	I	X	E	N		U	S	E
S		S	U			I		E		B	A	D	E
U	L	T	I	M	A	T	E		B	A	D	E
E		R		P			M		O		O	
D	U	O		A	P	T		S	N	U	G	
	N			T		O		K			M	
Z	E	R	O		E	L	F		C	A	B	
I		A		I			I		L		I	
S	P	R	Y		C	A	T	C	H	I	N	G
I		A		A		U		H		Q		
F	R	O		B	A	N	J	O		U	T	E
T		T		S		T		W	O	E		R

SOLUTION 205

RELATIVES

SOLUTION 206

1	2	5	7	3		3	2	9
3	2	4	1	9	6	8	8	1	7
1	2	1	7		2	1	3	5
3	1	7	9		6	8	7	9
9	8	2		2	1	3	4	6	2	1
7	9	1		2	4	5		1	3
7	3	1	2	4		3	9	2	7
7	2	9		2	3	1

SOLUTION 207

SOLUTION 208

SOLUTION 209

SOLUTION 210

SOLUTION 211

1. Jupiter
2. Uranus
3. Neptune
4. Cupid
5. Venus

SOLUTION 212

SOLUTION 213

SOLUTION 214

C	F	U		D		
H	R	T	I	E	R	
N	O	T	E		C	N	N
O	W	E	D		C	I	A
S	O	S		W	R	E	N
E		T			E	D	D
A	S	A		B	E	D	
		P		A		I	R	E
I	T	E	M	S		B	O	A
M		Y	I	E	L	D	S
L	I	L	A	C		E	S	T

SOLUTION 215

FAMILY GATHERINGS

SOLUTION 216

B	G	F	A	D	H	E	C
D	A	E	H	C	F	G	B
A	H	C	E	G	B	D	F
H	C	B	F	E	G	A	D
E	F	G	B	A	D	C	H
F	E	D	G	H	C	B	A
G	D	H	C	B	A	F	E
C	B	A	D	F	E	H	G

SOLUTION 217

3	2	1	5	6	4
4	1	2	6	3	5
1	4	3	2	5	6
2	6	5	4	1	3
6	5	4	3	2	1
5	3	6	1	4	2

SOLUTION 218

C	L	A	I	M	E	D		A	V	E	R
P		A	N	N		M	E	A			A
A	R	T	I	C	L	E		E	R	R	O	R
S		E		O	R		L	A			E
S	I	R	E	N		G	R	O	U	N	D
I			S	Y		D	D		M		
V	I	O	L	I	N		A	R	G	A	L	I
E		V		S	S		A				S
S	E	T	T	E	E		M	E	A	N	T
A		R	E		C	A		B	A		
F	E	L	O	N		O	U	T	L	O	O	K
A		A		T		N		I	U		E
R	A	P	S		E	D	U	C	A	T	E

SOLUTION 219

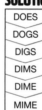

SOLUTION 220

D	A	E	C	F	B
E	C	F	B	A	D
F	B	A	D	C	E
A	D	C	E	B	F
C	E	B	F	D	A
B	F	D	A	E	C

SOLUTION 221

8	9	4	3	2	7	1	6	5
2	6	1	4	9	5	7	8	3
3	7	5	1	8	6	2	9	4
6	3	7	8	1	2	5	4	9
4	1	2	5	6	9	8	3	7
5	8	9	7	3	4	6	2	1
7	2	6	9	5	3	4	1	8
9	5	8	2	4	1	3	7	6
1	4	3	6	7	8	9	5	2

SOLUTION 222

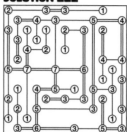

SOLUTION 223

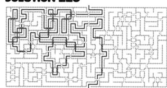

SOLUTION 224

DOES
DOGS
DIGS
DIMS
DIME
MIME

SOLUTION 225

CELEBRATE

There are around 70 words in total

SOLUTION 226

SOLUTION 227

OVERBALANCES

There are around 90 words in total

SOLUTION 228

65	93
52	62
39	3
26	95
182	19
196	171

SOLUTION 229

SOLUTION 230

2	0	1	1	0	1	2	0
4	4	3	5	5	5	3	5
1	2	3	0	5	5	6	2
5	4	6	3	1	3	4	4
3	1	4	6	6	4	2	1
6	6	0	1	0	5	6	3
2	2	0	4	2	3	6	0

SOLUTION 231

SOLUTION 232

SOLUTION 233

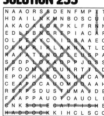

SOLUTION 234

SOLUTION 235

E	E	K		T		H		E	B	B	S
L		E		O	K	A	Y		I		K
B	A	Y	O	U		I	K	F	U	Z	Z	Y
O			G		K		E				W
W	A	R	E	H	O	U	S	E		E	R	A
	H		V		L		R		R	O	D
B	A	A		T	A	X	I	S			R
A		R	E			R			O		W
R	U	T		A	S	C	E	N	D	I	N	G
O			M			E		R			U
Q	U	I	T	S		S	I	F	T	S
U		N			J	E	S	T		A	T
E	A	S	Y		P				R	H	O

SOLUTION 236

CHESTNUTS

SOLUTION 237

	8	3	2		1	8	2	4	3		
9	8	3		1	3	9	5	2	8	4	
	1	2	4	8		4	1	3		8	6
4	8	3	9		3	8		9	7
2	1		1	2	3	6	4		7	6	1
5	6		5	3		3	9	8		1	5	2
	2	8	5	6		9	1	3	8	7
	9	7	5		8	2	1	3	

SOLUTION 238

(number-path puzzle grid)

SOLUTION 239

(grid puzzle with 5, 4, 6, 3, 2, 7, 8, 12, 20, 6)

SOLUTION 240

1	2	6	5	4	3
3	5	1	2	6	4
4	6	2	3	5	1
5	4	3	6	1	2
6	3	4	1	2	5
2	1	5	4	3	6

SOLUTION 241

4	3	6	5	2	1
6	2	1	4	5	3
2	1	3	6	4	5
1	4	5	3	6	2
3	5	4	2	1	6
5	6	2	1	3	4

SOLUTION 242

1. 1996
2. Nintendo
3. Game Gear
4. Xbox 360
5. GameCube

SOLUTION 243

2	5	4	3	1	6	7
6	3	7	4	5	2	1
7	6	5	1	4	3	2
1	4	3	2	7	5	6
5	1	6	7	2	4	3
3	2	1	5	6	7	4
4	7	2	6	3	1	5

SOLUTION 244

(path/loop puzzle grid)

SOLUTION 245

	L	I		T		S	
	I	S	O	L	A	T	E	S
F	E	E	T		C		A
		V	A	N	I	L	L	A
	P	E	S	E	T	A		L
	R		O		Z	O	O
P	O	E	M		P	Y	R	E
	C	L	E	F		A
	E	Y	E		A	N	T	I
	A		T	E	R	R	O	R
O	N	U	S		M	A	R	K

SOLUTION 246

WRAPPING PAPER

SOLUTION 247

F	H	A	G	D	B	E	C
E	A	G	D	C	F	B	H
B	C	H	E	A	D	F	G
A	F	E	B	G	C	H	D
G	D	C	H	B	E	A	F
C	G	F	A	E	H	D	B
H	B	D	C	F	A	G	E
D	E	B	F	H	G	C	A

SOLUTION 248

6	1	4	2	5	3
4	3	6	1	2	5
3	5	1	4	6	2
1	2	3	5	4	6
2	4	5	6	3	1
5	6	2	3	1	4

SOLUTION 249

A		T		P			S	D		S
C	I	R	C	U	I	T		C	L	E	A	N
C		E		T		E	R		S		A
E	W	E		R	E	M	A	I	N	I	N	G
S			I		P		M		G
S	W	A	R	D		E	X	P	A	N	D	S
E		C		R			E				I
D	I	O	R	A	M	A		D	A	R	E	D
	U		X		T		R				E
I	N	S	T	I	T	U	T	E		B	O	W
D		T		O	R		A		A		A
O	D	I	U	M		E	A	R	T	H	L	Y
L		C		S			Y		T		S

SOLUTION 250

SOLUTION 251

E	D	F	A	B	C
F	B	C	D	E	A
C	E	A	B	F	D
A	F	D	E	C	B
D	C	B	F	A	E
B	A	E	C	D	F

SOLUTION 252

5	3	2	4	1	6	8	9	7
8	1	9	5	3	7	2	4	6
4	6	7	9	8	2	3	5	1
2	5	6	8	4	1	9	7	3
7	8	3	6	9	5	1	2	4
9	4	1	7	2	3	6	8	5
3	9	5	1	7	8	4	6	2
1	7	8	2	6	4	5	3	9
6	2	4	3	5	9	7	1	8

SOLUTION 253

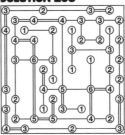

SOLUTION 254

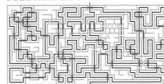

SOLUTION 255

SLOW
SLOT
SOOT
SOON
SOWN
DOWN

SOLUTION 256

TRADITION

There are around 35 words in total

SOLUTION 257

SOLUTION 258

INTERACTIONS

There are around 110 words in total

SOLUTION 259

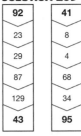

92	41
23	8
29	4
87	68
129	34
43	95

SOLUTION 260

(crossword: POEM, DRAGON, UTOPIA, ONCE, ASSEMBLY, SUSCEPTIBLE, STEREOTYPED, CALCULUS, ECHO, COMMON, ESCAPE)

SOLUTION 261

3	3	5	0	4	2	4	2
5	5	0	5	1	5	6	0
2	6	1	4	0	6	1	3
1	3	1	1	5	5	1	3
0	3	2	6	3	1	6	5
2	6	4	2	4	2	6	0
0	4	3	4	4	2	6	0

SOLUTION 262

(9×9 number grid)

SOLUTION 263

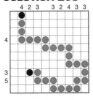

SOLUTION 264

SOLUTION 265

SOLUTION 266

	C	V		I	M	P	O	R	T	S
Q	U	E	E	N		E		R		E
S	U	D		T		B	E	J	E	W	E	L
	I		K	O	I		T		H	O
D	E	L	I		O			D	I	V	A
T		L	E	T		S	W	I	M		F
	L			A	S	H		G		O
A		E	E	L	S		R	O	E		O
F	U	N	D			U		S	I	Z	E
A		D		A		B	O	T		O
R	E	S	I	G	N	S		B		G	N	U
Y		F		O			P	I	X	I	E
P	E	R	S	O	N	S		T		N

SOLUTION 267
EPIPHANY

SOLUTION 268

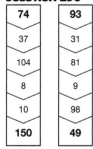

SOLUTION 269

SOLUTION 270

SOLUTION 271

SOLUTION 272

SOLUTION 273
1. *Carcassonne*
2. *Settlers of Catan*
3. Boardwalk
4. *Clue*
5. 32

SOLUTION 274

SOLUTION 275

SOLUTION 276

	B		T	Y		R	
	A		A		O	U	S	T
S	N	O	B		D	P	I
	A	N	O	R	A	K		U
L	E	O			E	A	R
			S	T	E	R	N
M	E	W		U		P	C	S
	R	O	O	M			H
	E	R	R		T	H	I	N
	R	E	C	E	I	V	E
J	A	Y	S		E	P	E	E

SOLUTION 277
GREETING CARDS

SOLUTION 278

A	C	B	D	F	H	E	G
D	E	G	A	H	F	B	C
E	H	F	B	A	G	C	D
G	F	C	H	E	B	D	A
C	B	H	G	D	A	F	E
F	A	E	C	G	D	H	B
B	G	D	F	C	E	A	H
H	D	A	E	B	C	G	F

SOLUTION 279

SOLUTION 280

N	O	R	M	A	L		E	R	A	S	E	R
U		E		S			A		K	E	
C	U	P		A	D	V	A	N	C	I	N	G
L		R		P		I		D			R	
E	G	O	S		G	E	N	O	C	I	D	E
I		D		O		W		M		R	T	
	U	N	P	O	P	U	L	A	R	
G		C		P		O	Y		I		S	
R	H	E	T	O	R	I	C		S	T	A	T
A			N		N		P	A		O	
P	R	E	S	E	N	T	L	Y		T	A	R
H		O		N			R		E	E	
S	O	N	A	T	A		C	E	A	S	E	D

SOLUTION 281

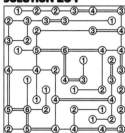

SOLUTION 282

F	C	B	D	E	A
B	E	A	C	F	D
A	F	D	E	B	C
D	B	C	F	A	E
C	A	E	B	D	F
E	D	F	A	C	B

SOLUTION 283

6	7	5	2	1	4	8	3	9
2	1	9	3	8	5	6	4	7
4	8	3	7	6	9	1	2	5
3	6	4	9	7	8	2	5	1
8	5	2	6	3	1	7	9	4
1	9	7	5	4	2	3	8	6
7	4	1	8	5	3	9	6	2
9	3	6	4	2	7	5	1	8
5	2	8	1	9	6	4	7	3

SOLUTION 284

SOLUTION 285

SOLUTION 286

FALL
FULL
FURL
FURS
OURS
OUTS

SOLUTION 287
SHEPHERDS
There are around 50 words in total

SOLUTION 288

SOLUTION 289
PRESENTATION
There are around 95 words in total

SOLUTION 290

74		93
37		31
104		81
8		9
10		98
150		49

SOLUTION 291

E	D	I	T		R	E	I	N	D	E	E	R
	E		R		A		N		O		W	
A	B	S	O	R	B		U	N	U	S	E	D
	A		U		B		T		B		
S	T	A	B		I	D	E	N	T	I	F	Y
	A		L		R				A		
O	B	J	E	C	T	I	O	N	A	B	L	E
	L		R		R		L			
K	E	Y	B	O	A	R	D		T	B	S	P
		A		N		I		I		H	
R	O	U	T	E	S		A	N	C	H	O	R
		U		H		N		L		R	
G	R	E	E	N	T	E	A		E	A	T	S

SOLUTION 292

6	5	2	1	2	4	0	4
2	0	5	5	1	4	4	3
5	5	0	6	0	0	3	3
0	2	3	2	4	3	5	4
0	1	4	6	6	5	2	6
3	6	2	6	0	1	2	3
1	1	1	6	5	1	4	3

SOLUTION 293

1	7	3	6	5	8	9	4	2
5	6	4	9	3	2	1	7	8
9	2	8	7	4	1	5	3	6
2	5	1	3	7	6	4	9	8
8	3	9	2	1	4	6	7	5
6	4	7	8	9	5	3	2	1
3	9	5	1	8	7	2	6	4
4	8	2	5	6	3	7	1	9
7	1	6	4	2	9	8	5	3

SOLUTION 294

SOLUTION 295

(word-search grid)

SOLUTION 296

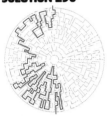

SOLUTION 297

(crossword grid) COS · PAY · JAR · WOMAN · PIC · CUB · OIL · CAMEL · FORECASTS · ANY · FEARS · ETA · OWL · LEA · EGG · UMBRA · TUX · ABS · PAD · EVE

SOLUTION 298

CHIMNEYS

SOLUTION 299

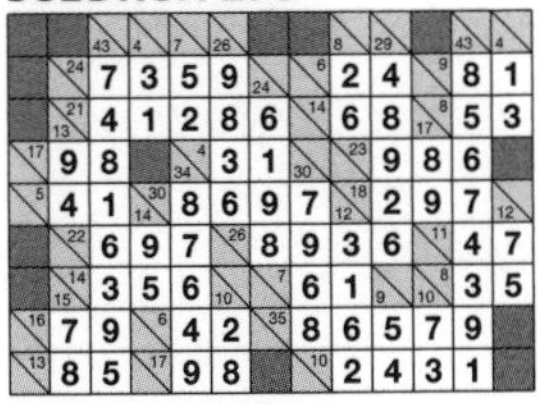

(number grid)

SOLUTION 300

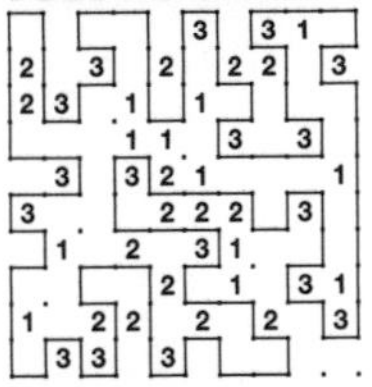

(link/number grid)

SOLUTION 301

(grid)

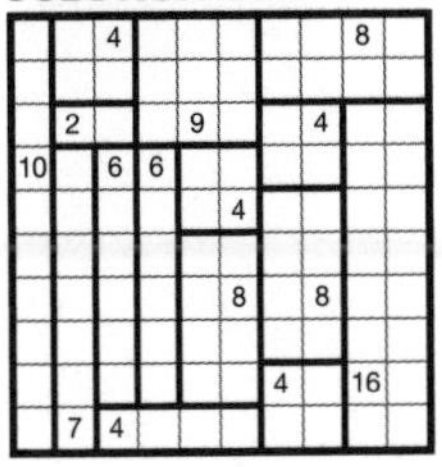

SOLUTION 302

3	2	1	6	5	4
4	5	3	1	2	6
5	6	2	3	4	1
6	3	5	4	1	2
2	1	4	5	6	3
1	4	6	2	3	5

SOLUTION 303

6	4	3	5	1	2
4	5	1	2	3	6
3	2	4	1	6	5
1	3	2	6	5	4
5	1	6	4	2	3
2	6	5	3	4	1

SOLUTION 304

1. Pixar
2. Industrial Light and Magic
3. *MASSIVE*
4. Computer-generated imagery
5. Weta Digital

SOLUTION 305

6	3	2	7	4	5	1
5	4	3	2	1	7	6
4	1	7	6	2	3	5
2	7	6	5	3	1	4
7	6	4	1	5	2	3
1	2	5	3	6	4	7
3	5	1	4	7	6	2

SOLUTION 306

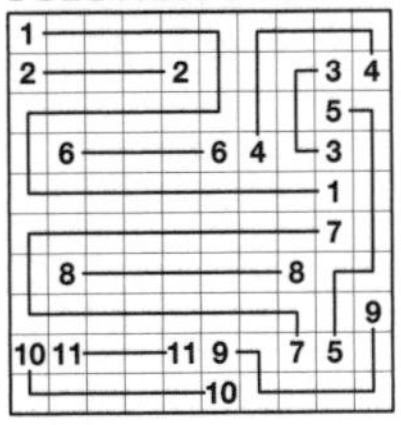

(number-link grid)

SOLUTION 307

(crossword grid) S · C · P · R · LOE · ESPY · PARR · ATM · VARY · RY · EKE · AIDE · PRESERVES · YP · KEN · NOV · G · PLANETARY · ADS · CUP · CONSTANTS

SOLUTION 308

SINGING CAROLS

SOLUTION 309

H	D	A	F	G	E	B	C
A	B	F	H	C	D	G	E
B	G	D	E	A	C	F	H
G	E	C	A	H	F	D	B
C	H	B	D	E	G	A	F
D	F	E	G	B	H	C	A
F	A	H	C	D	B	E	G
E	C	G	B	F	A	H	D

SOLUTION 310

	3	4	3			
6	4	5	2	1	3	
1	6	4	3	2	5	
3	5	2	1	6	4	
2	1	3	5	4	6	
4	3	6	1	5	2	

SOLUTION 311

(crossword) SHAMPOO NEEDS · ENLIGHTENMENT · FEATURES CLEF · WITNESSES · ONUS UPDATING · MANUFACTURERS · BESET WHISPER

SOLUTION 312

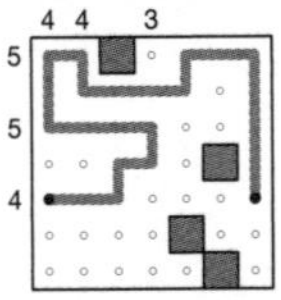

SOLUTION 313

D	E	F	C	A	B
B	C	A	D	F	E
F	D	B	E	C	A
E	A	C	F	B	D
C	B	D	A	E	F
A	F	E	B	D	C

SOLUTION 314

4	3	5	6	2	1	8	9	7
2	9	1	5	7	8	6	3	4
8	6	7	4	9	3	2	1	5
7	4	3	1	6	2	9	5	8
5	1	2	7	8	9	3	4	6
6	8	9	3	5	4	7	2	1
3	2	6	8	4	5	1	7	9
9	7	4	2	1	6	5	8	3
1	5	8	9	3	7	4	6	2

SOLUTION 315

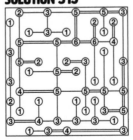

SOLUTION 316

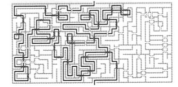

SOLUTION 317

SOCK
SACK
HACK
HARK
HARE
HERE

SOLUTION 318

CHOCOLATE
There are around 40 words in total

SOLUTION 319

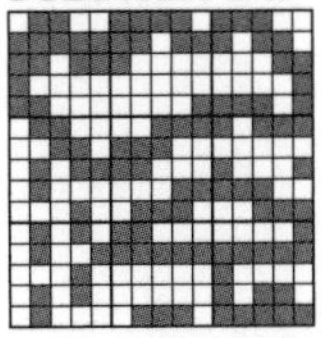

SOLUTION 320

FRANKINCENSE
There are around 70 words in total

SOLUTION 321

67		49
134		42
173		3
104		16
130		128
65		194

SOLUTION 322

(crossword) LETTER METRIC · GET PERFORMED · NOISE BEHAVES · WENSLEYDALE · FUCHSIA OPERA · ECONOMICS ADO · DREARY MYSELF

SOLUTION 323

5	2	0	4	4	1	1	3
3	5	2	0	1	3	6	3
2	6	4	2	0	1	5	4
4	1	3	0	1	2	0	4
1	6	3	5	0	5	2	2
5	0	6	4	4	3	1	6
5	5	0	0	3	5	4	1

SOLUTION 324

7	8	5	3	6	9	4	1	2
4	2	3	8	1	5	9	6	7
1	6	9	4	2	7	3	5	8
3	1	6	5	7	2	8	4	9
9	7	2	6	4	8	5	3	1
5	4	8	9	3	1	7	2	6
2	9	7	1	8	3	6	4	5
6	3	1	7	5	4	2	8	9
8	5	4	2	9	6	1	7	3

SOLUTION 325

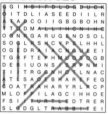

SOLUTION 326

SOLUTION 327

SOLUTION 328

SOLUTION 329
CHRISTMASTIDE

SOLUTION 330

SOLUTION 331

SOLUTION 332

SOLUTION 333

SOLUTION 334

SOLUTION 335
1. Helium
2. Alkali metals
3. Au
4. 6
5. Xenon

SOLUTION 336

SOLUTION 337

SOLUTION 338

SOLUTION 339
BUILDING SNOWMEN

SOLUTION 340

F	A	C	H	B	D	E	G
E	D	A	G	F	C	H	B
C	H	B	E	G	F	A	D
A	B	G	C	D	H	F	E
H	E	F	B	C	G	D	A
D	F	H	A	E	B	G	C
G	C	D	F	A	E	B	H
B	G	E	D	H	A	C	F

SOLUTION 341

SOLUTION 342

SOLUTION 343

SOLUTION 344

F	D	A	E	B	C
E	B	F	C	A	D
C	A	E	D	F	B
D	F	C	B	E	A
B	E	D	A	C	F
A	C	B	F	D	E

SOLUTION 345

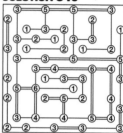

6	8	2	3	9	7	4	5	1
7	5	3	4	1	8	6	9	2
1	9	4	2	5	6	8	7	3
4	1	8	5	2	3	7	6	9
9	2	6	1	7	4	5	3	8
5	3	7	8	6	9	2	1	4
2	7	5	9	8	1	3	4	6
8	4	9	6	3	5	1	2	7
3	6	1	7	4	2	9	8	5

SOLUTION 346

SOLUTION 347

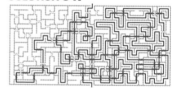

SOLUTION 348

| COOK |
| COOT |
| COAT |
| MOAT |
| MEAT |
| MEAD |

SOLUTION 349
STOCKINGS
There are around 30 words in total

SOLUTION 350

SOLUTION 351
MARSHMALLOWS
There are around 55 words in total

SOLUTION 352

34	13
17	156
39	78
26	6
13	97
99	52

SOLUTION 358

SOLUTION 365

6	1	3	5	4	2	28
3	4	2	1	6	5	16
4	3	1	2	5	6	5
5	2	4	6	1	3	3
2	5	6	4	3	1	4
1	6	5	3	2	4	

SOLUTION 366

1. DNA
2. The cell
3. Kingdom
4. Chlorophyll
5. 206

SOLUTION 367

1	4	2	3	7	5	6
5	2	3	6	4	1	7
7	6	4	1	3	2	5
2	5	1	7	6	4	3
4	3	6	2	5	7	1
6	1	7	5	2	3	4
3	7	5	4	1	6	2

SOLUTION 373

GAFFE ADVERSE
N A D I X U
MISCHIEF TARO
M U S F R P
DAHLIA EMAIL
T P R U
PITY PIE PESO
N O N A
CORGI TATTOO
L A N I I P
NUMB TRAVESTY
D B E L N I
PERIODS STICK

SOLUTION 374

SOLUTION 375

F	E	C	A	B	D
B	D	F	E	C	A
E	C	A	B	D	F
A	B	D	F	E	C
D	F	E	C	A	B
C	A	B	D	F	E

SOLUTION 353

LEMON JUDGED
U M R P P O A
STANDARDS RAN
U I E E E I K
ABLER LITTLE
L E I L Y
FUNDAMENTAL
N I U A
BURDEN CELEB
M S U A L Y
I O U VARIETIES
N A E Y A N S
DILATE DRUGS

SOLUTION 354

3	1	5	2	2	4	2	5
1	6	6	1	6	3	6	6
3	0	2	0	4	2	1	2
3	0	0	5	1	6	1	3
1	5	4	4	5	5	1	3
4	4	4	2	6	2	5	4
3	5	0	0	6	0	3	0

SOLUTION 359

E G O HOE C
Q VISA AJAR
LURE WAR U
I RACK NOSE
EPIC A E ERE
L OUR ADO G
FILM OIL PROP
T EBB LET O
ICY O O IBEX
HOUR SWUM A
K RHO INTO
PESO OYEZ E
S WET EON

SOLUTION 360

SHEPHERDS

SOLUTION 361

SOLUTION 376

6	1	7	3	8	5	9	4	2
2	4	8	9	1	7	3	5	6
3	9	5	6	2	4	1	7	8
5	2	9	8	4	3	7	6	1
8	6	4	1	7	9	5	2	3
7	3	1	2	5	6	8	9	4
4	5	3	7	6	1	2	8	9
9	8	6	5	3	2	4	1	7
1	7	2	4	9	8	6	3	5

SOLUTION 355

4	2	9	7	3	5	6	1	8
6	3	5	1	8	2	7	4	9
1	7	8	6	9	4	3	2	5
3	6	4	2	5	7	8	9	1
9	1	2	4	6	8	5	3	7
5	8	7	4	1	9	2	6	3
8	5	6	3	7	1	9	7	4
2	4	1	9	7	6	5	8	3
7	9	3	5	4	6	1	8	2

SOLUTION 362

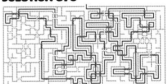

SOLUTION 377

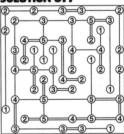

SOLUTION 356

SOLUTION 363

					6	4	
6				3			
	2	8			3		
3		6		10			
	4	6			6	3	14
						3	
3			4			6	

SOLUTION 364

5	2	4	3	1	6
6	5	3	4	2	1
1	3	2	6	4	5
3	4	5	1	6	2
2	1	6	5	3	4
4	6	1	2	5	3

SOLUTION 371

B	H	E	G	C	F	A	D
A	F	D	B	H	C	G	E
F	G	A	D	E	B	H	C
E	C	H	F	D	A	B	G
C	A	G	E	F	H	D	B
D	B	C	A	G	E	F	H
H	D	B	C	A	G	E	F
G	E	F	H	B	D	C	A

SOLUTION 372

6	5	4	1	2	3	4
3	6	2	4	1	5	2
4	1	3	6	5	2	
5	4	1	2	3	6	
2	3	6	5	4	1	4
1	2	5	3	6	4	

SOLUTION 357

MQEOLOGLAETDOAP
ERIEPRNAEEHAREN
LTRASHSLRGLORRI
ESPILLECGISAGEE
ALTENHQLUPONLEE
ALGTMTTUDEASOLI
NRYNENIMUNPOTG
INMPMRYPVIRNE
RAPAJGEEDGTAAU
SADONDEPMPNLSC
OOERONTRIANGLEE
LGREHUDELNEER
RIEDNONXEHNYEAQ
RDIAMONDVYNPXAM

SOLUTION 368

						1	
1			2	3			4
		5					
		6	2	7			
	5		4				
				3			
7							
	8						
6	8						

SOLUTION 369

U S M N
REPEATED
ENVY G W
E ENDED
R B EARL
REWROTE C
MIA I L
CIRCUIT
ANKLE SKA
ELF EEL
CEDE ADSL

SOLUTION 370

HANGING GARLANDS

SOLUTION 378

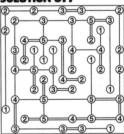

SOLUTION 379

| HEAT |
| HEAD |
| HELD |
| HOLD |
| HOOD |
| FOOD |

SOLUTION 380
CHRISTIAN
There are around 60 words in total

SOLUTION 381

SOLUTION 382
DEPRECIATION
There are around 60 words in total

SOLUTION 383

18	50
3	94
9	47
6	24
66	168
42	21

SOLUTION 384
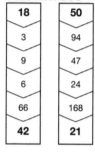

SOLUTION 385

3	4	0	2	5	1	0	0
3	4	0	3	1	4	4	4
3	1	0	6	1	0	3	1
2	3	2	6	0	4	0	3
5	5	1	6	5	6	6	1
6	2	5	6	5	2	5	4
2	6	4	1	3	2	5	2

SOLUTION 386

SOLUTION 387

SOLUTION 388
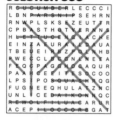

SOLUTION 389
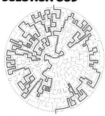

SOLUTION 390

	L	E	G	A	L	L	Y		E	C	H	O	
I		X		U		E		V		A			
V	I	P	E	R		S	Q	U	E	E	Z	E	
O		L		A		S		N			E		
R	I	O	T		F	O	O	T	B	A	L	L	
Y		R		S		N		I		L			
	W	I	T	C	H		A	D	M	I	T		
N				U		U		Y		G		S	
L	I	G	H	T	I	N	G		K	N	O	T	
N		H		U		B		M			M		
O	F	F	S	E	T	S		E	N	E	M	Y	
	E		A		E		A		N		S		
C	R	U	X		A	D	J	U	S	T	S		

SOLUTION 391
NUTCRACKERS

SOLUTION 392

SOLUTION 393

SOLUTION 394

SOLUTION 395

10× 2	1	5	18× 3	6	20× 4
4- 1	4	12× 3	6	2	5
5	6	1	7+ 4	9+ 3	2
48× 6	2	4	6+ 5	1	3
1- 3	5	2	1	4	6
4	3	6	8× 2	5	1

SOLUTION 396

17ᒣ	7ᒣ	9ᒣ	8ᒣ	5ᒣ	
4	3	1	2	6	5	Lᒤ18
4ᒣ 5	6	4	1	3	2	Lᒤ16
8	6	1	3	5	2	4	Lᒤ16
13ᒣ 1	5	2	6	4	3	Lᒤ9
8ᒣ 2	4	6	3	5	1	Lᒤ6
17ᒣ 3	2	5	4	1	6	
ᒪ3	ᒪ4	ᒪ10	ᒪ21	ᒪ12	

SOLUTION 397
1. *Cats*
2. 1960s
3. *Little Shop of Horrors*
4. *Evita*
5. *Martin Guerre*

SOLUTION 398

7	2	1	3	4	5	6
1	3	6	4	5	2	7
4	7	5	2	6	3	1
2	6	3	5	1	7	4
6	5	2	1	7	4	3
3	4	7	6	2	1	5
5	1	4	7	3	6	2

SOLUTION 399

SOLUTION 400

	S		N		M		R		
	I		E		A	M	E	N	
I	N	P	U	B	L	I	C		
	C	A	R		I	N	O	N	
	E	R	A	S		N	G	O	
	R		L			O	N	O	
S	E	P		H		W	I	N	
	L	O	C	A	L		Z		
	Y	E	A	H		S	I	M	
	T	S	A		I	N	A		
C	Y	S	T		E	R	G	O	

SOLUTION 401
CANDY CANES

SOLUTION 402

A	C	D	E	B	F	G	H
F	E	B	G	H	C	A	D
H	D	G	C	A	B	F	E
C	H	A	D	E	G	B	F
E	G	F	B	D	H	C	A
B	A	C	H	F	D	E	G
D	B	E	F	G	A	H	C
G	F	H	A	C	E	D	B

SOLUTION 403

	5		4	3			
3	1	4	2	3	6	5	
	2	3	4	1	5	6	
	4	6	3	5	2	1	4
3	3	2	5	6	1	4	2
	5	1	6	4	3	2	4
	6	5	1	2	4	3	
	1		2		3	3	

SOLUTION 404

P		G	O		O	P		L		S		
R	A	R	E	R		F	R	A	G	I	L	E
E		A		A			R		O		V	
F	I	D	D	L	E	S		T	E	N	S	E
E		U		E		I			R			
R	E	A	L	I	S	T	I	C		U	T	E
E		T		N				N				
R	O	E		V	A	R	I	E	T	I	E	S
E				I			O		Q		I	
S	M	A	R	T		U	N	U	S	U	A	L
I		U		I			T		R	E	E	
S	T	R	A	N	G	E		N	Y	L	O	N
T		A	G		S		S		Y		T	

SOLUTION 405

SOLUTION 406

E	D	A	B	F	C
B	F	C	E	D	A
D	A	B	F	C	E
F	C	E	D	A	B
A	B	F	C	E	D
C	E	D	A	B	F

SOLUTION 407

2	7	3	8	9	5	4	1	6
4	9	6	1	2	7	5	3	8
1	8	5	6	4	3	9	7	2
3	5	2	4	1	9	6	8	7
9	4	8	7	6	2	3	5	1
6	1	7	5	3	8	2	4	9
8	6	9	3	7	4	1	2	5
7	3	1	2	5	6	8	9	4
5	2	4	9	8	1	7	6	3

SOLUTION 408
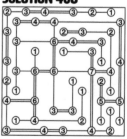

SOLUTION 409
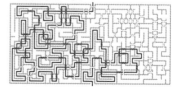

SOLUTION 410

BAKE
BIKE
BITE
BITS
PITS
PIES

SOLUTION 411
MISTLETOE
There are around 80 words in total

SOLUTION 412

SOLUTION 413
ADVANCEMENTS
There are around 75 words in total

SOLUTION 414

14		59
196		177
139		97
191		194
176		160
88		168

SOLUTION 415

S	P	O	U	S	E		I	N	S	U	L	T
	O		M		N		L		K		O	
P	L	E	B		L	O	L	L	I	P	O	P
	A		R		U		L		L		K	
A	R	R	A	N	G	E	S		L	A	S	H
I			H		T		E					
A	S	S	E	R	T		R	E	D	U	C	E
	A			E		A						O
T	H	I	S		N	A	T	I	O	N	A	L
A		M		I			U		T			
A	L	T	E	R	E	G	O		T	R	I	O
	V		S		N		N		D			N
S	E	X	T	E	T			S	T	O	O	G	E

SOLUTION 416

1	5	2	6	0	5	1	6
4	2	1	6	6	6	3	5
3	0	5	0	4	4	4	4
0	3	2	6	0	1	4	2
4	5	3	1	6	5	0	0
6	5	3	0	2	3	2	3
2	5	1	4	1	1	2	3

SOLUTION 417

SOLUTION 418

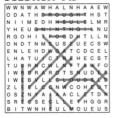

SOLUTION 419

SOLUTION 420

SOLUTION 421

E		O		T		G			I	V	Y	
T	A	X	P	A	Y	E	R		E		E	E
A		E		R		E		O	R	B	S	S
E	N	J	O	Y			G	A	B		S	S
E		A			A	U	K				E	
F	L	O	W	C	H	A	R	T		K	I	N
I		A		Y		C		O		O		C
L	O	T		E	M	P	H	A	S	I	Z	E
B			O	W	N			K				
E		A	W	E			T	W	I	S	T	
R	I	P	E		P		I		E			S
T		E		Q	U	I	C	K	E	S	T	
	O	D	E		G		K		D			Y

SOLUTION 422
LIGHTING

SOLUTION 423

SOLUTION 424

SOLUTION 425

SOLUTION 426

SOLUTION 427

SOLUTION 428
1. *Mosaic*
2. *Netscape*
3. Hypertext transfer protocol
4. Tuvalu
5. *Safari*

SOLUTION 429

SOLUTION 430

SOLUTION 431

	A		O	P		N	
	K	A	N	G	A	R	O	O
N	A	B	S		S	U	
		N	E	P	T	U	N	E
B	O	T	H	E	R		W
	R		I		D	U	E
S	E	M	I		B	U	G	S
	L	A	S	T		L	
A	L	L		A	R	I	D
T		E	C	H	O	E	D
M	E	S	S		A	I	R	S

SOLUTION 432
OPENING PRESENTS

SOLUTION 433

C	F	B	A	G	H	D	E
H	G	C	E	A	B	F	D
D	A	G	F	B	E	C	H
B	E	H	D	F	C	G	A
F	H	D	C	E	G	A	B
E	C	A	B	D	F	H	G
G	D	E	H	C	A	B	F
A	B	F	G	H	D	E	C

SOLUTION 434

3	4	5	1	2	6	3	
	6	1	2	3	5	4	
	2	6	3	1	4	5	
	5	3	4	6	2	1	3
	1	4	6	5	3	2	4
3	3	2	5	4	1	6	

SOLUTION 435

M	O	U	N	T		A	S	S	I	S	T
E		N		E		F		U	L		I
D	I	S	A	S	T	E	R	S		L	E	D
I		E		T		A		H	E	Y	
T	U	T	T	I		T	H	I	N	G	S
S		N		U			A				
	D	A	N	G	E	R	O	U	S	L	Y
	M			E		T			U	
T	U	N	N	E	L		T	O	N	E	S
P	S		O		E		O		A	
L	E	I		O	B	S	E	R	V	I	N	G
O		N		S		S		L		S	E
D	E	G	R	E	E		T	Y	P	E	D

SOLUTION 436

SOLUTION 437

C	D	F	E	B	A
B	E	C	A	D	F
D	A	B	F	E	C
E	F	D	C	A	B
A	C	E	B	F	D
F	B	A	D	C	E

SOLUTION 438

7	9	3	2	5	1	6	8	4
5	1	4	3	8	6	2	7	9
6	8	2	9	7	4	3	1	5
1	7	9	6	4	8	5	2	3
2	4	8	5	3	7	9	6	1
3	6	5	1	2	9	8	4	7
4	3	7	8	6	5	1	9	2
9	5	6	7	1	2	4	3	8
8	2	1	4	9	3	7	5	6

SOLUTION 439

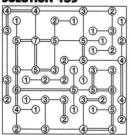

SOLUTION 440

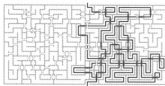

SOLUTION 441

HOLD
BOLD
BALD
BALE
BABE
BABY

SOLUTION 442
COMMUNITY
There are around 20 words in total

SOLUTION 443

SOLUTION 444
INACCURATELY
There are around 75 words in total

SOLUTION 445

61		89
160		71
40		146
36		73
105		53
55		133

SOLUTION 446

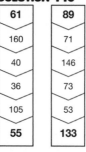

S	I	T	U	P	S		A	P	P	E	A	R
H		R		L		A		E		R		E
E	M	U		A	M	B	I	T	I	O	U	S
N		N		S		S		E				E
T	A	K	E	N		T	O	U	R	I	S	T
S				T		R		N		O		
	E	S	T	I	M	A	T	I	O	N	S	
	A		F		C	F		R		R		
B	E	N	E	F	I	T		O	T	H	E	R
Y		D		I		I		R		E		O
T	R	A	N	S	F	O	R	M		A	N	N
E		L		E		N		L		R		L
S	Y	S	T	E	M		M	Y	S	T	I	C

SOLUTION 447

3	6	4	6	0	0	3	6
6	2	5	4	1	5	2	0
1	2	6	3	4	4	1	0
3	2	2	1	3	3	1	0
3	5	5	5	6	6	4	0
1	2	4	3	1	5	5	0
2	6	0	2	4	5	1	4

SOLUTION 448

2	8	3	7	9	6	5	4	1
7	4	9	3	5	1	2	8	6
5	6	1	2	8	4	3	7	9
8	2	4	1	3	7	6	9	5
6	3	5	9	4	2	7	1	8
1	9	7	6	5	8	4	3	2
4	7	8	5	1	9	2	3	6
9	1	6	4	2	3	8	5	7
3	5	2	8	7	9	1	6	4

SOLUTION 449

SOLUTION 450

SOLUTION 451

SOLUTION 452

		G	M	F		M	S	T	
	G	A	T	E	A	U	O	B	E	S	E
		R		T	R	A	J	L		L
R	O	B	B	E	R		O	F	F	A	L
A			E		T		A		R		
R	I	V	E	R	S		A	N	T	I	C
E				P	O	X		L		S	
W	A	F	E	R			I	T	A	L	I	C
A		E		Y		R			R		A
F	R	O	Z	E		D	E	T	E	C	T
I		K		B	E	D		D	M		
S	C	R	U	B		U	N	I	Q	U	E
H		A		S			O		T		S

SOLUTION 453
GINGERBREAD

SOLUTION 454

(grid puzzle)

SOLUTION 455

(grid puzzle)

SOLUTION 456

(grid puzzle)

SOLUTION 457

5	3	2	6	4	1
3	5	6	2	1	4
4	2	1	3	6	5
2	1	3	4	5	6
1	6	4	5	3	2
6	4	5	1	2	3

SOLUTION 458

4	3	1	5	6	2
3	4	2	1	5	6
2	1	4	6	3	5
1	6	5	4	2	3
5	2	6	3	4	1
6	5	3	2	1	4

SOLUTION 459
1. Maria Sharapova
2. Roger Federer
3. Rafael Nadal
4. Monica Seles
5. Stefan Edberg

SOLUTION 460

6	5	1	7	4	3	2
5	7	2	4	3	1	6
1	3	4	2	6	7	5
2	6	5	3	1	4	7
7	4	3	6	5	2	1
4	1	7	5	2	6	3
3	2	6	1	7	5	4

SOLUTION 461

(grid puzzle)

SOLUTION 462

	L	O		B	K		
E	X	P	L	A	I	N	S
U	N	I	T		C	I	
		S		S	T	I	F	F
M		A		E	K	E	D
P	R	E	P	A	R	E	A
I	M	P		I	S		
	B	A	N	A	N	A	S
B	U	R	R	O		A	L	I
		Y	E	T		M	A	R
I	D	O	L		B	E	D	S

SOLUTION 463
GIVING GIFTS

SOLUTION 464

D	C	G	F	B	A	E	H
B	E	H	C	A	D	G	F
F	G	A	H	E	C	B	D
H	A	D	E	F	B	C	G
G	H	B	A	D	E	F	C
C	D	E	G	H	F	A	B
E	F	C	B	G	H	D	A
A	B	F	D	C	G	H	E

SOLUTION 465

1	3	6	5	2	4
2	1	3	4	5	6
3	2	4	6	1	5
6	4	5	2	3	1
5	6	1	3	4	2
4	5	2	1	6	3

SOLUTION 466

S	W	A	T		I	N	F	E	C	T	E	D
A		O		S		A		R		N		
G	L	O	B	A	L		S	T	A	N	D	S
L		A		E		H		M				
E	P	I	C		T	A	I	L	P	I	P	E
A		C				O				R		
O	P	P	O	R	T	U	N	I	T	I	E	S
		E		R				I		S		
B	R	O	C	C	O	L	I		C	R	E	W
		L		U		S		K		R		
S	U	P	E	R	B		S	H	E	L	V	E
		K		A		L		U		T		E
R	E	T	R	I	E	V	E		S	A	S	H

SOLUTION 467

SOLUTION 468

D	E	C	A	B	F
A	B	F	D	E	C
F	D	E	C	A	B
E	C	A	B	F	D
B	F	D	E	C	A
C	A	B	F	D	E

SOLUTION 469

6	1	3	7	8	2	5	4	9
7	2	4	1	5	9	6	3	8
9	8	5	6	3	4	7	1	2
8	4	2	9	6	7	3	5	1
3	7	9	5	1	8	4	2	6
5	6	1	2	4	3	9	8	7
1	5	8	4	9	6	2	7	3
2	3	6	8	7	5	1	9	4
4	9	7	3	2	1	8	6	5

SOLUTION 470

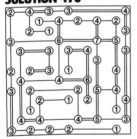

SOLUTION 471

SOLUTION 472

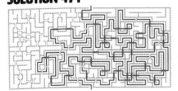

GIVE
DIVE
DIME
DIMS
AIMS
ALMS

SOLUTION 473
NOSTALGIA
There are around 85 words in total

SOLUTION 474

SOLUTION 475
REFRIGERATOR
There are around 55 words in total

SOLUTION 476

42	35
70	5
20	10
16	89
160	86
48	43

SOLUTION 477

S	E	Q	U	E	L		E	D	I	T	E	D
K		U		L		I		E			E	
E	T	A		A	S	S	I	S	T	A	N	T
T		L		N		H		T				
C	H	I	C		P	O	L	I	S	H	E	S
H		F		S		R		N		A		T
		I	D	E	N	T	I	C	A	L		
A	E		P		E		T			F		I
C	U	R	T	A	I	N	S		O	B	O	E
I		R		E		A		A		L		
D	O	G	E	A	T	D	O	G			K	O	I
I		O		T				U			E		U
C	E	A	S	E	S		S	E	L	D	O	M

SOLUTION 478

1	3	2	2	6	0	5	1
4	1	5	0	6	6	2	1
5	1	5	1	2	4	4	3
0	3	3	2	4	2	0	3
4	6	4	0	6	5	0	3
6	6	1	5	2	3	0	5
0	2	4	4	5	3	6	1

SOLUTION 479

5	7	6	8	1	4	2	9	3
1	3	2	6	9	7	8	4	5
4	8	9	5	3	2	6	1	7
6	9	4	3	8	5	7	2	1
7	1	5	2	6	9	4	3	8
8	2	3	4	7	1	9	6	5
9	5	8	1	4	6	3	7	2
3	6	1	7	2	8	5	4	9
2	4	7	9	5	3	1	8	6

SOLUTION 480

SOLUTION 481

SOLUTION 482

SOLUTION 483

	O		S		R				C	O	O		
	S	H	E	R	I	F	F		H		V		
	T		Q		N		I		O	P	A	L	
G	R	O	U	N	D		B	O	O		R		
	I		E				S	A	Y	S		
S	C	A	L	E	S		E	V	E			
	H			P	A	L				D		
		E	R	A		K	E	E	P	E	R	
T	W	I	N			X				F		
H			J	O	Y		S	E	I	Z	E	D
C	I	A	O		E		E		S		N	
	C		Y		S	W	E	A	T	E	D	
H	A	S					M		S		S	

SOLUTION 484
WINTERTIME

SOLUTION 485

SOLUTION 486

SOLUTION 487

SOLUTION 488

20+	4	5	3	2	6	1
	5	1	4	3	2	6
6+	6	4	2	5	1	3
	1	3	6	4	5	2
7+	2	6	5	1	3	4
	3	2	1	6	4	5

SOLUTION 489

	1	6	2	5	3	4	21
	6	2	1	4	5	3	17
	2	3	4	1	6	5	14
	5	1	3	2	4	6	2
	4	5	6	3	2	1	2
	3	4	5	6	1	2	

SOLUTION 490

1. Johann Sebastian
2. 17th
3. Sibelius
4. Tchaikovsky
5. Mozart

SOLUTION 491

4	5	2	3	7	1	6
6	1	3	7	2	4	5
7	4	1	6	5	3	2
1	3	4	5	6	2	7
2	7	5	4	3	6	1
5	2	6	1	4	7	3
3	6	7	2	1	5	4

SOLUTION 492

SOLUTION 493

	S		C		M		A	
	T		A		E	N	D	S
Y	U	A	N		M	O	A	
	F	L	O	W	E	R		S
	F	E	E			M	U	M
				E	R	A	S	E
D	T	P		E		L	E	E
	L	O	C	K			L	
	C	P	R		O	W	E	S
		P	U	R	P	O	S	E
O	N	Y	X		S	O	S	O

SOLUTION 494
TWELFTH NIGHT

SOLUTION 495

B	F	A	D	E	G	C	H
G	C	H	B	D	E	A	F
A	E	F	G	C	H	D	B
E	H	C	F	A	B	G	D
D	B	G	E	F	A	H	C
H	G	D	A	B	C	F	E
C	D	E	H	G	F	B	A
F	A	B	C	H	D	E	G

SOLUTION 496

	4			2		
5	1	2	3	4	6	5
	3	5	4	6	1	2	2
	6	4	5	2	3	1	4
3	2	3	6	1	5	4
2	4	6	1	5	2	3
2	5	1	2	3	4	6	1
			3			

SOLUTION 497

```
N E E D F U L N E S S
A   L   W   N E   P   D
D I F F E R E N T I A T E
M   L   V   S   G   P
I N S U L T E D   T H A T
T   H   I   N   S E   H
W O U N D   G U S T O
P   R   G   C   N   T   G
I O T A   F L A B B I L Y
N   E   M   O   A   P
C O N V E R S A T I O N S
H   E   N   E   H   U   Y
A D J U S T M E N T S
```

SOLUTION 498

SOLUTION 499

F	B	D	E	C	A
E	C	A	F	B	D
A	F	B	D	E	C
D	E	C	A	F	B
C	A	F	B	D	E
B	D	E	C	A	F

SOLUTION 500

8	9	1	6	3	2	5	4	7
2	7	5	1	9	4	8	6	3
3	6	4	8	7	5	1	9	2
4	2	8	7	6	3	9	5	1
9	5	7	4	1	8	2	3	6
6	1	3	5	2	9	7	8	4
5	8	2	3	4	7	6	1	9
1	3	9	2	5	6	4	7	8
7	4	6	9	8	1	3	2	5

SOLUTION 501

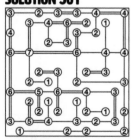

SOLUTION 502

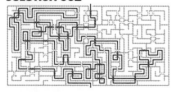

SOLUTION 503

STAR
SEAR
NEAR
NEAT
NEST
REST

SOLUTION 504
SNOWBALLS
There are around 40 words in total

SOLUTION 505

SOLUTION 506
WEATHERPROOF
There are around 45 words in total

SOLUTION 507

71		44
77		11
55		78
22		6
11		34
66		17

SOLUTION 508

```
P   A U       S O   E
A L M A N A C   T I M I D
T   I   E   O   A   N   G
  T E D   V A L E N T I N E
E   E   E   D   D   V
R I P E N   B I S H O P S
N   R       L   R   U
S C O R P I O   U S E R S
  G   O     O N     P
P E R S U A D E S   U A E
U   A   R   E   A   P   C
F E M M E   D E F R O S T
F   S   D       E   N   S
```

SOLUTION 509

5	0	6	0	4	2	1	0
5	0	5	1	5	3	3	4
4	2	1	5	5	2	6	0
2	6	3	6	6	6	1	3
2	6	1	0	5	3	0	2
3	2	1	3	1	4	2	0
4	4	6	1	3	4	4	5

SOLUTION 510

5	3	7	8	2	6	4	1	9
8	9	6	5	1	4	2	3	7
4	2	1	7	3	9	8	6	5
9	6	5	4	7	3	1	8	2
7	4	2	1	5	8	6	9	3
3	1	8	9	6	2	7	5	4
1	5	4	3	8	7	9	2	6
6	7	3	2	9	5	3	4	8
2	8	9	6	4	1	5	7	1

SOLUTION 511

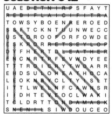

SOLUTION 512

```
U A E D E T N I R P S F A Y T
R E B I F L A I C I F I T R A
T O W S Y B O E N E R E O E D
S E T C K N T J U N W E C C
K R R O O F O R F O W D E
L F H E T R L E A T H E R
N C N R R E F V W D Y E E
T T R O I I S Y W D A R R
E D S U L O R A H S C A
L I   T L W E N F C A W I S R
I   D H T E T O C L W A K I
T C L D R T T O   D A M A S K
S N E N I L S I W D O U C E O
```

SOLUTION 513

SOLUTION 514

```
S Q U A S H   A T T A I N
E   N   A     W   H   O
C A W   C O G N I Z A N T
U   E   S   E   L     A
R O L E   E N G I N E E R
E   C   I   E   G   X   Y
    O W N E R S H I P
S M   M   C   A   T   L S
U S E F U L L Y   Y O K E
D     R   L   I   S   L
D E S T R O Y E D   I C E
E   U   E     L   V   C
N O B O D Y   R E J E C T
```

SOLUTION 515
SNOWFLAKES

SOLUTION 516

SOLUTION 517

SOLUTION 518

SOLUTION 519

4	1	6	3	2	5
6	2	4	5	3	1
5	6	2	4	1	3
2	5	3	1	6	4
3	4	1	2	5	6
1	3	5	6	4	2

SOLUTION 520

6	3	2	4	5	1
1	2	5	3	4	6
2	5	1	6	3	4
3	1	4	5	6	2
5	4	6	1	2	3
4	6	3	2	1	5

SOLUTION 521

6	2	5	3	4	1
5	6	1	2	3	4
3	1	2	4	5	6
1	4	3	5	6	2
4	5	6	1	2	3
2	3	4	6	1	5

SOLUTION 522

6	7	2	5	1	4	3
4	6	1	2	5	3	7
3	1	4	7	2	5	6
2	3	5	1	6	7	4
1	5	7	4	3	6	2
5	4	6	3	7	2	1
7	2	3	6	4	1	5

SOLUTION 523